# Catholic Schools: Mission, Markets and Morality

Faith-based schooling is the focus of much contemporary political and policy discussion and yet, as a research field, it is relatively undeveloped.

In this ground-breaking book, Gerald Grace addresses the dilemmas facing Catholic education in an increasingly secular and consumer-driven culture. The book combines an original theoretical framework with research drawn from interviews with sixty Catholic secondary headteachers from urban areas. Issues discussed include the Catholic meanings of academic success, tensions between market values and Catholic values, threats to the mission integrity of Catholic schools and the spiritual, moral and social justice commitments of contemporary Catholic schools.

This book will be equally valuable to leaders of Catholic and other schools and to all those interested in values and leadership in schooling.

**Gerald Grace** is a Professorial Research Fellow at the Institute of Education, University of London. He is also Director of the Centre for Research and Development in Catholic Education, based at the Institute of Education.

Cover image: The icon, *Sedes Sapientiae*, by Father M. I. Rupnik, presented by Pope John Paul II to the university world on 10 September 2000. Reproduced by kind permission of the Congregation for Catholic Education, Rome.

# Catholic Schools: Mission, Markets and Morality

Gerald Grace

London and New York

First published 2002
by RoutledgeFalmer
11 New Fetter Lane, London EC4P 4EE

Simultaneously published in the USA and Canada
by RoutledgeFalmer
29 West 35th Street, New York, NY 10001

*RoutledgeFalmer is an imprint of the Taylor & Francis Group*



Typeset in Bembo by Taylor & Francis Books Ltd
Printed and bound in Great Britain by TJ International Ltd, Padstow, Cornwall



*British Library Cataloguing in Publication Data*
A catalogue record for this book is available from the British Library

*Library of Congress Cataloging-in-Publication Data*
Grace, Gerald Rupert.
Catholic schools: mission, markets and morality / Gerald Grace.
p. cm.
Includes bibliographical references and index.
1. Catholic Church–Education. 2. Education–Philosophy. 3. Catholic schools–England–Case studies. I. Title.

LC47 .G73 2002
371.0712–dc21 2001058703



ISBN 0–415–24324–6 (hbk)
ISBN 0–415–24325–4 (pbk)

# Contents

# Acknowledgements

The inspiration for this book came when I attended a seminar on Catholic education organised by Dr Terry McLaughlin and Dr Bernadette O'Keeffe at St Edmund's College, Cambridge, in 1993. At this seminar I met Father Joseph O'Keefe SJ from Boston College, an active researcher of Catholic schooling in the USA, and Professor Anthony Bryk from Chicago, one of the authors of the research study which we were discussing at the seminar, i.e. *Catholic Schools and the Common Good*. I was so impressed with the scholarly excellence of this study and so dismayed at the relatively undeveloped state of Catholic education research in the UK at the time that I felt impelled, or as Catholics would say, 'called', to do something about it. From this defining moment my ideas for a Centre for Research and Development in Catholic Education began to take shape and also the general conception of this book on Catholic secondary schools in urban deprived communities. Terry, Bernadette, Joe and Tony Bryk provided this initial context for inspiration and I thank them for this.

The subsequent foundation of the Centre for Research and Development in Catholic Education (CRDCE) in 1997 at the Institute of Education, University of London, was made possible because of the imaginative and creative educational leadership of its then Director, Professor Peter Mortimore. As a leading educational researcher, Peter recognised that the whole field of Catholic schooling needed to be opened up to systematic enquiry and investigation. With his encouragement and support, CRDCE began its operations with the considerable advantage of being located within a world-class institute for educational research. I hope that he will take the view that this book has, in part, repaid his trust.

The funding of the research and scholarship necessary for the production of this book has come from two sources. A Leverhulme Trust Fellowship awarded for 1997–2000 financed the costs of the research fieldwork. I thank the Trustees for this crucial support and also Mrs Jean Cater, Secretary to the Research Awards Advisory Committee, for her personal encouragement and help. The scholarly resources of CRDCE were essential to this project and these were made possible thanks to the sponsorship of the Centre by a number of religious orders and charitable foundations. These included: The Society of Jesus, De La Salle Brothers, Christian Brothers, Faithful Companions of Jesus, Sisters of Charity of St Paul (Selly Park), Salesians of Don Bosco, Benedictines of Ampleforth, Sisters of Notre Dame, Society of the Holy Child Jesus, Missionaries of the Sacred Heart (Dublin), Sisters of Mercy, Institute of the Blessed Virgin Mary, La Retraite Sisters, Servite Sisters Charitable Trust, Congregation of Our Lady of the Missions and the Jane Hodge Charitable Foundation (Cardiff).

In the conduct of the fieldwork and in the transcription of the research interviews I received great help from CRDCE's secretary, Mary Atherton, and also from members of my family, June Grace, Helena Grace and Claire Gracethorne. This is more than an acknowledgement of research efficiency. It is to thank them all for valuable discussions about the direction of the project and the possible significance of its findings.

As many who read this will know, the actual writing of a book requires some form of protected space in which reflection is possible. I was fortunate to obtain a Visiting Professorial Fellowship at the University of Sussex Institute of Education from October 1999 to May 2001 which provided the necessary conditions for sustained writing. I thank the Vice-Chancellor and the then Director of the Institute, Professor Joan Bliss, for making this opportunity possible.

In what amounts to a five-year research and writing project so many professional, personal and intellectual debts are acquired that it becomes difficult to acknowledge all of them. I apologise therefore for any omissions. My most fundamental debts are to the Catholic headteachers, diocesan officials and senior school students who generously gave of their time to assist with this enquiry. The fact that the headteachers in particular were prepared to assign one and a half hours for interview/discussions on various aspects of Catholic urban schooling was in itself a small miracle, given the highly pressurised environment in which they worked. The accounts which many of them gave about their work and vocation in Catholic school leadership were not only informative but deeply impressive as evidence of Christian service to the common good in challenging circumstances.

For various forms of intellectual support, feedback on draft materials and general encouragement for the work I thank Archbishop Vincent

Nichols, James Arthur, Peter Boylan, Tony Bryk, Wilfred Carr, Tony d'Arbon FMS, Tony Edwards, Matthew Feheney FPM, Michael Fielding, Harvey Goldstein, Andrew Greeley, David Halpin, Alan Harrison SJ, Michael Hornsby-Smith, Val Klenowski, Denis Lawton, Loreto Loughran, Tony Mackersie, Peter and Jo Mortimore, Andrew Morris, Sally Power, Albert Price, Richard Pring, John Sullivan, Sally Tomlinson, Sister Mary Peter Traviss OP, Paddy Walsh, Maurice Whitehead, Geoff Whitty and Richard Zipfel.

I have also learned much in discussions with participants at AERA, BERA and NCEA Conferences, with my colleagues in the Curriculum Studies Group at the Institute of Education and with participants in Catholic education conferences organised by a number of dioceses and organisations in England, Wales, Scotland and Ireland. A particularly fruitful relationship with the Catholic Institute of Education in South Africa and with its Programme Director, Mark Potterton, has done much to widen and deepen my understanding of the Catholic education mission. Visits to Rome, facilitated by Dominic Grace, have kept me in touch with some of the central agencies of Catholic education while I have investigated the impact of Vatican guidance on education in a specific national setting. Anna Clarkson of RoutledgeFalmer has been an encouraging and hospitable mentor of this project and I thank her for her sustained support.

These acknowledgements demonstrate that in keeping with Catholic tradition this book is the outcome of a communal effort and not simply of an individual. It is to be hoped that also in keeping with Catholic teaching it will make some useful contribution to the realisation of the common good in education.

## Permissions

Acknowledgement is made by the author and the publishers for kind permission to reproduce quotation extracts used in Chapter 3 of this book from the following:

Extracts from: *A Portrait of the Artist as a Young Man* James Joyce, Jonathan Cape: © Estate of James Joyce; *There's Something about a Convent Girl* (ed.) J. Bennett and R. Forgan (M. Binchy, C. Boylan, C. Callil, G. Greer, M. Kenny, M. O'Malley, J. Walsh, M.. Warner), Virago Press, Little, Brown and Company; *Frost in May*, Antonia White, Virago Press, Little, Brown and Company; *Memories of a Catholic Girlhood*, Mary McCarthy, Heinemann: used by permission of the Random House Group Limited; *Catholic Boys* (ed.) Jim Sullivan, Penguin Books, New Zealand; *Convent Girls* (ed.) Jane

Tollerton, Penguin Books, New Zealand; *Jesuit Child*, Macdonald Hastings, Michael Joseph, Trustees of M. Hastings; *Angela's Ashes*, Frank McCourt, HarperCollins Publishers Ltd; *Reading in the Dark*, Seamus Deane, published by Jonathan Cape, © Seamus Deane 1996, used by permission of the Random House Group Limited; *Our Kid*, Billy Hopkins, Headline Book Publishing Ltd; *Alone of All Her Sex*, Marina Warner, Picador Books, used by permission of Orion Publishing Group Ltd.

# Introduction

It is often assumed that issues to do with Catholic education and schooling are relevant only to Catholics and therefore may be regarded as marginal to mainstream educational research and discourse. This assumption becomes apparent in any detailed scrutiny of the literature on globalisation and education, policy studies, school effectiveness studies and school leadership studies, or in the conference programmes of organisations such as the American Educational Research Association or the British Educational Research Association. While Catholic schools, in some societies, may have come 'out of the ghetto' in terms of their relationships with external agencies[1] this process does not seem to have happened to the same extent in educational scholarship and research. There still seems to be 'a secret garden of Catholic education research' known, in general, only to the cognoscenti.

There are many reasons for this secret garden phenomenon including, of course, the relatively limited number of scholars and researchers active in the Catholic education field. However, there are at least four other factors internationally which account for this situation. The first is the idea, especially strong in the USA, that Catholic schools as private schools have cultures and leadership challenges which are of a very different kind from those which characterise state or publicly provided schooling. From this perspective, Catholic schools are perceived as a somewhat privileged sector of any schooling system. While this first assumption is true for the USA and for a number of other countries, this 'private sector' image has tended to overshadow different relationships in other societies. In Belgium, Germany, New Zealand, The Netherlands, England, Scotland and Ireland, Catholic schools receive significant support from public funds and, as a consequence, are an integrated (although distinctive) sector of publicly provided education.

The Catholic secondary schools in London, Liverpool and Birmingham, which are the focus of this study, are not private schools. Their formal status in England is that of 'voluntary-aided' schools, which means in practice that they are non-fee-paying institutions and an integrated part of the free secondary education system. Such Catholic schools, especially those located in inner-city and deprived community areas, frequently have student populations registering high levels of poverty as indicated by entitlement to free school meals. They have arisen out of a tradition of Catholic working-class schooling in England and they remain largely in the service of that class, albeit with greater ethnic and cultural diversity than in the past. Catholic schools in England are front-line providers of quality education in many working-class and ethnically mixed communities, especially in urban areas.

The second assumption of the secret garden perspective is that Catholic schools exist to serve Catholics only. Viewed internationally this is an erroneous assumption. In a number of societies Catholic schools have enrolments in which Catholic students are the minority.[2] Of the sixty Catholic secondary schools which are the focus of this study only twelve schools reported a 100 per cent Catholic student enrolment. In varying proportions, the other Catholic schools admitted students from a pluralistic range of religious cultures, and in five of the schools Catholic students constituted only 50 per cent of the enrolments. Catholic schools, as Bryk *et al.* (1993) and others have argued, can legitimately claim to be in the service of the common good in education and not simply that of the specific good of Catholic communities.

A third mis-perception is based upon outdated but still tenacious images of traditional Catholic schooling as a process of authoritarian indoctrination rather than a process of education *per se*. These images have been widely disseminated and amplified in autobiographical accounts and influential literary creations. The existence of what might be called the Antonia White, James Joyce or Frank McCourt versions of a Catholic schooling have obscured the extent to which new forms of Catholic education have developed as one consequence of the reforms of the Second Vatican Council (1962–5).

Finally, the generally low-profile representation of all faith-based schooling, including Catholic schooling, in educational enquiry can be seen to be an outcome of what Gallagher (1997, p. 23) has referred to as 'secular marginalisation' in contemporary intellectual culture, i.e. 'especially in the academic and media worlds, a secular culture reigns with the results that religion is subtly ignored as unimportant'. Major studies of globalisation and education, policy struggles in education, school effectiveness investigations and school leadership analysis take place as if the existence of faith-based schooling systems was peripheral to the central questions being raised.[3]

This study is a limited attempt to counter some of these misconceptions, dated images and secular marginalisations related to Catholic schooling, at least in the English urban context. In Part I, 'Theoretical frameworks', Catholic schooling is positioned in terms of foundational distinctions between the sacred and the secular and an attempt is made to construct the social field of Catholic education using theoretical insights derived from the influential writings of Pierre Bourdieu and Basil Bernstein. In Part II, 'Historical, cultural and research contexts', two chapters contrast the traditional images of Catholic schooling, pre-Vatican II, with the findings of systematic research on Catholic schooling conducted in the USA, Canada, Australia, England, Scotland and Ireland.

In Part III, 'Catholic secondary schools in three English cities', the results of a fieldwork investigation with sixty secondary headteachers in the period 1997–2000 are reported. Five chapters in this part give an account of the research approaches used and provide a critical analysis of the headteachers' responses to changing conceptions of the Catholic educational mission and issues of leadership; their explanations for the relative academic 'success' or 'failure' of their schools; their policies in relation to the impact of more competitive market relations in schooling; and their reflections upon the spiritual, moral and social effectiveness of the schools and the nature of the Catholicity being realised in contemporary educational practice. Also considered in this part are reflections upon the influence of race and gender relations in Catholic culture and schooling.

Wider perspectives on the schools were obtained by analysis of the reports of external inspectors (Office for Standards in Education (OFSTED) and diocesan reports), by interviews with diocesan education officials and by focus-group discussions with fifty senior students in five London schools.

The conclusion, Chapter 10, argues that dynamic spiritual capital has been the distinctive feature and animator of Catholic schooling in the past and the question of what forms its renewal will take in contemporary settings is a major issue for the future vitality and integrity of the system.

Catholic schools of the future and their school leaders and teachers have to devise ways, in changing conditions, of remaining faithful to the principle of St Thomas More: that they should be 'the King's good servant, but God's first'. It is hoped that this book may assist them in meeting this considerable challenge.

# Part I

# Theoretical frameworks

# 1 The Catholic school

## The sacred and the secular

The future of the Catholic voluntary-aided school in England and Wales looks bright and is, from one perception, an occasion for celebration. Catholic schools, both primary and secondary, have been well placed in the public league tables of academic and test results which are, in contemporary society, an important source of the making or breaking of a school's reputation and public image.[1] In addition to support from local Catholic communities, the schools are much sought after by parents of other Christian faith communities and by those of other faiths. In many areas therefore Catholic schools are filled to capacity and are in fact over-subscribed by parents attracted by the Catholic school's reputation for academic success, 'good' discipline and for taking spiritual and moral education seriously. Speaking of 'The Church's Mission in Education', Cardinal Hume argued that:

> Today, Catholic schools are increasingly popular, not only because of the good academic results they often achieve, but also because many parents sense that a Catholic school might help their children to develop the self-discipline, moral resilience and spiritual maturity so necessary in surviving exposure as young adults to the winds of secularism and materialism in our society.
>
> (1997, pp. 25–6)

The decision by the British Prime Minister (an Anglican) and his wife (a Catholic) to send their children to Catholic secondary schools in London appeared to confer public and political legitimacy upon a schooling system that has, even as late as the 1970s, been subject to ideological critique from some sections of the Left and to calls for its abolition on the grounds of social divisiveness, covert selection and a general undermining of the reputation and effectiveness of the state system of schooling.[2]

The contemporary 'success' and legitimacy of Catholic schools now appear to be assured. The schools have most of the surface and visible indicators of success and effectiveness and most of them enjoy a strong position in the competitive internal market for schooling which developed in the 1980s. In an educational culture and discourse in which 'improvement', 'quality assurance', 'stakeholder confidence', 'success', 'effectiveness' and 'excellence' are dominant categories for the making of public judgements, Catholic schools have moved from a previously marginal[3] to a currently centre-stage position of public and official endorsement.

While there is cause for celebration among the Catholic community in England and Wales for the present achievements of a schooling system which began with the efforts of the Catholic Poor-School Committee in 1847, the paradox is that this very evident success generates its own contemporary threats to the integrity of the holistic mission caused by undue emphasis upon part of the mission; the potential to become preoccupied by the visible and measurable in education to the detriment of the invisible and more intangible outcomes of schooling; the potential for Catholic schools to be incorporated into a secular marketplace for education which may weaken their relation with the sacred and the spiritual and the distinctive culture of Catholicity itself. As the Sacred Congregation for Catholic Education observed in 1977:

> Today, as in the past, some scholastic institutions which bear the name Catholic, do not appear to correspond fully to the principles of education which should be their distinguishing feature.
>
> (p. 50)

If this situation was perceived in 1977, it seems very likely that over two decades later, following the impact of instrumentalist and radical reforms in education, the gap between the theory and the practice of Catholic schooling may have increased. Part of the intention of this present study is to attempt to illuminate this issue by reference to contemporary fieldwork data. However, before this is attempted, the enterprise of Catholic schooling must be located in relation to its theoretical, historical and cultural contexts. From what I have called, in other places, a policy scholarship perspective,[4] there can be no significant understanding of contemporary Catholic schooling which does not involve some engagement with its theological–social rationale and some awareness of the historical and cultural contexts which have shaped and influenced its development. It seems evident that the analytical priority has to be given to what I have called the *theological–social rationale* of the Catholic school and in particular to the Catholic school's relation to concepts of the sacred, the profane and the secular; to its relation to contemporary educational principles and practice; and to its relation to the institutional Roman Catholic Church.

## The Catholic school and the culture of the sacred

It may be said that one of the prime purposes of the Catholic school and perhaps its fundamental rationale is to keep alive and to renew the culture of the sacred in a profane and secular world. This, in itself, is a massive and daunting educational challenge since the nature of the sacred is not easily articulated and represents 'a struggle to conceive the inconceivable, to utter the unutterable and a longing for the Infinite'.[5] Durkheim, in his classic study *The Elementary Forms of the Religious Life* (1971), made a sustained attempt, from the standpoint of religious sociology, to understand the nature of the sacred and of its relation to the profane in human societies. For Durkheim, that which was sacred in a society referred to things which were superior in dignity and power to the elements of mundane life, to things 'set apart', to notions of the transcendent and divine, of souls and of spirits and of the ultimate destiny of persons. The sacred was a representation of the Other in human existence, 'something added to and above the real',[6] that which was holy, ineffable and mysterious. Religion, for Durkheim, was the social and cultural form which regulated relations with the sacred and prescribed the necessary rites 'of oblation and communion, imitative rites, commemorative rites and expiatory rites'.[7] But religion, in the societies which Durkheim studied, had other profound social and intellectual functions in that it was perceived to be constitutive of categories of thought, the nature of society and constructs of an ideal world. Thus Durkheim concluded in a powerful and evocative passage:

> We have established the fact that the fundamental categories of thought … are of religious origin … Nearly all of the great social institutions have been born in religion … If religion has given birth to all that is essential in society, it is because the idea of society is the soul of religion.[8]

Given Durkheim's conviction that 'the idea of society is the soul of religion', it is not surprising that he was opposed to forms of radical individualism and there can be little doubt about what his response to Mrs Thatcher's assertion that 'there is no such thing as society' would have been.[9] For Durkheim, religion constituted not only what society was but crucially also what it could be in a perfected and ideal form. While the concept of 'utopia' is not explicitly used in *The Elementary Forms of the Religious Life*, it is clear that Durkheim saw religion as contributing to the formation of an ideal world.[10]

In this analysis, religion is seen to be an essential cultural relay between the sacred and the profane but the categories themselves are sharply differentiated:

> In all the history of human thought there exists no other example of two categories of things so profoundly differentiated or so radically opposed to one another … The sacred and the profane have always and everywhere been conceived by the human mind as two distinct classes, as two worlds between which there is nothing in common. To move from one world to another requires initiation rites in a long series of ceremonies.
>
> (1971, pp. 38–9)

At the basis of this sharp distinction between the sacred and the profane is the notion that the profane, viewed as the mundane exigencies of everyday living, has the potential to pollute and devalue the purity and the integrity of that which is sacred. From this perspective the polluting potential of the mundane world has to be counteracted by the creation of social distance, ritual formulation, strong cultural insulators and physical structures designed to protect the integrity of the sacred. The forms of religious culture and practice are designed to connect the world of the sacred with the world of the profane while ensuring, through a whole array of cultural insulations and boundaries, that the sacred is not devalued by this connection.

This concept of the sacred and of its associated rituals and modes of realisation are manifested in Roman Catholic religious culture in particular ways. The centrality of the Mass as a dramatic realisation of the sacred in the mundane world is that which is most distinctive of the Catholic Christian tradition. Durkheim, who viewed Catholic Christianity from his own location within Judaic culture, observed that Catholicism was:

> inconceivable without the ever-present idea of Christ and his ever-practised cult; for it is by the ever-living Christ, sacrificed each day, that the community of believers continues to communicate with the supreme source of the spiritual life.
>
> (p. 33)

The institutional Roman Catholic Church has for centuries been the repository of 'the sacred mysteries' of Christianity, of its ritual modes and of its regulatory structures, of relations with other faiths and with non-faith and of its whole relationship with the profane world. While the history of Roman Catholicism provides many examples of the sharp separation between the sacred and the profane noted by Durkheim (the enclosed religious life of monasteries and convents being just one illustration), Catholic Christianity has always been characterised by two contrasting forms of relation to the external world. On the one hand there has been the notion that 'retreat from the world' may be necessary if the fullness of spiritual integrity and wisdom is to be obtained. On the other hand, there has been the imperative, from Christ Himself, to 'go out and convert all nations'. The history of Catholic practice thus illustrates forms of cultural retreatism (for the perfection and protection of the sacred) existing at one and the same time with forms of cultural imperialism (for disseminating the knowledge of the sacred to a wider world). In the formal discourse of the Church what sociologists might style 'cultural imperialism' is perceived and expressed in a discourse of 'mission'. From a Catholic perspective, the Church has a sacred mission to take the message of Christ to the ends of the earth. The dialectic of 'retreat' and 'mission' in Catholic religious culture generates some internal tensions and contradictions which have to be worked out in different historical periods, social and cultural settings and within the social institutions of the Church. The Catholic school, as one of the most significant social institutions of the Church, has been caught up in tensions between 'retreat' and 'mission' both in its historical circumstances and in its present role in modern society.

## The Catholic school: retreat and mission

The dialectic of retreat and mission has shaped and patterned Catholic schooling in England and the USA in particular ways, although the discourse and the concepts have themselves developed across different historical periods. It is a commonplace of Catholic educational history that Catholic schools in England, the USA and Australia were, in their origins, constructed and constituted as citadels and fortresses for the preservation of the faith in a hostile external environment characterised by a dominant Protestant order, continuing anti-Catholic prejudice and the growing influence of secularisation. Whereas various schemes were proposed for the integration of Catholic children and youth into state and publicly provided educational systems, the Catholic bishops and the Catholic religious orders were clear that the preservation of Catholic religious culture required separate provision. As a policy imperative this can be seen in the declaration of the first synod of the province of Westminster, following the restoration of the Catholic hierarchy in 1850:

> The first necessity ... is a sufficient provision of education adequate to the wants of our poor. It must become universal ... to ... prefer the establishment of good schools to every other work ... We should prefer the erection of a school, so arranged as to serve temporarily for a chapel, to that of a church without one.[11]

The Catholic school in England from its origins was clearly intended to be a cultural and faith bastion against the potentially polluting effects of hegemonic Protestantism and secular rationalism. The Catholic school was constituted as another form of church and its duty was to transmit and renew the sacred truths of the Catholic faith and an understanding of its discourse, symbols and ritual practices among its largely poor and working-class adherents. In addition, Catholic schooling faced the particular challenge at this time of providing a socio-cultural and religious provision for a large influx of Irish immigrants whose distinctive Catholic faith had to be 'saved' from potential corruption in Protestant England. Thus it was that Catholic schools were constructed at first in a mode of cultural retreatism, defence and separation from a profane world that was seen to threaten their integrity. The concept of the integrity of the Catholic school, which is a main theme of this present study, surfaced early in the discussions between the Catholic hierarchy and government representatives. Cardinal Manning made it very clear to the British Prime Minister in 1870 that:

> the integrity of our schools as to (i) Doctrine (ii) religious management and the responsibility of the Bishops in these respects, cannot be touched without opening a multitude of contentions and vexations.[12]

Given these concerns to preserve the integrity of Catholic religious and educational culture it is not surprising that the dominant model of the Catholic school became that of 'retreat from the world'. As McLaughlin *et al.* (1996) remark:

> The bishops were single-minded in their attempt to maintain a religious subculture against perceived threats of an increasingly secular society and what they saw as an emerging secular state school

> system. As a result the Church carried out its educational role in relative isolation from the wider state maintained education system.
>
> (pp. 4–5)

A similar imperative shaped the formation of Catholic schools in the USA as McLaughlin *et al.* (1996) point out:

> Bishop Bernard McQuaid of Rochester typifies the attitude that won out. He saw schools as protective walls. In order 'to protect children from the "wolves of the world" who were destroying countless numbers of the unguarded ones' he committed the Church to building those walls and he added, 'if the walls are not high enough, they must be raised; if they are not strong enough, they must be strengthened'.
>
> (p. 9)

Bishop McQuaid's statement provides a dramatic exemplification of the policy imperatives for the first stages of Catholic schooling in England and in the USA. To escape the depredations of the 'wolves of the world', Catholic children and youth needed to be safe in the cultural retreat of the Catholic school, with strong cultural insulations from the external, profane world. While therefore the dominant characteristic of early Catholic schooling was a form of cultural retreatism and defence, this did co-exist with a conception of educational mission. However, the mission of this period (i.e. the nineteenth and early twentieth centuries) may be described as one of *internal mission*.

The internal mission of Catholic schooling in England was primarily to the industrial working class in the major conurbations of London, Liverpool, Lancashire, Birmingham, Manchester, Newcastle and the North-East, a considerable proportion of whom were of Irish origin.[13] It is symbolic of this distinctive educational mission to the poor that one of the key agencies of the Catholic Church in matters of educational policy and provision in the period 1847 to 1906 was the Catholic Poor School Committee, the forerunner of the contemporary Catholic Education Service. Before the deliberations of the Second Vatican Council (1962–5) gave particular emphasis to the notion of 'a preferential option for the poor' as a defining characteristic of Catholic social and educational activity, a very clear option for the poor already existed in Catholic schooling provision in England. This was a necessary option for the poor (rather than a preferential one) and arose from the demographic fact that the Catholic community in England was largely poor, working class and immigrant Irish. The crucial internal mission of

Catholic schooling in England in the nineteenth and early twentieth centuries was to provide religious, personal and educational formation for the children of the Catholic poor in elementary schools of reasonable quality. Cardinal Manning[14] was a noted champion of working-class causes in the latter part of the nineteenth century. As Roberts (1996) notes:

> The Catholics, under the leadership of Cardinal Manning, provided a vast range of social institutions to help the poor, destitute and handicapped in human society.
>
> (p. 128)

A key social institution was the Catholic elementary school and the mission for the Cardinal and the bishops was to attempt to provide a place in a Catholic school for every Catholic child. This *mission of universal access* was regarded by the Catholic hierarchy as not only a sacred duty but also a prudential one. Failure to make such provision could lead to Catholic parents sending their children to locally provided Board schools which gave a technically secular education but were viewed by the bishops as Protestant in ethos. The mission of Catholic elementary schooling was, among other things, to save the Catholic poor from the potential corruptions of secularism and of Protestantism.

While the overwhelming and dominant educational mission of the Catholic Church in England was the provision of universal and adequate elementary education for its working-class adherents, some thought had to be given to the education of other Catholic social classes. Beales (1950, p. 367) has pointed out that whereas the 'mission of universal access' was the preoccupation of the Catholic bishops, what may be called the 'mission of leadership' was largely the work of the religious orders.[15] Catholic independent schools and Catholic grammar schools were established in the nineteenth and early twentieth centuries to provide an education for leadership for the sons and daughters of the relatively small Catholic upper and middle classes. Catholic grammar schools which offered free secondary education after 1944 to Catholic boys and girls who demonstrated 'scholarship' merit and talent were to become an important channel for upward social mobility in the Catholic community. This educational mission of leadership formation resulted in the creation of a more substantial Catholic middle class which was to have a significant influence in public and professional life, in the life of the Church and in the future development of the Catholic educational mission.[16]

## The Catholic school and secularisation

In Durkheim's (1971) analysis, profane culture has the potential to pollute and devalue sacred culture but its potential to do this is always constrained. It is constrained by the fact that in Durkheim's study, sacred culture is in an acknowledged position of hierarchical superiority to that of profane culture. That which is profane is subservient to and contained within the jurisdiction of the rules and the principles of the sacred. The integrity of the sacred is also preserved by the existence of strong cultural insulations from the world of the profane. While these conditions remain, sacred culture is not fundamentally threatened by the existence of profane culture.

However, the development of secularisation in the modern world from the Enlightenment to the present day presents the agencies of sacred culture with a more powerful and sharper challenge. Secularisation represents the denial of the validity of the sacred and of its associated culture and its replacement by logical, rational, empirical and scientific intellectual cultures in which the notion of the transcendent has no place. Secularisation involves a significant change in the cultural power relations of any society. Berger, in his influential study *The Social Reality of Religion* (1973), expresses it in this way:

> By secularization we mean the process by which sectors of society and culture are removed from the domination of religious institutions and symbols … Secularization manifests itself in the evacuation by the Christian churches of areas previously under their control and influence.
>
> (p. 113)

While secularisation changes intellectual culture and power relations, it also operates to affect the world view of many individuals so that religious concepts, religious discourse and religious sensitivities are simply irrelevant to the everyday business of life. This is what Berger (1973) refers to as 'a secularisation of consciousness':

> Put simply this means that the modern West has produced an increasing number of individuals who look upon the world and their own lives without the benefit of religious interpretations.
>
> (p. 113)

Protestantism, in Berger's perspective, has left itself open to the depredations of secularisation because it has historically involved itself in a process of reducing the scope and the symbolism of the sacred in its religious practice. Catholicism, on the other hand, is for Berger a stronger adversary of secularisation because of the internal richness of its sacred culture:

> The Catholic lives in a world in which the sacred is mediated to him through a variety of channels … the sacraments of the church, the intercession of the saints, the recurring eruption of the 'supernatural' in miracles … a vast continuity of being between the seen and the unseen.
>
> (p. 117)

Berger is actually making a large assumption here that most Catholics are in fact 'living' in the richly symbolic world of the sacred which he describes. While at a theological and historical level the notion of 'a vast continuity of being between the seen and the unseen' is distinctive of Catholic religious culture, the extent to which most Catholics are immersed in that culture, whether in the Church or in the school, is more problematic in contemporary settings.

There is debate about the wider cultural and intellectual significance of the process of secularisation in modern society. For some, it represents the liberation of humanity from the myths and obscurantism of religious domination; in short, a true form of human enlightenment in which reason comes to occupy the place formerly assigned to God. For others, secularisation represents a crucial loss of the sense of transcendence in human existence and with it the sense of ultimate meaning and purpose for humanity. The domination of 'reason' from this perspective represents the arrival of a potentially calculative, bloodless and inhumane cultural form.

White (1995) in *Education and Personal Well-Being in a Secular Universe* celebrates the arrival of secularisation and of the growth in intellectual and personal maturity which, from his perspective, it represents. For White:

> The replacement of a Christian by a secular utilitarian ethic by the end of the eighteenth century meant abandoning all notions of other-worldly felicity.
>
> (pp. 4–5)

In this major cultural and intellectual transformation, the realisation of personal autonomy as independence from the idea of God, from tradition and social custom and from significant others became a new form of personal maturity, allowing new forms of self-determination:

> Collectively, we are not given ethical direction by forces outside ourselves, whether these are natural or transcendental; we have worked this out over millennia from our own resources.
>
> (pp. 8–9)

Recognising the need for new sources of personal well-being (in the absence of other-worldly felicity) and for an awareness of a secular cosmic framework (in the absence of a divine framework), White argues that schools could find in aesthetic education[17], understood in its widest sense, a powerful alternative to religious education and that philosophy of education could have a key role 'in illuminating the place of a non-religious … Cosmic framework in the education of our children' (pp. 18–19).

If secular humanist philosophers such as White are concerned to provide a viable and meaningful framework for secular education, others, such as Hirst (1974, 1976, 1994) have argued that the whole idea of a Christian education (or of any faith-based education) is not defensible in the modern world. Hirst's argument is that with an Enlightenment emphasis upon the primacy of rationality, logic, empirical evidence and manifest truth criteria, the search for knowledge and understanding, which is education, cannot be based upon the unverifiable propositions of the Christian faith or of any faith. The autonomy of education, as with the autonomy of the person, cannot be constrained by the prior formulations, dogma and catechism of religious belief. The educational enterprise must be entirely free of the limiting effect of ideological commitment whether that commitment is religious or political in nature. Hirst's prime target is, however, religious ideology[18] in education:

> Just as intelligent Christians have come to recognise that justifiable scientific claims are autonomous and do not, and logically cannot, rest on religious beliefs, so also, it seems to me, justifiable educational principles are autonomous. That is to say, that any attempt to justify educational principles by an appeal to religious claims is invalid.
>
> (1976, pp. 155–7)

What this argument fails to recognise is that there has not been, and in human society, cannot be, a school or an educational experience which is entirely autonomous, objective, neutral and ideologically free. Schools in Europe were first formed in the ideology (or faith) of Catholic Christianity, whereas the vast majority of them are now located in the ideology (or faith) of secular humanism. Schools are not scientific laboratories. They are, crucially, person-forming, citizen-forming and society-forming social institutions, and as such they always have been, and they are likely always to be, influenced by external ideologies of various types – religious, secular, humanist, political, atheist. If therefore the historically and politically formed enterprise of schooling (as opposed to the abstract and theoretical notion of education) will always be located within a given ideological and cultural framework, then other means have to be found to protect the integrity and relative autonomy of intellectual and educational processes.[19] Secular schools as opposed to religious schools are not ideologically free zones. Secularism has its own ideological assumptions about the human person, the ideal society, the ideal system of schooling and the meaning of human existence. While these assumptions may not be formally codified into a curriculum subject designated 'secular education' as an alternative to 'religious education', they characteristically permeate the ethos and culture of state-provided secular schools and form a crucial part of the 'hidden curriculum'.[20]

Writers and researchers such as McLaughlin (1990, 1992, 1996) and Bryk *et al.* (1993) have argued that contemporary Roman Catholic schooling (as opposed to pre-Vatican II forms of schooling) provides a viable and defensible mode of liberal education in a secular age, although one marked by tensions and dilemmas. Bryk *et al.* (1993) conclude their detailed empirical study of Catholic schooling in the USA with these observations:

> Catholic educators must struggle to discern the valuable contributions of this larger, secular culture, while maintaining fidelity to the religious ideals that have vitalized Catholic schools since Vatican II. Such *openness with roots* [my emphasis] inevitably creates organisational tensions and dilemmas.
>
> (pp. 334–5)

Bryk *et al.* recognise that this new Vatican II principle of 'openness with roots' in Catholic schooling faces an internal reaction and backlash from those Catholics who fear the effects of openness and who wish to return to the certainty and security of pre-Vatican II theological, liturgical and educational roots. However, the authors of *Catholic Schools and the Common Good* (1993) believe that Catholic schooling as a form of defensible liberal education in a secular culture must continue to develop the Vatican II emphasis upon openness:

> An alternative conception – one that we have stressed here – envisions Catholic schools as a realization of the prophetic Church that critically engages contemporary culture. Anything that even remotely smacks of 'indoctrination in the mind of the Church' can seriously undermine this more public function ... From this perspective, Catholic education represents an invitation to students both to reflect on a systematic body of thought and to immerse themselves in a communal life that seeks to live out its basic principles.
>
> (p. 335)

The notion that a secular form of liberal education is the only defensible educational experience which can be offered in modern society has been criticised from a philosophical perspective by McLaughlin. For him, it is clearly a right of parents in a democratic and pluralist society to shape the early education of their children according to the beliefs, values, principles and ideologies which they regard as important. It is also clearly a democratic right of parents to commit their children to faith-based schooling of a religious nature. However, McLaughlin is also aware of the rights of children and young people as they mature, to come to their own reasoned position on religious and ideological issues, morality and principles for living, i.e. to aspire to relative autonomy. In his view, a modern form of Catholic schooling characterised by 'openness with roots' can be a synthesis of these two legitimate positions:

> Such schooling can be seen to be compatible with liberal, democratic principles, not least by providing a particular substantial starting point for the child's eventual development into autonomous agency and democratic citizenship.
>
> (1996, p. 147)

The positions of both Bryk *et al.* (1993) and McLaughlin (1996) on the possibilities for a Catholic schooling in a secular age which synthesises both 'roots' and 'critical openness' may seem to external observers to be unduly optimistic about changes in educational culture brought about by the new spirit of Vatican II. Pervasive historical myths and images of Catholic schooling, such as the well-known statement attributed to the Jesuits, 'Give me the child until he is seven, and I will give you the man', make many external observers believe that Catholic schooling is, in practice, a strong and effective form of indoctrination.[21] At the level of the institutional Roman Catholic Church, the stance of Pope John Paul II does not seem to be one of encouraging critical openness in the religious and social institutions of the Church. It is a commonplace of Catholic communities in the UK and in the USA to observe that the new spirit of openness inaugurated by Vatican II in the 1960s is no longer in the ascendant in the institutional Church.[22] What are the implications of this for the educational cultures and practices of contemporary Catholic schools? Given the paucity of detailed school-based educational research on Catholic schooling, it is difficult to answer this question.[23] We do not know, in any comprehensive sense, what the effects of post-Vatican II religious and cultural change have been on the internal cultures of Catholic schools. Neither do we know what the consequences for Catholic schools have been as a result of the very different external conditions – religious, socio-economic and ideological – in which they now operate. Part of the intention of this study is to probe some of these important issues.

If the relative underdevelopment of empirical educational research into the nature and effectiveness of Catholic schooling in a secular age is surprising, the relative underdevelopment of a Catholic philosophy of education in a secular age is even more surprising. It might have been expected that, with attacks upon the legitimacy and defensibility of Catholic schooling produced by secular humanist philosophers, a countervailing defence would have been constructed by Catholic philosophers. In fact, this has not happened in any comprehensive sense. One of the reasons for this would seem to be that many Catholic educators in the past (largely priests and members of religious orders) were confident that they had an authoritative exposition and defence of Catholic education in the writings of St Thomas Aquinas.

Writing in 1964, Archbishop Beck commented upon 'the vitality of thought' of the 'Angelic Doctor' and of the continuing relevance of his 'Christianized Aristotelianism' to contemporary Catholic education. In particular, he argued that St Thomas's greatest work, the *Summa Theologica*, could be regarded as 'an educational document of the highest importance' because it involved an exposition of a complete philosophy of the person derived from the fundamental proposition 'God is the first principle of things' (p. 114).

It seems likely that the religious and intellectual pre-eminence of St Thomas Aquinas[24] overshadowed and partly inhibited subsequent attempts to rearticulate and recontextualise a Catholic philosophy of education to face the challenges of secularism.

Reviewing the field in 1995, Carr *et al.*, while acknowledging that 'Important resources for the rational articulation and defence of a distinctively Catholic conception of education are indeed to be found in the philosophy of St Thomas' (p. 176), called for new efforts to produce a contemporary Catholic philosophy of education. Such an attempt would involve drawing upon the wisdom of St Thomas but also integrating this with the work of neo-Thomists such as Maritain (1961, 1964) and the work of contemporary Catholic philosophers such as MacIntyre[25] (1981, 1988, 1990) and Taylor[26] (1989). In the absence of a fully articulated Catholic philosophy of education for modern culture, Catholic educators have in practice used as a resource the formal publications and declarations on Catholic education of the institutional Church. These publications, mediated by the Sacred Congregation for Catholic Education, later renamed the Vatican Congregation, have provided the main source of theological, philosophical and educational guidance for lay Catholic educators. In so far as contemporary Catholic schooling, in England at any rate, can lay claim to an articulated theoretical framework, it has been derived from these 'documents for guidance' rather than from the developed insights of formal scholarship.

## The Roman Catholic Church and the rationale for Catholic schooling

This analysis will concentrate upon the modern forms in which the mission of the Catholic school has been articulated and it will attempt to draw out the key constructs and the commended principles for the Catholic educational mission in the modern world. In what is generally regarded as the foundation document of a Vatican II conception of the Catholic school, the *Declaration on Christian Education* (Gravissimum Educationis)[27] 1965, a more open and liberal mode of Catholic schooling is announced:

> The Church's role is especially evident in Catholic schools. These are no less zealous than other schools in the promotion of culture and in the human formation of young people. It is, however, the special function of the Catholic school to develop in the school community an atmosphere animated by a spirit of liberty and charity based on the Gospel. It enables young people, while developing their own personality, to grow at the same time in that new life which has been given them in baptism … Accordingly, since

> the Catholic school can be of such service in developing the mission of the People of God and in promoting dialogue between the Church and the community at large to the advantage of both, it is still of vital importance.
>
> (Flannery 1998, pp. 732–3)

This new discourse of the Catholic school can be contrasted with the cultural characteristics of the Catholic citadel school of the pre-Vatican II era. While an emphasis upon the spirit of charity would be common to both, radical developments are apparent in references to a spirit of liberty, development of the personality and a dialogue with the wider world. The declaration, *Gravissimum Educationis* (1965), was therefore calling for a new mode of Catholic schooling to meet the challenges of a modern and secular culture and of the needs and expectations of young people growing to maturity in such a culture. A great deal was being asked of Catholic educators in terms of the transformation of an educational ethos. Many of those who received this new agenda had themselves been schooled and socialised in Catholic educational institutions which were authoritarian, enclosed and repressive of individual personality.[28] The declaration emphasised that:

> Teachers must remember that it depends chiefly on them whether the Catholic school achieves its purpose.
>
> (Flannery 1998, p. 733)

What was not fully recognised was that considerable programmes of educational and professional reorientation of Catholic educators would be required if new forms of Catholic liberal education were to be realised in practice rather than simply in a new Vatican II discourse of schooling.

While *Gravissimum Educationis* articulated a principle of openness for Catholic schooling, it, at the same time, articulated a principle of special concern for certain groups in the community:

> The sacred Synod earnestly exhorts the pastors of the Church and all the faithful to spare no sacrifice in helping Catholic schools to become increasingly effective, especially in caring for the poor, for those who are without the help and affection of family and those who do not have the Faith.
>
> (Flannery 1998, pp. 734–5)

The emphasis upon the educational mission to the poor was a powerful rearticulation of a traditional concern of Catholic schooling. The emphasis upon those in family difficulties was a recognition of a growing problem in modern society but in terms of the traditional expectations of Catholic schooling, the reference to 'those who do not have the Faith' was most dramatic in its implications. It could be taken to mean that the Church recognised a growing loss of believers within its own communities, as a consequence of secularisation and therefore a need for a renewed internal mission, or it could be taken to mean that Catholic schooling should emphasise its external mission, in an evangelical and ecumenical sense, to those of other faiths and of no faith. This latter interpretation, if implemented, would constitute a radical extension of the concept of the Catholic school in those societies where Catholic schools were traditionally for Catholics only.[29]

Three subsequent documents from the institutional Church developed and supplemented the educational and religious principles commended in *Gravissimum Educationis. The Catholic School* (Sacred Congregation for Catholic Education 1977) reasserted the role of education as part of the saving mission of the Church to 'reveal to all ages the transcendent goal which alone gives life its full meaning' (p. 13). The influence of Catholic social teaching is particularly evident in this document where the principle of special concern for the deprived in education is again emphasised:

> First and foremost the Church offers its educational service to the poor.
>
> (p. 44)

And a more general principle of service for the community and for the common good is highlighted:

> Knowledge is not to be considered as a means of material prosperity and success, but as a call to serve and to be responsible for others ... A policy of working for the common good[30] is undertaken seriously as working for the building up of the kingdom of God.
>
> (pp. 43–6)

In 1982, recognising the continual decline in the number of priests and members of religious orders working in Catholic schools, the Sacred

Congregation for Catholic Education issued *Lay Catholics in Schools: Witnesses to Faith.* This document provided a theorisation of the vocation of the lay Catholic educator and of the concept of an educational professional as a form of vocation. The 1982 document, *Lay Catholics*, is, in essence, a strong reassertion of the principle of vocational calling in education. As the Church observed the decline in the number of school leaders and teachers with a formal religious vocation to the service of Catholic education, it was clearly necessary, against the secularised and utilitarian spirit of the age, to reassert the conception of a lay vocation to teach and to be a member of the teaching profession.

The discourse constructs an ideal model of the lay Catholic educator which is daunting in its expectations:

> The Catholic educator must be a source of spiritual inspiration … The Lay Catholic educator is a person who exercises a specific mission within the Church by living the faith, a secular vocation in the communitarian structure of the school: with the best possible professional qualifications, with an apostolic intention inspired by faith, for the integral formation of the human person, in a communication of culture, in an exercise of that pedagogy which will give emphasis to direct and personal contact with students.
>
> (p. 14)

Although the document later admits that 'realism combined with hope' has to be a feature of modern Catholic schooling, there is a sense in which the discourse of idealism for the lay Catholic educator overpowers a sense of realism. It will be noted, later in this work, that unduly high expectations for the role of Catholic school leaders and teachers may have a counter-productive effect on actual recruitment and succession patterns.

Concern about the impact of secularisation in the wider world and within Catholic communities prompted the publication *The Religious Dimension of Education in a Catholic School* (Vatican Congregation for Catholic Education 1988). For the 1988 document, secularisation has in practice produced a world devoid of ultimate meaning and purpose, with disastrous consequences in particular for modern youth:

> Many young people find themselves in a condition of radical instability … They live in a one-dimensional universe in which the only criterion is practical utility and the only value is economic and technological progress … Not a few young people, unable to find any meaning in life or trying to find an escape from loneliness, turn

> to alcohol, drugs, the erotic, the exotic etc. Christian education is faced with the huge challenge of helping these young people discover something of value in their lives.
>
> (pp. 8–10)

In response to this challenge of meaninglessness in modern society, the Vatican Congregation for Catholic Education called upon all Catholic schools to review the vitality of the religious ethos of the school, both in relation to the quality of formal religious education programmes and the religious education provided by the whole culture and life of the school. It also suggested the need for more 'study, research and experimentation' (p. 87) to be undertaken on the effectiveness of the religious culture of Catholic schools.[31]

For the 1988 document, the challenge for the Catholic school is not only to attempt to give meaning and purpose to the lives of contemporary youth but also to take a stance, with the Church, in a larger struggle for the soul of the world:

> The Lord calls us to an endless struggle to resist the forces of evil … The call to be a Christian involves a call to help liberate the human family from its radical slavery to sin and therefore from the effects of sin in the cultural, economic, social and political orders.
>
> (pp. 68–9)

This principle of endless struggle against evil and sin in their various manifestations was subsequently given dramatic amplification by Pope John Paul II in 1994:

> Against the spirit of the world, the Church takes up each day a struggle that is none other than the struggle for the world's soul. If in fact, on the one hand, the Gospel and evangelisation are present in this world, on the other there is also present a powerful anti-evangelisation which is well organised and has the means to vigorously oppose the Gospel and evangelisation. The struggle for the soul of the contemporary world is at its height where the spirit of the world seems strongest.
>
> (p. 112)[32]

The Vatican Congregation for Catholic Education was, in its 1988 declaration, reminding Catholic schools that the effectiveness and vitality of their religious cultures and the outcomes of this for Catholic youth were a crucial part of the struggle for the soul of the contemporary world.

A considerable challenge is presented here for Catholic educators. It is widely accepted in educational studies and in teacher education programmes that being in rapport with contemporary culture and the interests of modern youth is regarded as an important constituent of pedagogic effectiveness. In other words, some engagement with the spirit of the modern world seems to be a necessary part of a modern Catholic education, while at the same time the call to be 'against the spirit of the world' appears to be in contradiction to that aim. What this situation does in practice is to place a considerable responsibility for discernment[33] and professional judgement upon Catholic teachers and school leaders. They have to make crucial decisions about what aspects of the spirit of the world they can legitimately accommodate to and what aspects they must be clearly against. The Church gives its guidance on such matters as secularism, atheism, capitalism and communism, consumerism and hedonism, the structures of sin, personal and sexual morality and the responsibilities of citizenship and of family life. However, in each individual school situation the school leaders, teachers and parents have to interpret and implement this hierarchical guidance. In practice, the culture of Catholic schools is not a simple reflection of, or in one-to-one correspondence with, the authoritative teaching and declarations of the Roman Catholic Church. Some examples of this lack of correspondence will be noted later in this study.

In the Congregation for Catholic Education's most recent declaration on Catholic education, *The Catholic School on the Threshold of the Third Millennium* (1998), an earlier principle of 'realism combined with hope' can be discerned. While celebrating the many achievements of Catholic education across the world there is a realistic assessment of the problems which Catholic educators face in many societies and in particular locations:

> The school is undoubtedly a sensitive meeting-point for the problems which besiege this restless end of the millennium. The Catholic school is thus confronted with children and young people who experience the difficulties of the present time. Pupils who shun effort, are incapable of self-sacrifice and perseverance and who lack authentic models to guide them often even in their own families. In an increasing number of instances they are not only indifferent and non-practising but also totally lacking in religious or moral formation. To this, we must add – on the part of numerous pupils and families – a profound apathy where ethical and religious formation is concerned, to the extent that what is in fact required

> of the Catholic school is a certificate of studies or, at the most, quality instruction and training for employment.
>
> (pp. 37–8)

In commenting on the growth in indifference and apathy towards religious and spiritual formation alongside a growing emphasis upon the technical and utilitarian outcomes of education[34], the 1998 declaration expressed, in stark terms, some central contemporary challenges to the distinctive mission of the Catholic school. How these challenges are being responded to in various urban locations in England will be examined in later chapters.

This chapter has attempted to locate the Catholic school in relation to conceptions of the sacred, the profane and the secular, in what might be called its primary theoretical context.[35] Some examination has also been made of historical and cultural developments in conceptions of the Catholic school and of its educational rationale and of the documents and discourse of the institutional Catholic Church which have projected the Church's aspirations for schooling in the period 1965–98.

In the next chapter, Catholic education as a social and cultural field will be analysed using theoretical insights derived from the work of two leading theorists of culture and education, Pierre Bourdieu and Basil Bernstein.

# 2 The field of Catholic education

## Perspectives from Bourdieu and Bernstein

### Sociology and Catholic culture

In the 1998 pronouncement of the Vatican Congregation for Catholic Education the following statement occurs:

> The Catholic school is not a merely sociological category, it has a theological foundation as well.
>
> (p. 46)

The statement itself is a rearticulation of an order of priorities within the Catholic Church when reviewing its educational institutions. Primacy is given to the theological foundations of such institutions, to their 'fundamental reason for existing' and to their sacred mission in the world. It is in relation to these sacred purposes that Catholic education can also be described as 'a merely sociological category', at work in the profane world. 'Merely sociological' is part of the formal discourse of the Catholic Church and encoded in this discourse is not only a relatively low evaluation of sociological concepts and research but also a guarded and cautious attitude to the sociological enterprise in general. That this should be so is hardly surprising. For the Catholic Church, theological matters and the culture of the sacred must always take precedence over profane studies of all types. However, in the case of the social sciences, as with the natural sciences, challenges to sacred truths and to hierarchical authority may result from the outcomes of empirical analysis and enquiry. The outcomes of such enquiry are unpredictable and may have potentially disturbing consequences for the faithful. For this reason, relations between the institutional Church and the practice of sociology have been marked by cultural distance, cultural insulation and cultural suspicion.

Wexler (1997), in a provocative discussion of relations between social theory, education and religion, has suggested a reason for such cultural distancing. Taking the classic argument of Weber (1930) expressed in *The Protestant Ethic and the Spirit of Capitalism*, of the affinities between these two forms, Wexler extends the argument to produce, in effect, a thesis of the Protestant ethic and the spirit of sociology:

> sociology, as a modern project, is a secularization ... If the mainstream of social theory is a secularization of religious interests ... the main tendency in that secularization was a translation or recontextualization of ascetic Protestantism into secular sociology.
>
> (p. 9)

In so far as Wexler's argument is accepted, it provides good reasons why the Catholic Church should have kept a strong cultural insulation between its own culture and that of secular sociology.

The effect of this separation has been, in practice, that the sociological study of Catholic education has been relatively undeveloped and marginalised. While there have been significant empirical sociological research texts produced, especially in the USA, by writers such as Greeley (1982), Coleman and Hoffer (1987), Lesko (1988) and Bryk *et al.* (1993), much less work has been undertaken on the social field of Catholic education in general, i.e. on the attempt to apply particular aspects of social theory to a deeper understanding of the field of Catholic education. In the following pages some attempt has been made to make a contribution to this neglected field using concepts and insights derived from two major contemporary social theorists, Pierre Bourdieu and Basil Bernstein.

## Perspectives from Pierre Bourdieu: constituting Catholic education as a 'field'

In commending Pierre Bourdieu's prolific writings as an important intellectual resource for those working in education, Harker (1990) has argued that:

> there are two tasks in front of educationalists who would seek to use Bourdieu theoretically ... First, it is necessary to catch up with Bourdieu theoretically, by seeing his work as a method of enquiry, rather than a completed theoretical edifice; and second, to work out the method in relation to their own social space and the particular 'field' of education within it.
>
> (p. 99)

This is precisely the intention here, i.e. to take some of the intellectual tools provided by Bourdieu in concepts such as 'field', 'habitus', 'symbolic power' and to apply these to a more theorised understanding of Catholic education.[1]

Bourdieu's concept of field demarcates a social and cultural space as a focus for enquiry and in his own research and writing he has examined the field of cultural production, the field of schooling, the field of higher education and the scientific field, among many others. For Bourdieu, a field is a social and cultural space characterised by a particular activity which, while it may enjoy partial autonomy from other fields, is internally marked by struggles and conflicts over what is to be transformed within it and what is to be conserved. While a field may appear to have democratic consensus on the one hand or the total domination of one authority on the other, there is always, from this perspective, a relation of forces, sites of resistance as well as of domination and consensus. In his detailed examination of the concept, Swartz (1997, p. 123) points out that 'fields are arenas of struggle for legitimation' and for the exercise of symbolic power. In addition to this, Bourdieu emphasises that the influence of the class structure of societies is always apparent in any given field but that such influence is mediated through the particular culture and structure of a field. In what senses can these ideas be applied to the Catholic Church and to the 'field' of Catholic education?

There have always been struggles for legitimation and for symbolic power within the institutional Church and a rich historical record exists which documents such conflicts between popes and anti-popes, orthodoxy and heresy, reaction and reform, bureaucracy and charisma, hierarchy and laity, magisterium and collegium.[2] Catholic history reveals an internal field of struggle of remarkable complexity and it is significant that Bourdieu explains that the origin of the concept of 'field' emerged from his reading of the history and sociology of religion (Swartz 1997, p. 118). Catholic culture is historically replete with examples of the whole range of analytical concepts which Bourdieu has developed in his social theory, i.e. 'field of forces', 'habitus', 'cultural capital', 'symbolic power', 'symbolic violence', etc. While their applications are clear in the documented historical record of the Catholic church, what might be their relevance for a deeper understanding of Catholic education? The formal discourse of Catholic education has always stressed vocation, idealism, consensus, service and unity and it has either avoided or repressed the recognition of internal struggles and conflicts as unedifying and as potentially disturbing to the faithful. This profound inhibition of the articulation of internal troubles, conflicts and struggles (which exist for a number of reasons) has had various consequences. One of these has been the projection of an image of Catholic education that is too consensual and too idealised. The value of applying Bourdieu's concept of 'a field of forces' to Catholic education is that it compels Catholic educators to face the deeper internal struggles which actually exist below the surface structure of consensual unity. While this may be an uncomfortable exercise, part of the Catholic tradition involves a requirement to face personal and institutional failures as a necessary prelude to 'amendment of life'.

When Bourdieu's theoretical schema is applied to Catholic education as a field, it reveals at least two arenas of struggle, which may be called *legitimation struggles* and *control struggles*. It also provokes questions about the ways in which the wider power relations of society, relating to class, race and ethnicity and gender, are, in practice, mediated within the field of Catholic education.

## Legitimation struggles and Catholic education

External attacks on the legitimacy of Catholic education raised by secular humanist philosophers such as Hirst (1976, 1994) can be answered in 'Catholic' terms (see Chapter 1) but internal attacks raised by Catholic intellectuals and educators have represented, and where they still exist, do represent, a more serious challenge to the legitimacy of the whole enterprise. These are the arguments raised by those who from an institutional Church perspective are educational heretics, questioning the fundamental rationale and orthodoxies of Catholic schooling. Such criticisms were particularly salient following the ferment of ideas stimulated by the Vatican II Council although they were in practice confined to a small and radical intellectual elite, some of whom had the interesting and apparently contradictory status of Catholic Marxists. Prominent among these was Terry Eagleton who in an article entitled 'Catholic Education and Commitment' published in 1967 made sharp and wide-ranging attacks upon the legitimacy of Catholic education. The essence of Eagleton's critique was that holding on to a separate system of Catholic schooling was to remain within a stance of theological, social and educational exclusivity when what the new spirit of Vatican II required was a stance of greater inclusivity. Therefore he claimed that Catholic education as it was currently constituted was 'an inauthentic expression of the sacramental Christian community' and that the only possible course of action was to abolish it (p. 8). With abolition would come a larger and more authentic sense of mission:

> I want to emphasise that it seems to me that the burden of justification, after Vatican II, lies not with those who want to dissolve the Catholic educational system, but with those who want to maintain it. I think its supporters have to demonstrate how the maintenance of a separate and enclosed system of this kind can be reconciled with the radically worldly theology which we now assent to, at least intellectually, as characterising the Church's mission. Either we are serious about world engagement or we aren't: what we can't do, I think, is to compromise. A compromise solution, half in and half out of the world, seems to me very much the emphasis of much of our current thinking.
>
> (p. 10)

Radical intellectual Catholics such as Terry Eagleton, Bernard Tucker, Michael Hennessy and others became an oppositional force within the field of Catholic education especially in the years immediately following the Vatican II Council, and their views were amplified and disseminated in a critical journal entitled *Slant* which was published in the years between 1965 and 1970. The essence of their argument was that the new spirit of openness in the Church required Catholics to come out of the enclosed and defensive structures of Catholic educational institutions and act as a 'leaven' in the secular world. In practice this meant integrating Catholic youth, Catholic teachers, Catholic priests and members of religious orders within the culture and the structures of state schooling. The integration of Catholics within state-provided systems of education would, it was claimed, have many benefits. It would help to break down religious, social and cultural bigotry and divisiveness, it would widen the educational and intellectual horizons of both Catholics and non-Catholics and it would constitute a modern form of 'witness' in an increasingly secular world. The integration argument appeared to be strengthened by research findings from the USA which suggested that from a value-added faith perspective, Catholic schools simply enhanced the Catholicity of youth from strong faith homes and had insignificant effects on those from lapsed or nominal faith homes.[3] If this was the case, then the internal critics could argue that Catholic schools were operating on a principle articulated in St Matthew's Gospel (25: 29), 'unto him that hath, it shall be given'. While such a principle appeared to have a biblical mandate, it also seemed to be in sharp contradiction to a Vatican II emphasis of reaching out to those who were far from the faith.

Arthur (1995, p. 100) points out that in the face of these challenges to the legitimacy of the field of Catholic education, the strategy of the institutional Church in England followed a classic form of hierarchical authority, i.e. ignoring the existence of critics and of their arguments:

> the bishops did not feel the need to make any official response to them ... The bishops continued to expand the school system despite these criticisms and the CEC Reports and Handbooks during the 1960s never referred to any opposition to the policy of the bishops.

The legitimation struggle was in practice confined to a relatively small group of intellectual Catholics who wanted to generate an internal debate and dialogue about the justification for a separated system of Catholic schooling, given a Vatican II emphasis upon a greater openness to the external world. Neither the hierarchy nor the Catholic community in general were ready for such a debate. For the hierarchy, evidence of internal dissent about the value of Catholic education was too dangerous a phenomenon to be amplified or even recognised by serious debate. For the majority of the laity, too much effort, finance and faith had been invested in the building up of a Catholic system of schooling across a hundred years to have its credentials seriously questioned by a 1960s' spirit of reform. The habitus of Catholic education, understood to be its deep-structured cultural dispositions, was not to be easily shaken. Bourdieu (1990, pp. 60–1) notes that habitus can generate 'avoidance strategies' to 'protect itself from crises and critical challenges' by 'rejecting information capable of calling into question its accumulated information'. This response was apparent in the Catholic educational community in the UK in the 1960s and 1970s when faced with internal challenges to the legitimacy of Catholic schooling. Such avoidance strategies had two consequences. In the first place, an alienated sector of the educated Catholic middle class broke their loyalty ties to the Catholic system and began to send their children to multi-faith state comprehensive schools. In the second place, fundamental questions about the contemporary legitimation of Catholic schools in changed social, cultural and educational circumstances were not seriously addressed. The Catholic system continued to run in practice on its nineteenth-century justifications. A contemporary question of some significance is whether or not the habitus of Catholic education has now changed sufficiently to allow more open debate and dialogue about the nature of Catholic schooling and of its justifications. As later chapters will show, the Catholic headteachers involved in this study were clearly ready to be informed and thoughtful participants in any such debate.

## Symbolic power, control struggles and Catholic education

Bourdieu's concept of symbolic power was partly derived from Weber's sociology of religious leadership (Swartz 1997, p. 93) and it has a particular value in illuminating the internal control struggles which have characterised Catholic education at different historical periods. For Bourdieu, symbolic power is constituted by culturally significant attributes such as prestige, status and authority and it functions in practice as a powerful means of communication and of potential domination. Symbolic power is 'a way of talking about the legitimation of power relations through symbolic forms'[4]

The hierarchy of the Catholic Church represents an agency of considerable symbolic power and the Catholic bishops have used this power to develop, shape and control Catholic education in specific ways. Catholic bishops have spoken and acted with a powerful authority, which for Catholics represents a mediated form of the symbolic power of the Pope, viewed as the Vicar of Christ on earth. Symbolic power could hardly have a more dramatic and universal manifestation. However, despite this array of awesome authority, episcopal jurisdiction within Catholic schooling has never achieved total hegemonic domination and examples of power and control struggles exist. Once again it has been regarded as unedifying to draw attention to them but both the historical and the contemporary record of Catholic schooling demonstrate an internal politics of struggle and control which modifies any simple story of consensus and unity of purpose. There have been and are different conceptions about what forms of Catholic schooling should be provided, by what agencies and under what modes of governance.

An early example of control struggles can be seen in the relation between the educational planning and priorities of the English Catholic bishops and the relatively independent educational planning of some religious orders, notably the Jesuits. Religious orders with an educational mission had a tendency to make their own decisions about what sort of Catholic schools they would provide and in what locations. This was irksome to the bishops who wanted to concentrate educational resources, in the first instance, on the provision of Catholic elementary schools in urban centres. While this early struggle was resolved in favour of the bishops (by an appeal to Rome), it has remained the case that the religious orders in education have continued to exercise forms of relative autonomy in their educational decision making which have impacted upon wider educational planning.

## Clergy–laity relations in Catholic education

The most fundamental internal control struggles in Catholic schooling have, however, occurred, as might be expected, in clergy–laity relations. Indeed, one of the most enduring of the socio-historical images of Catholic schooling is that of a priest-dominated system especially in the elementary and primary school sectors. As with many enduring images, there is a core of truth in this perception and yet, at the same time, it oversimplifies a complex and changing set of relations.

Arthur (1995) points out that the first initiative for the establishment of Catholic elementary schools came from the aristocratic and lay-dominated Catholic Institute of Great Britain, which campaigned for public funds in support of Catholic schools, comparable with those already available since 1833 for Church of England schools. However, by 1847 the Catholic bishops had asserted their authority in the field, replacing the Catholic Institute with the Catholic Poor School Committee consisting of two laymen and eight clerics. Ecclesiastical authority was thereafter a dominant feature of Catholic schooling in the UK for the greater part of the nineteenth and twentieth centuries. Catholic cardinals such as Manning, Vaughan and Wiseman were not only the agents of great symbolic power in education but also manifest political negotiators in the endless struggles between Church and state over funding, inspections, governance and the curriculum of Catholic schools in the first phases of development. At a later period, Cardinals Hinsley, Heenan and Hume continued this significant conjunction of symbolic power and 'hands-on' political negotiation for what they defined to be the interests of Catholic education.

In what might be described as the *historical praxis of symbolic power* cardinals were the influential agents of Church–state relations, archbishops and bishops exercised diocesan leadership and jurisdiction, while at the parish level, priests had a powerful role in the constitution of Catholic primary and secondary schools, especially where the priest was also the chairman of the school governors.

## Symbolic power, the strong state and parentocracy

Bourdieu stresses that one of the important ideological consequences of symbolic power is that 'the dominated accept as legitimate their own condition of domination' (Swartz 1997, p. 89). This describes very well the general pattern of response by the Catholic laity to clerical leadership in schooling until the late 1980s. The deference shown to such clerical leadership by the great majority of Catholics was the cultural outcome of a long historical tradition of hierarchical relations within the Church, mediated by class relations (where the majority of Catholics were working class) and by the influence of symbolic power. The impact of the latter was registered even by non-Catholic government ministers as late as the 1980s. Kenneth Baker, as Secretary of State for Education in the 1980s, has given, in his memoirs, a dramatic account of his experience of such symbolic power in action:

> I was conscious that I was not dealing merely with a local authority, or merely a trade union, or even the British Cabinet, but with one of the great and enduring institutions of Western civilisation … [Cardinal Hume] conveys a sense of holiness, kindliness and courtesy, and it is not easy to argue with such a saintly man. But within that scarlet and purple apparition was the sinewy force of a prelate concerned with temporal as well as spiritual power … The Cardinal in effect was arguing that all Catholic schools should be excluded from the provisions of the Government's legislation … In the Anglican tradition I argued for the supremacy of Parliament, for at the end of the day, the issue was who should determine the law relating to the education of English children in England … I … found the Cardinal the most formidable of my opponents, since he reflected the settled authority of centuries.
>
> (Baker 1993, pp. 217–18)[5]

Despite Baker's recognition that he was dealing with 'the settled authority of centuries' when discussing the proposed radical legislation in the Education Reform Bill (1988), government policy was largely unaffected by this. The 1980s and the 1990s in the UK were to demonstrate, quite dramatically, the limitations of Catholic symbolic power in education in changed cultural, ideological and political conditions.

In a more utilitarian and secularised context and facing the reform programmes of the administrations of Margaret Thatcher and John Major (1979–97), ecclesiastical authority and historical traditions of consultation and partnership in educational policy counted for little. The institutional Catholic Church had to conform its educational arrangements to policies devised by governments strongly influenced by New Right ideologies of market forces, competition, individualism and consumer choice in schooling. However, control struggles with the state had been a constant feature of Church–state relations in the nineteenth and early twentieth centuries and the symbolic power of the Catholic hierarchy had suffered setbacks on a range of educational issues. Although the educational issues of the 1980s and 1990s were radical and disturbing, they were, in one sense, within a known context of struggle. The Church, as a relatively autonomous institution of symbolic power, was accustomed to varying degrees of tension, struggle and overt conflict with state agencies in education. What it was *not* accustomed to was serious dissent and resistance to its educational policies and leadership from within its own community. The rejection of the symbolic power of the hierarchy by the state was one thing, but its rejection by sectors of the Catholic community was more serious and more threatening. Loyalty and obedience among the laity were historical cultural expectations of long standing (although severely tested and broken in some cases by the effects of Vatican II reforms). One of the great strengths of Catholic educational policy and strategy had been, as Arthur's (1995) research demonstrates, a capacity to unite hierarchy and laity in concerted political and interest-group action on educational issues. This political conjunction had been very effective in advancing the Catholic cause in the past. The 1980s and 1990s saw the breaking of this conjunction in significant ways and the making visible of internal control struggles over education policy within the Catholic community.

Chadwick (1997) and Arthur (1994a, 1995) have examined the nature of internal dissension within the Catholic community over issues of educational policy. Although there was a range of issues on which dissension became apparent, the fundamental principle which was at stake in all of the struggles was the relative influence and control potential of the symbolic power of the Catholic hierarchy *vis-à-vis* a newly empowered laity (especially parents) in the determination of educational policy and practice. Using the authority of canon law, the Catholic bishops wanted to insist during the education reform process of the 1980s and 1990s that they were the guardians of the distinctive mission of Catholic schooling. It followed from this that they would be the articulators of the Catholic position on controversial issues such as the nature of the National Curriculum, the status of religious education within the National Curriculum, admission policies for schools, the preservation of a Catholic ethos within schools, the desirability of grant-maintained schools and issues of governance and control in Catholic schools.[6] This had been the praxis of symbolic power in the past and it had been an effective strategy. However, in the last two decades of the twentieth century, the bishops encountered radically new forms of power and ideology in education which significantly curtailed their influence. As part of the education reform process, Conservative governments had enacted a vast array of statutory powers, producing an unprecedented degree of central state control in education in England and Wales. This was a manifestation of the 'strong state' in education on a scale which Catholic bishops in the past had not encountered. In practice, statute law in education took precedence over canon law in education and the whole context for educational policy negotiations and even 'consultation' had been transformed. Such state powers had been taken to overcome the resistance of oppositional groups to the government's plans for education. These groups included the teaching profession, the local education authorities and educational bureaucracies of all types. From this perspective, the Catholic hierarchy was constituted as an educational bureaucracy with oppositional potential, and not as an honoured partner of the 'dual system' of schooling.

Gamble's (1988) text, *The Free Market and the Strong State*, expresses, in its title, the apparent contradictions of government policy in education at this time. On the one hand, strong state legislative power was being exercised to compel change and to constrain opposition. On the other hand, and under the influence of New Right ideology, the governments of the time were celebrating and empowering parental choice in schooling, the application of market forces to enhance competition among schools and the generation of a 'customer' culture in education, with, as one of its outcomes, the attempted commodification of educational processes and 'products'. In this situation therefore, the Catholic bishops of England and Wales faced not only the imperatives of strong state regulation but also the influence of New Right ideology as manifest in a strongly individualist, consumerist, market-driven and 'parental power' strategy in education.

Brown (1990) has shown that 'the ideology of parentocracy' which rose to dominance in English schooling in the 1980s is a complex phenomenon which can be appropriated to serve various social and political ends. The governments of Margaret Thatcher and John Major used 'parent power' as a mechanism to diversify the school system, to stimulate market-driven competition among schools, to stimulate greater school effectiveness and efficiency and to counter-balance the perceived dominance of professional 'vested interests' in the governance of education. This meant, in policy terms, that if a significant number of Catholic parents decided that grant-maintained status would be advantageous to their children's schooling, they could effect such a change, even against the advice of their bishop. Similarly, greater parental power in the governance of schools meant that such parents could change the Catholic character of the school in various ways and that they could oppose diocesan reorganisation plans designed to restructure the system of Catholic education in a given area.

The rise of the ideology of parentocracy in schooling therefore presented to the Catholic hierarchy two major challenges. In the first place, parents as a group were given precedence in educational decision making over the whole Catholic community of which they were only a part. Secondly, control of the governance of specific Catholic schools could pass from clerical leadership to parental leadership, with radical implications for the Catholic ethos of the school.

## The common good, parents' rights and grant-maintained schools

The strategy of the Catholic bishops when faced by the growing influence of the ideology of parentocracy was to define a Catholic position realised in statements issued by the Catholic Bishops Conference of England and Wales or by the Catholic Education Service.[7] This Catholic position emphasised commitments to community and common good considerations in educational policy as having precedence over individual or even group parental rights and decision making. As Arthur (1994a) has put it:

> the Church's dispute with both government and some of its own members can be located in the differing interpretations of parental rights. The government's stress on parental involvement and choice gives predominance to 'the market' and emphasises individual rights over the rights of the community as a whole. By contrast, the Church's distinctive mission places greater emphasis on the right of the whole Catholic community in determining the future of Catholic schools. The Church does not recognise that the rights of parents and pupils already placed in Catholic schools can override the rights of the whole Catholic community.
>
> (p. 188)

There are some interesting theoretical paradoxes and contradictions which are apparent in this sector of the field of Catholic education. On the one hand, an essentially authoritarian and hierarchical leadership takes the role of defender of community and 'common good' rights in educational decision making. On the other hand, groups of school governors and parents could claim, through the process of a ballot, to be the democratic voice of lay involvement on the future of Catholic schools. In fact, objections could be made to the legitimacy of both positions. The assumption by the Catholic hierarchy that it could speak for the rights of 'the whole Catholic community' could be interpreted as a covert means of maintaining clerical control of the schools. The assumption by some Catholic school governors and parents that they were the newly empowered voice of democratic community or of 'the consumer interest' could be countered by pointing to their limited, sectoral representation of the wider community.

The seriousness of this internal control struggle within Catholic schooling in England and Wales in the 1980s and 1990s can be judged by the fact that Cardinal Hume made an appeal to Rome for a clarification of the issues (a strategy which had worked effectively in earlier internal conflicts). Cardinal Baum, Prefect of the Congregation for Catholic Education, responded with an authoritative Roman judgement:

> Individual Catholics who are 'governors' of Catholic schools in the 'dual system' must not only know and fulfil their statutory obligations but must also know and fulfil their ecclesial rights and obligations. In other words they are to respond to the State's and the Church's legitimate expectations of them in such a way as to fulfil their responsibilities both as citizens and as Catholics. The management of one Catholic school should be conducted with due regard for the needs of other Catholic schools and for the interests of Catholic education in general as determined by the bishop of the diocese.[8]

The references to the 'ecclesial obligations' of Catholic parents and school governors and to the role of diocesan bishops made it clear that on the many contested policy issues of the time, Rome expected that Catholics would follow the guidance of their bishops.[9] It gives some measure of the transformations which were taking place in the attitudes of Catholic parents and in the power relations between clerics and laity in the 1980s and 1990s to note that the Roman judgement had little effect on subsequent events. In his detailed studies of lay participation in Catholic education structures, Arthur (1994a, 1994b) has shown that groups of Catholic parents and governors defied episcopal authority by voting for grant-maintained status for schools such as Cardinal Vaughan, the London Oratory and La Retraite (all in London) and St Francis Xavier (Liverpool). The most dramatic and bitter struggle occurred in the Cardinal Vaughan case where resort to the courts made such conflict visible and public. Cardinal Hume attempted a sustained resistance to the Cardinal Vaughan School's application for grant-maintained status and, as Arthur records, 'the parents threatened to take Cardinal Hume back to the courts … And the Cardinal threatened to place himself in contempt of the courts' (1995, p. 153).

The final withdrawal of the Cardinal from this struggle marked the triumph of the ideology of parentocracy in this case and in a number of others.[10] While the number of Catholic schools which took the disapproved route to grant-maintained status was small (140 in 1995) the socio-cultural significance of the struggle within the Catholic community was large. Not only had a group of Catholic headteachers, school governors and parents defied the advice of their Cardinal and their bishops on a key issue of educational policy but some of them had been prepared to 'take the Cardinal to court' on the issue. Such events were unprecedented within the English Catholic community and they made visible the limitations of clerical symbolic power when faced by the alliance of 'strong state' and 'strong parentocracy'. Under the new education reforms and the new statutory powers of the 1980s and 1990s, the guardianship of the distinctive Catholic mission and ethos of a school had passed, in practice, from the bishops to empowered school governors and parents. The long-term implications of this shift in power for the future direction and nature of Catholic schooling were clearly of great potential significance.

Using Bourdieu's concept of 'a field of forces' shows that Catholic education, like state education, has an internal dynamic and politics as well as a set of external relations and struggles. By this analytical device a more in-depth understanding of the Catholic educational system can be obtained, which in turn illuminates the nature of contemporary schooling debates and conflicts.

A similar analytical value, at the cultural level, can be obtained by using Bourdieu's concept of 'habitus' and this will be considered in the following pages.

## The habitus of Catholic education and socialisation

It has been mentioned earlier that one understanding of habitus is of deep-structured cultural dispositions within a community or an institution. In other places, Bourdieu refers to habitus as 'cultural unconscious', 'habit-forming force' and 'mental habit' and takes the view, as Swartz (1997) points out, that:

> Habitus is fairly resistant to change, since primary socialization in Bourdieu's view is more formative of internal dispositions than subsequent socialization experiences.
>
> (p. 107)

This is not to say that habitus cannot change but to recognise that it is an adaptive mechanism which 'always addresses present situations in terms of past experiences'.[11] The resonances of this concept with popular understandings of Catholic culture are very clear, e.g. 'give me the child until he is seven and I will give you the man' and 'once a Catholic, always a Catholic'. These observations might be seen as a popular sociology of habitus in action. However, to construct a more systematic and nuanced account of the habitus of Catholic education and of Catholic socialisation is a complex exercise. Part of the complexity arises because the experience of Catholic education and socialisation, of acquiring deep-structured cultural dispositions, is always mediated by different locations of class, race, gender, region and culture. While there is a Catholic habitus which will be a constant in all of these locations, there will also be specific variants of the habitus influenced by these locational characteristics. Qualitative differences will be apparent in the cultural dispositions of 'good Catholic boys' when compared with 'good Catholic girls'; of Irish Catholics in relation to English Catholics, of Liverpool Catholics *vis-à-vis* London Catholics and of Catholics from an upper-class public school setting when compared with Catholics from a working-class comprehensive school. The cultural dispositions of black Catholics may be different from those of white Catholics. There is, in short, no simple unitary habitus of Catholic socialisation despite the institutional Church's claim to be one and universal.

A further complexity arises because any attempt to specify or characterise forms of Catholic habitus meets the same challenge as those who attempt to analyse its related concept of culture.[12] Both concepts lack the specificity of structure and attempted analysis of them can often appear as diffuse and overgeneralised. What is attempted here is therefore a problematic exercise and one open to challenge, but it is premised on the conviction that some systematic analysis of the varieties of Catholic habitus should be a focal point of current Catholic scholarship.

## The habitus of convent schools

Codd (1990) observes that:

> the habitus of a group or class exists in the dispositions (capacities, tendencies, abilities to recognise and to act) of individuals such that these dispositions are an embodiment within each individual of objective regularities, relations and structures that pre-exist the individual and have been socially constituted.
>
> (p. 139)

An evocative account of such 'objective regularities' is given in White's (1999, pp. 44–6) description of her pre-Vatican II education in the Convent of the Five Wounds:

> The Junior School day was modelled on the same rigid pattern as that of the Senior School and the community itself. As soon as the Rising Bell had clanged through the cold dormitory, each child publicly dedicated the day to the service of God, in the words, 'O Jesus, wounded on the cross for me, help me to become crucified to self for love of Thee' .... She learnt the elaborate technique of dressing according to Christian modesty ... The whole day was punctuated by prayers. Besides the morning and evening devotions and the thrice-recurring Angelus, every lesson began with an invocation to the Holy Ghost and ended with a recommendation to Our Lady. Before supper, the whole school assembled to recite five decades of the rosary and there was usually a novena in preparation for an important feast ... The day ended with prayers in the chapel and an elaborate examination of conscience under the heading of sins against God, against one's neighbour and against oneself ... On Saturdays every child in the school went to confession and in the evening ... There were special devotions in the vestibule of Our Lady of Good Success ... As a result of all this, Nanda developed a nice sense of piety.

Here are exemplified some of the features of a particular form of Catholic education and socialisation and of a Catholic habitus which will have influenced (in various ways) generations of girls and women in this century until the reforms of Vatican II modified these practices. Convent education of this type generated a habitus characterised by an all-pervasive sense of the sacred in the midst of the profane; a sense of consecrated service; a discipline of time and study; a discipline of the body and mind; a strong awareness of sin (and its associated guilt); and a reflexivity about the ultimate purposes and final end of human existence. The *convent school habitus* of Catholic education and socialisation has been historically a class-patterned cultural form being more associated with the education of upper- and middle-class girls, at least in England, than with that of working-class girls. As a result of the strong literary emphasis of convent school education and of the class origins of many of the girls who experienced it, the convent school habitus has been comprehensively portrayed in novels, plays, autobiographies and reflective accounts (see Chapter 3). It has probably had an influence on popular images of Catholic education out of all proportion to its sectoral strength. The category, convent school habitus, can in fact only act as a general description, because more fine-grained analysis will show that the charism of each religious order of women will have produced qualitative differences in habitus. Thus, more precisely, one would have to speak of the habitus of the Sacred Heart, of the Dominicans, of La Sagesse, of La Retraite, of the Institute of the Blessed Virgin Mary, and so on.

## The formation of Catholic boys

The same fine-grained qualitative analysis would also be necessary in describing the various forms of habitus associated with the schools of religious orders of men and of orders of teaching brothers. Here it would involve attempts to specify the habitus in the schools of the Jesuits[13], the Benedictines, the Xaverians, the Salesians, the Marists, the De La Salle Brothers and the Christian Brothers as examples. A further complication inheres in the fact that there will be changes in habitus across different historical periods and, within the Catholic community, the impact of Vatican II reforms has been considerable in changing forms of habitus. One of the few ethnographic studies available in this sector and particularly relating to a general category which may be called a *Brothers school habitus*, is Angus's (1988) account of 'Christian Brothers College' (CBC) in Newburyport, Australia. Angus points out that the habitus of the College was constituted by a complex attempt to hold together a press for social and economic mobility, a strong transmission of the Catholic faith, a strict disciplinary regime and a competitive ethos in study and sport. For Angus, such a habitus was characteristic of Christian Brothers schools in general:

> Along with most Christian Brothers schools … CBC had historically, a distinctive working-class location. But rather than reproduce the working class culture of its pupils, the aim has historically been to transform their cultural identity in order to establish and maintain a Catholic middle class.
>
> (pp. 2–3)

This was a habitus of robust, manly, assertive Catholicism which intended to make an impact on the personal, academic and spiritual formation of Catholic boys and through such formation to have an impact upon the wider society. As Brother Manion (1977, vii) expressed it in *Christian Brothers Studies*:

> The objective of the school was to hand on the Faith intact and ready to fight; to raise the working class boy to a position of prestige in Public Service or Profession; and to attain high levels of examination success in open competition. Also, another objective, only slightly lower in estimation than the first, was the ability to challenge the domination of better endowed schools in any field, scholastic or sporting.
>
> (Quoted in Angus 1988, p. 3)

One of the final conclusions of Lawrence Angus's research which has a particular resonance for this present study is his view that the complex and balanced matrix of CBC's objectives and habitus had by the 1980s moved out of balance because of the domination of academic success over other goals. CBC, in this analysis, had become too successful in its secular mission of scholastic success and social mobility to the detriment of its spiritual mission:

> religious education is shifted into discrete timetable slots which least interfere with the timetabling of the 'academic' subjects … such examples have convinced many teachers that CBC's academic emphasis has clear priority over its seemingly waning commitment to religious education.
>
> (p. 176)

Here we have an example of a changing school habitus which can be expected to have implications for the deep-structured cultural dispositions of the pupils within it. Such issues will be taken up in later chapters of this book because such changes seem likely to be universal features of contemporary Catholic secondary schooling.

The habitus of religious order schools and those of teaching brothers have been experienced by many Catholic women and men now prominent in the Church and the professions, in education and the media, in government and public service, in finance and corporate enterprise, and in voluntary service and charitable agencies of various kinds. Religious order secondary schools have had a significant influence upon the constitution of a Catholic middle class in many countries and through the activities of their alumni the position of the institutional Church has been strengthened in some areas.

## Habitus in new contexts: diocesan comprehensive schools

For many Catholics, especially working-class Catholics, access to a *diocesan school habitus* is likely to have been a more typical experience. In so far as religious order secondary schools had entry criteria relating to levels of scholarship or ability to pay fees, their engagement with working-class Catholics tended to be at the level of the aspirant working class. While the class dispositions of Catholic secondary schools vary internationally in significant ways, for some societies the normal educational route for a Catholic working-class child would be from a diocesan primary school to a diocesan secondary school (grammar, comprehensive or secondary modern in England and Wales).

One description of a diocesan school habitus has been given by Burgess (1983) in his study of 'Bishop McGregor School', a Roman Catholic comprehensive school in a city in the English Midlands. What is apparent from Burgess's ethnographic account of this large, working-class comprehensive school which opened in 1969 is that its Catholic identity and habitus was more attenuated and vulnerable than that of long-established convent and religious order schools. The Catholic habitus of the school was not constituted by the spiritual and cultural capital of a religious order but had to be constituted by the dedicated commitment of the headteacher and senior staff, supported by the practising Catholic teachers. However, their efforts to construct a Catholic habitus at Bishop McGregor's were not always supported by a significant sector of the staff. As Burgess (1983, p. 35) noted:

> We have already seen that the church considered that the Catholic character of a school could be established and maintained by the appointment of Catholic teachers. Accordingly, Mr Goddard [the headteacher] attempted to recruit the maximum number of Catholic teachers. However, a dearth of applicants from Catholics resulted in almost half the appointments going to non-Catholics. In an interview with me Mr Goddard admitted that this concerned him as he wanted to give the school a distinct Catholic character.
>
> Mr Goddard took a key role in developing religious education within the school … Most Wednesday mornings he attended the school Mass and each week he took a share of religious education classes … Goddard therefore demonstrated to all that religion was for him a crucial element of school life. But the same could not be said for his staff. Many did not attend the weekly mass … while less

> than half the staff in my house regularly attended the morning assembly.

Even allowing for the relative newness of Bishop McGregor School, it is clear from Burgess's account that the pupils experienced a fragmented and divided habitus. In the jurisdiction of the headteacher, the senior staff and the practising Catholic staff, the pupils experienced the teachings, rituals and symbolism of the Catholic faith. In the jurisdictions of other teachers they experienced a more pragmatic, utilitarian and work-focused regime in which Catholicism *per se* was marginalised and possibly even commented upon in cynical terms.[14]

From the perspective of the institutional Catholic Church the ideal context for the development of a strongly defined Catholic habitus in schooling was that which Goffman (1961) has defined as a 'total institution'. Within the total institution the individual is comprehensively immersed in cultural teachings and beliefs, rituals, symbols and practices designed to produce deep-structured cultural dispositions in the individual arising out of an intense process of socialisation and formation. Many convent schools in the past and schools of religious orders and teaching Brothers approximated to this model, especially in the case of boarding schools. However, the conditions for the generation of a total institution experience were simply not available to large, working-class, diocesan comprehensive schools. Recognising the danger to Catholic ethos and habitus in such schools, the Catholic Church insisted that the school leadership must always be Catholic (i.e. the headteacher, senior staff and the majority of school governors) and that wherever possible a high proportion of the teachers should be Catholic.

Viewed in sociohistorical perspective it can be seen that the institutional Church has attempted to recontextualise the Catholic habitus of its religious order schools in the larger constituency of its new diocesan schools, primary and secondary, by a strong Catholic teacher and headteacher recruitment strategy. In so far as many of these teachers and headteachers had received their own educational socialisation in schools and colleges of religious orders and teaching Brothers, they could act as a cultural relay for Catholic habitus in new and more pluralistic situations. In other words, if a distinctive Catholic habitus was to be maintained, especially in large, urban comprehensive schools, then a practising Catholic leadership and teaching force were regarded as crucial. As studies such as Burgess's demonstrate, this policy was easier to achieve at leadership level than at the level of classroom teachers. Catholicity, understood as the realisation of a distinctive Catholic habitus, was therefore always more problematic in large urban diocesan comprehensive schools than in other types of Catholic school and the consequences for the cultural dispositions of pupils within such schools were also more uncertain.

Bourdieu's concept of habitus[15] shows itself to have considerable analytical value in understanding Catholic education both historically and in its contemporary forms. The detail of some of its contemporary forms will be examined in the later fieldwork chapters of this book, with especial reference to urban comprehensive schools in England.

## Perspectives from Basil Bernstein: knowledge and pedagogy

In the Preface to *Knowledge and Pedagogy: The Sociology of Basil Bernstein*, Sadovnik (1995, p. vii) observes that 'Bernstein's work is acknowledged internationally as among the finest attempts to construct a systematic theory of school and society', and he argues that Bernstein's theoretical work has great potential to illuminate diverse fields of culture, education and socialisation. In texts such as *Knowledge and Pedagogy* (1995) and *Discourse and Reproduction* (Atkinson *et al.* 1995) some of these possibilities have been explored, but, in general, applications within the field of Catholic education remain undeveloped.[16]

The argument of this section is that valuable connections can be made between Bernstein's theorising and issues in Catholic education. A limited attempt to make these connections will be made here. Particular attention will be given to those aspects of Bernstein's writings on knowledge and the curriculum and on pedagogy and discourse which have a resonance with major themes in the culture of Catholic education.

*Pedagogy, Symbolic Control and Identity*, Bernstein's major text of 1996, has such resonances with Catholic education both historically and in terms of its contemporary challenges and dilemmas. In this text, Bernstein focuses upon critical changes in the classification and framing of educational knowledge and in the forms of consciousness and identity which are being generated in contemporary school situations. He focuses upon changes in forms of pedagogy and of pedagogical discourse. Above all, he locates his analysis of such changes in a larger socio-cultural and ideological context which examines major transformations in the realm of the sacred and the secular in society.

Bernstein has provided theoretical concepts which can be applied with particular effect to a deeper understanding of Catholic education. These concepts include the classification and framing of educational knowledge; pedagogies, visible and invisible; symbolic control and the pedagogic device; and the secular market curriculum. Of all of these, the most far reaching in terms of challenges for contemporary Catholic education is that of the emergence of a market curriculum and of a secular pedagogy.

## The market curriculum and a secular pedagogy

Bernstein outlines a major cultural transformation which can be discerned in Europe from a faith-based conception of knowledge and pedagogy to a secular, market-based conception of education. In this analysis official knowledge and the curricula derived from it in Europe were historically realisations of Christian religious culture in pursuit of a greater understanding of God:

> The Christian God was a god you had to think about. It was a god that not only was to be loved but to be thought about. And this attitude created an abstract modality to the discourse.
>
> (Bernstein 1996, p. 83)

The abstract modality of educational discourse in the medieval university or 'school' involved exploration of the word and exploration of the world, 'word and world held together by the unity of Christianity' (ibid.). The fundamental regulative principle of 'school' knowledge and pedagogy was the existence of God whose nature could be partly apprehended by the study of sacred texts and partly apprehended by exploration of the created universe.

This religious regulative principle was, in Bernstein's view, progressively replaced during the Renaissance and the Enlightenment by a 'humanizing secular principle' and this principle is now being replaced by 'a dehumanizing principle' of market commodification of knowledge and pedagogy. This argument is elaborated in the following passage:

> Today, throughout Europe … there is a new principle guiding the latest transition of capitalism. The principles of the market and its managers are more and more the principles of the policy and practices of education. Market relevance is becoming the key orientating criterion for the selection of discourses … This movement has profound implications from the primary school to the university … Of fundamental significance, there is a new concept of knowledge and of its relation to those who create it and use it. This new concept is a truly secular concept. Knowledge should flow like money to

> wherever it can create advantage and profit. Indeed knowledge is not like money, it *is* money ... Knowledge, after nearly a thousand years, is divorced from inwardness and literally dehumanized. Once knowledge is separated from inwardness, from commitments, from personal dedication, from the deep structure of the self, then people may be moved about, substituted for each other and excluded from the market.
>
> (Bernstein 1996, p. 87)

Accompanying this secularisation, commodification and marketisation of knowledge in contemporary settings, there are comparable transformations in pedagogic discourse and communication. Pedagogy is not simply a means for the transmission of knowledge, it is also a powerful regulator of consciousness and a formative influence upon personal identity. Pedagogy in the secularised, market curriculum has itself become dominated by output measures of specific competences and skill acquisition, by performance models of comparative achievement levels and by efficiency and effectiveness criteria relating to the 'delivery'[17] of the required objectives of a prescribed National Curriculum. It follows from this analysis that pupil consciousness and sense of identity and personal worth will be affected in particular ways by what Bernstein (1996, p. 80) describes as 'a virtually secular pedagogic discourse'. The pedagogy of a faith-based curriculum has to acknowledge, at least at the formal level, the Christian value and dignity of every pupil and student regardless of achievement. The pedagogy of the market curriculum has no similar principled constraint and its potential danger is that pupils and students may become differentially valued as output assets.

To the extent that Bernstein's analysis of these major transformations in knowledge, curricula and pedagogy is accepted, then their implications for Catholic education are profound. At one level, the fundamental regulative principles of Catholic education have a continuity with and a lineage from the educational cultures of the medieval 'schools'. Catholic education exists as an attempt to know God and God's purposes in the world. At another level, Catholic educational institutions are caught up in the working of the secular, market curriculum, a performance-based pedagogic regime and a system of accountability and evaluation where measurable and visible outcomes are dominant. The question of how contemporary Catholic secondary schools in England cope with such dilemmas and contradictions will be the focus of later chapters.

## The classification and framing of Catholic schooling

Singh and Luke (1996, p. xii) have argued that Bernstein's 'concepts of classification and framing remain among the most powerful and illuminating theoretical tools for those of us working in the field of curriculum studies'. A similar claim could be made by those working in the field of Catholic education, given that the concepts of classification and framing are central to the illumination of that field. In the concept of classification, Bernstein is referring to the dominant power relations which establish boundaries and degrees of insulation. The boundaries and insulations may be between subject categories in a school curriculum or more generally 'between agencies, between agents, between discourses, between practices'.[18] In situations of strong classification there is a strong insulation of categories one from another, generating distinctive spaces and relative autonomy for agents within them. When classification is weakened and insulation is broken, then Bernstein (1996, p. 20) argues:

> a category is in danger of losing its identity, because what it is, is the space between it and another category. Whatever maintains the strengths of the insulation, maintains the relations between categories and their distinctive voices.

The relevance of this theorising to the contemporary scholarship of Catholic education is very clear. Catholic education has historically been, in many societies, strongly classified and insulated from the mundane and secular world. In the formation of its curriculum priorities, modes of pedagogy and assessment, school ethos and habitus of values and practice, Catholic education has preserved its distinctive voice and character behind strong boundaries of cultural insulation. In more recent times, this strong classification and insulation has weakened as a result of a complex of factors including ideological, social, educational and political change. The weakening of classification and insulation has arisen partly as the outcome of Vatican II reforms and the call to a greater openness to the external world: partly as a result of educational change which has celebrated relating the world of school more closely to 'real life', 'the world of work', 'youth culture', etc.; partly as a result of the decline in the number of priests and religious and the distinctive habitus which they represented in schools, and partly as a result of the imperatives of strong state reforms in education which have required compliance from the Catholic system. There can be no doubt that Catholic education institutions are now more weakly classified and insulated from external agencies than in earlier historical periods. The problematic issue which this generates for contemporary analysis is: does this represent a progressive development of the mission of Catholic schools and a fruitful realisation of the openness principles of Vatican II reforms, or does it represent a loss of distinctive voice, character and integrity for the Catholic faith in the modern world?

Comparable and problematic questions are also raised when Bernstein's concept of framing is applied to contemporary Catholic schooling in England and Wales. In the concept of framing, Bernstein is talking about the power relations which shape knowledge, the curriculum, pedagogic practice and evaluation. Thus, 'classification establishes voice, and framing establishes the message'.[19] Framing is about who controls what in the pedagogic process: 'where framing is strong, the transmitter has explicit control over selection, sequence, pacing, criteria and the social base'[20] of curriculum and pedagogy in the educational process.

Once again, the relevance of this for the study of Catholic education is apparent. Historically, the framing of Catholic curricula, pedagogy and evaluation was determined by the institutional Church, the charism and traditions of religious and teaching orders and by diocesan headteachers, teachers, inspectors and advisers. While the curriculum, pedagogy and evaluation procedures of Catholic schools had to be in a functional relation with the requirements of external agencies, the degree of relative autonomy for a distinctively Catholic framing of priorities was large. It was possible to talk of a Catholic curriculum and even of a Catholic pedagogy.[21]

However, the educational reforms of the 1980s and 1990s in England and Wales demonstrated that the 'transmitter' (in Bernstein's terms) of the messages and priorities of the curriculum was now the state which imposed a strong framing regime on all schools regardless of religious character. As a consequence of such state action the realm of autonomy for Catholic schools has been severely constrained. The problematic question which this situation raises for contemporary study is: what remains distinctive in the cultural messages carried by Catholic schools? Have the 1980s and 1990s state-imposed curriculum and assessment requirements dealt a fatal blow to concepts of a Catholic curriculum and pedagogy or has it been possible for Catholic schools to find ways of rendering to Caesar that which is Caesar's while rendering to God that which is God's?

## Catholic pedagogy: visible and invisible

Bernstein's concepts of visible and invisible pedagogy first articulated in 1977 have proved fruitful in empirical research in various educational settings (Sadovnik 1995) and have subsequently been developed (Bernstein 1990) and reproduced in major theoretical collections (Halsey *et al.* 1997).

For Bernstein (1990) a visible pedagogy:

> will always place the emphasis on the performance of the child, upon the text the child is creating and the extent to which that text is meeting the criteria … A visible pedagogy puts the emphasis on the external product of the child.
>
> (p. 70)

Visible pedagogies may be realised in different modalities and in different educational settings. For instance, in a traditional grammar school context, a pupil's mastery of the text and demonstration of scholarly knowledge is the desired outcome of a visible pedagogy. In contemporary market-driven schooling, a pupil's measurable performance in prescribed competences and skills becomes the objective of a visible pedagogy. The first may be called the visible pedagogy of scholarship and the second the visible pedagogy of the market. By contrast, invisible pedagogies:

> are less concerned to produce explicit stratifying differences between acquirers … Their focus is not upon a 'gradable' performance of the acquirer but upon procedures internal to the acquirer.
>
> (p. 71)

Invisible pedagogy refers to a holistic process of educational socialisation designed to produce changes in the dispositions, attitudes and behaviours of a child as a result of involvement in a particular educational environment. The pedagogy is invisible in the sense that both its procedures and its outcomes are more diffuse and intangible than those which characterise visible pedagogy. At the most general level, invisible pedagogy is designed to be person forming whereas visible pedagogy is designed to be product forming.

Bernstein has used these concepts to explore the social class assumptions of different forms of pedagogic practice and in particular to scrutinise the culture of progressive education at early childhood, primary and secondary levels. However, it is clear that these concepts have great theoretical and empirical potential for illuminating the field of Catholic education.

Catholic education has always utilised both visible and invisible pedagogies in the schooling of children and young people. A visible pedagogy of scholarship had its roots, as Bernstein points out, in the medieval university. Such a pedagogic tradition has been mediated and recontextualised in a variety of Catholic schools and colleges, in a variety of settings including contemporary Catholic schools serving inner-city populations. It is not surprising that many headteachers, school principals and teachers who were themselves socialised within the strong classifications and visible pedagogies of traditional schools and colleges in the Catholic network should have reproduced aspects of this academic culture within contemporary schooling. It is important to realise, however, that the visible pedagogy of scholarship in Catholic institutions had, in Bernstein's terms, 'the cover of the sacred'.[22] Scholarly outcomes, knowledge, achievement and skills were not an end in themselves. They were given significance and meaning in a relation to the sacred and in a relation to concepts of service to community and the public good. The emergence of a new form of visible pedagogy, that of the market, poses therefore considerable challenges to contemporary Catholic schooling. The danger of this new dominant form is that it dislocates knowledge from a relation to the sacred or to the community and replaces it with a utilitarian, commodified and individualistic relation. While Catholic schools may be 'successful' and 'effective' within this new visible pedagogy, such success will not articulate well with the principles enshrined in their mission statements. However, if there are problems for Catholic schools in the contemporary transitions of visible pedagogies, there are much larger problems in the sphere of invisible pedagogy.

## Invisible pedagogy and intangible outcomes

The key attribute of an invisible pedagogy, from Bernstein's perspective, is that it is concerned with a holistic process of personal formation rather than with the production of graded performances. In so far as Catholic schools have always aspired to be generators of spiritual and moral formation and transmitters of the Catholic faith, the role of an invisible pedagogy within them has always been important. A visible pedagogy of direct religious teaching and of instruction in the Catechism has always co-existed with an invisible pedagogy and hidden curriculum of Catholic personal formation in faith shaped by the whole-school environment, its ethos, rituals, symbols and value climate.

What is always problematic with an invisible pedagogy is that its outcomes and 'effectiveness' tend to be relatively invisible or intangible. While the production of test scores and examination results has a degree of visibility and concreteness, the formation of 'good Catholics' and of young people with greater spiritual, moral and civic maturity is less visible and tangible. The ultimate judgement of the effectiveness of Catholic schooling in this dimension can only be found in the subsequent lives, beliefs and practices of those adults who experienced a Catholic education (see Chapter 3). The invisible pedagogy is only made visible in the longer term.

Historically, Catholic schools faced with this dilemma have looked for 'outward and visible signs' of interior grace among their pupils. They have found these signs in a variety of proxy measures such as confirmation numbers, regular attendance at Mass and other liturgies, charitable and community service, membership of Catholic societies and vocations to the priesthood and the religious life. These visible signs have provided some sense of what the schools have achieved in what is, after all, their primary purpose for existing.

In contemporary contexts such traditional indicators of the success of the spiritual mission are relatively less visible than they were in the past and Catholic schools have to look for new signs of their spiritual, moral and social achievements. What has complicated this search is the fact that, in England at any rate, state policy in education and the extension of a market culture into the realm of education has given enhanced status and importance to the production of measurable academic results. The danger is that contemporary Catholic schools may find a greater sense of confidence, achievement and public recognition by concentrating their energies in the market curriculum rather than in the relatively invisible outcomes of their spiritual and moral curriculum.

## Social theory and the study of Catholic education

At the beginning of this chapter it was suggested that Catholic scholarship in education has kept social theory at arm's length from its concerns.[23] The argument of this chapter has been that such historical distancing is now outmoded and even obscurantist. Aspects of social theory applied to Catholic education have the potential to illuminate the field, to provide greater in-depth analysis of issues and to generate fruitful theoretical frameworks for future research and enquiry. In particular the explanatory potential of Pierre Bourdieu's concepts of field, habitus and symbolic power has been exemplified for a greater understanding of Catholic education in both its historical and contemporary contexts.[24] Similarly, the analytical power of Basil Bernstein's concepts of market curriculum and secular pedagogy, of classification and framing, and of visible and invisible pedagogies has been outlined. These concepts will inform the analysis of fieldwork data reported in the later chapters of this book and it is hoped that other researchers will take up these theoretical tools in their own enquiries.

While academic studies which draw upon appropriate social theory will constitute the field of Catholic education in new ways, it has to be recognised that they will provide only one form of account of the culture of Catholic schooling. Such accounts will have to be triangulated with other perspectives. In fact, three forms of account may be identified. The first, which has been the focus of this chapter and which will be developed in Chapter 4, may be called *social theory and research accounts*. The second, which in practice may be influential in shaping pervasive images of Catholic schooling, may be called *literary image accounts*. These are accounts of a Catholic schooling represented in novels, films and plays which disseminate and amplify particular versions of Catholic educational habitus. The third category, *personal reflective accounts*, are individual exercises in reflexivity, forms of oral history in which Catholic-educated adults look back upon their own education and personal formation to assess its positive and negative features. These accounts are not informed by particular theoretical stances but they provide rich sources of insight into the long-term effects of a Catholic education.

A sample of such literary image accounts and of personal reflective accounts will be examined in the following chapter to obtain more insight into the forms of traditional Catholic education.

# Part II

# Historical, cultural and research contexts

# 3 Images of Catholic schooling

## Pre-Vatican II

Hastings (1991, p. 525) has argued that:

> there can be no question that the Vatican Council (1962 – 65) was the most important ecclesiastical event of this century, not just for Roman Catholics but for all Christians. It so greatly changed the character of by far the largest communion of Christendom.

The reforms of the Vatican Council involved radical changes in the liturgy of the Mass and of other liturgical practices; in ritual cultures and traditional observances; in conceptions of the Church, with a new emphasis upon 'the people of God'; in relations with other Christians and other faiths; and in ideas about the nature of authority within the Church. While many Catholics welcomed the reforms inaugurated by the action of Pope John XXIII as involving a necessary renewal of the Church and a principled commitment to openness, dialogue, participation and more collegial authority, others saw dangers and difficulties. Among these critics, Archer (1986) suggested that the new cultural practices of Catholicism were a form of middle-class embourgeoisement of the Church which was likely to alienate working-class Catholics. The anthropologist Mary Douglas (1973, p. 67) saw dangers in a weakening of a sense of ritual,[1] mystery, sacredness and identity in Catholic culture:

> Now, the English Catholics are like everyone else.

There is a general consensus among writers that the Second Vatican Council of the 1960s marked a major cultural and religious transformation within Catholicism. Whether these transformations have strengthened or weakened the institutional Church and its associated agencies remains a subject of continued debate. In terms of these transformations and debates, it does seem valid to make distinctions between the pre- and post-Vatican II Church and between pre- and post-Vatican II Catholic schools. One of the intentions of this research study is to explore some of the differences between these two forms of Catholic schooling.

Much of what we actually know about the habitus of pre-Vatican II Catholic schooling is contained in the form of images created in literary accounts and personally reflective accounts by adults who experienced it. As Bernstein (1996, p. 7) notes:

> a school metaphorically holds up a mirror in which an image is reflected. There may be several images, positive and negative.

The problem with images of schooling, even when both positive and negative accounts are included, is that they tend to be class-specific constructions, i.e. more middle-class image accounts being available than working-class accounts.[2] A second problem is that images of schooling are subjective and partial accounts, since they are not constructed within the disciplines of social science enquiry.

If images of schooling have such limitations as evidence, the question may reasonably be raised as to why they should be included in any systematic study of Catholic schooling. The argument made in this chapter is that images of schooling, despite their limitations as reliable evidence, have an enduring power to affect both consciousness and behaviour. Widely disseminated images can have widely significant effects upon constructs of a particular educational setting. In effect, for many people, it is argued, 'image' becomes 'reality' and has continuing effects in contemporary situations. This is an exemplification of the classic observation of the social psychologist W. I. Thomas (1932) that situations which persons define as real are real in their consequences. The richness and widely disseminated nature of images of Catholic schooling provides not only an enduring element in what many people believe a Catholic education is, but also a useful background against which some sense of change in Catholic education can be constructed.

## Traditional Catholic schooling: some partial images

What is presented here is only a small sample taken from the rich field of Catholic school imagery contained in some published texts. In each case, an extract is used to exemplify particular dimensions of a pre-Vatican II school habitus. This is intended to be an indicative rather than a definitive account of some forms of traditional Catholic schooling.

## Strong discipline: 'Folly is bound up in the heart of a child but the rod of discipline drives it far from him' (Proverbs 22: 15)[3]

All forms of educational experience contain their own internal contradictions. In the case of traditional Catholic schooling one of the most widely disseminated images of contradiction has been that between a formal preaching of love, compassion and forgiveness, as emanating from the nature of Christ, and an educational practice involving, in some cases, brutal beating and sadistic psychological domination. In other words, in some traditional Catholic schooling contexts, the message of love from the New Testament was overpowered in practice by messages of retribution and punishment, derived from the Old Testament. Of all of the images of such contradictions perhaps the most widely disseminated and amplified has been that created by James Joyce in *A Portrait of the Artist as a Young Man*:

> The door opened quietly and closed. A quick whisper ran through the class: the prefect of studies. There was an instant of dead silence and then the loud crack of a pandybat on the last desk. Stephen's heart leapt up in fear. 'Any boys want flogging here, Father Arnall?' cried the prefect of studies. 'Any lazy idle loafers that want flogging in this class?'
>
> (1985, p. 49)

This dramatic account of the experience of discipline in a Catholic school for boys could be reproduced in many other schools, Catholic and non-Catholic, in that historical period. Traditional Catholic schools utilised traditional methods of school discipline which were taken-for-granted features of school life in the UK and Ireland in the first half of the twentieth century. Such punishments might be administered by Jesuits, Christian Brothers, De La Salle Brothers, Marists, Sisters of Mercy or lay Catholic headteachers and teachers. Such a regime was justified by an Old Testament mandate that the pursuit of knowledge and wisdom frequently involved the experience of ordeal and pain. It was also the case that a formal academic curriculum, experienced by many young people as arid, required an apparatus of strong discipline to maintain order and attention among the pupils. The critics of Catholic education and the rebels against it, however, maintained that the use of physical and psychological violence in what was supposed to be a Christian context of education was hypocritical and fatally undermined the integrity of its claimed distinctive mission.

Such accounts can be found in, for instance, the New Zealand Catholic Boys Oral History Project (Sullivan 1996) where Laurie O'Reilly, now the Commissioner for Children, records his criticism of the forms of discipline which he experienced:

> It was one of the few unhappy experiences I had in the Catholic school system and it may have been what decided me to become a lawyer and an opponent of corporal punishment.
>
> (pp. 135–6)

Other criticisms are to be found in oral history accounts of the education of Catholic girls and women (Bennett and Forgan 1991; Tolerton 1994). In general, such critical accounts of convent school life refer to forms of psychological violence rather than physical sanctions. In the light of her own experiences of suffering and 'mindless repression' in her convent school, Carmen Callil records her decision to found Virago Modern Classics and to publish Antonia White's *Frost in May* as a counter-blow to convent education:

> The world had to read the book again. It told everyone what it was like to be traumatised by nuns and have your life more or less ruined by them.
>
> (Bennet and Forgan 1991, pp. 55–6)

If there was, and is, 'an unacceptable face of capitalism', there has also been an unacceptable face of Catholic schooling, and it is a face which has been widely disseminated and amplified in these accounts. These are some of the negative images of Catholic schooling which still have some currency in contemporary settings. Such images raise questions about what has changed in the disciplinary climate of contemporary Catholic education. However, the images themselves are only partial constructions of the traditional story of Catholic education and they need to be balanced by other representations, images and experiences.

Literary images of strong Catholic school discipline and personal reflective accounts do not provide a complete account of the experiences of the majority of Catholic pupils in the past. As later accounts will show, there are countervailing images and constructs that place Catholic schooling of this period in a more positive light. Notwithstanding this, it seems likely that the contemporary reputations of many Catholic schools for 'good order' and 'structured environment' are the modern and mediated forms of these pervasive disciplinary images. The crucial difference is that cultures of order and structure are now created by more humane procedures in most contemporary Catholic schools.

## Faith of Our Fathers:[4] the catechism of Catholic doctrine

A widely held image of traditional Catholic schooling is that it had little relation with the concept of education *per se* (having to do with intellectual development by questioning and enquiry) but much more to do with a body of 'indoctrination in the mind of the Church'. Popular constructs of Catholic schooling, especially those informed by Protestant bigotry, emphasised a mechanical, rote-learning process of priestly domination, where the main focus of the pedagogy was not upon the work of God as realised in the Holy Bible but upon the word of the Roman Church as presented in the Penny Catechism. Academic critics such as the philosopher Paul Hirst have argued that traditional Catholic schooling had a major structural contradiction between its formal commitment to the development of rationality and intellectual enquiry on the one hand, and its formal commitment to the transmission of faith and doctrine by means of catechism. From this perspective, the learning of the catechism cannot be a valid part of an educational process but must take place in contexts external to the school, such as the parish and the home.

The centrality of learning the catechism and the forms of pedagogy associated with Catholic catechesis have been disseminated in literary images and in personal accounts. Once again, the images created by James Joyce in his description of the experience of Stephen Dedalus at a retreat have been powerful and evocative:

> A retreat, my dear boys, signifies a withdrawal for a while from the cares of our life, the cares of this workaday world, in order to examine the state of our conscience, to reflect on the mysteries of holy religion and to understand better why we are here in this world. During these few days, I intend to put before you some thoughts concerning the four last things. They are, as you know from your catechism, death, judgement, hell and heaven.
>
> (1985, p. 113)

This introduction is followed, as many readers will know, by one of the most terrifying descriptions of the nature of hell and of the torments of the damned that has ever been written. The catechetical teaching of death, judgement, hell and heaven was a central message of traditional

Catholic schooling. It was designed to focus the mind of the pupil upon the text, 'what doth it profit a man to gain the whole world if he suffers the loss of his immortal soul?' At the same time, having engendered the guilt and fear experienced by Stephen Dedalus, it was designed to hold out a message of hope and forgiveness, to be found in the sacraments of the Catholic Church.

The questions and answers of the *Catechism of Catholic Doctrine* were a distinctive and central part of the pedagogy of the pre-Vatican II Catholic school, a visible pedagogy of rote learning and repetition more frequently than one of discussion and dialogue. The 1951 version of the catechism, issued by the Irish bishops, for instance, had 443 questions and answers to be mastered, a major exercise in rote learning allowing little time for discussion. This was the Catholic version of a London taxi-driver's requirement to master 'the knowledge', although in this case the requirement was for a spiritual route map.

The struggles involved in learning the catechism have been represented with wit and humour in the novels of Frank McCourt, and by other writers.[5] In *Angela's Ashes: A Memoir of a Childhood*, McCourt gives his account of catechetical experience in an Irish parish school:

> The master tells us we have to know the catechism backwards, forwards and sideways. We have to know the Ten Commandments, the Seven Virtues, Divine and Moral, the Seven Sacraments, the Seven Deadly Sins. We have to know by heart all the prayers, the Hail Mary, the Our Father, the Confiteor, the Apostles' Creed, the Act of Contrition, the Litany of the Blessed Virgin Mary … He tells us we're hopeless, the worst class he ever had for First Communion but as sure as God made little apples, he'll make Catholics of us, he'll beat the idler out of us and the Sanctifying Grace into us. Brendan Quigley raises his hand … Sir, he says, what's Sanctifying Grace? The master rolls his eyes to heaven. He's going to kill Quigley. Instead he barks at him. 'Never mind what's Sanctifying Grace, Quigley. That's none of your business. You're here to learn the Catechism and do what you're told. You're not here to be asking questions. There are too many people wandering the world asking questions and that's what has us in the state we're in and if I find any boy in this class asking questions, I won't be responsible for what happens.'
>
> (1997, pp. 129–30)

The general emphasis upon the amount of knowledge to be learned and the discouragement of independent questioning was, it must be remembered, a feature of the culture of many categories of schooling in this historical period. It was not a characteristic only of Catholic schools. What was particular to Catholic schools was the nature of the knowledge that had to be learned and the assumption that Catholics could be 'made' by the learning of the catechism.

Warner (1990), in reflecting upon her Catholic education, has emphasised the sense of security which could be generated for the diligent and studious pupil in 'knowing the Faith' through the mastery of the pedagogy of the catechism. A strong sense of Catholic identity was forged by this process and, until the questionings of adolescence, a secure faith:

> Our religion was certainly untroublesome, because it consisted of simple certainties, outlined in the crisp rhetoric of the Catechism we learned by heart. And the Virgin was the chief of these certainties.
>
> (p. xx)

These simple certainties of the catechism, as many autobiographical accounts show, frequently came to crisis among those Catholic pupils who proceeded to higher education. Hastings (1996) has argued that the traditional Catholic pedagogy of catechesis produced, in practice, both spiritual and moral immaturity that could not withstand the pluralistic, questioning rationality of higher education institutions. The large number of ex-Catholics among university-educated professional people gives some credence to this thesis. For many Catholic women the encounters with feminist theory and analysis highlighted the patriarchal assumptions of the 'Faith of Our Fathers' and led to painful reappraisals of their childhood faith and beliefs. Warner (1990, p. xxi) has given a vivid account of the experience of loss of faith and of loss of iconic symbolism arising from new perceptions of Catholicism:

> The Virgin, sublime model of chastity, nevertheless remained for me the most holy being I could ever contemplate, and so potent was her spell that for years I could not enter a church without pain at all the safety and beauty of the salvation I had forsaken. I remember visiting Notre Dame in Paris and standing in the nave, tears starting in my eyes, furious at that old love's enduring power to move me. But though my heart rebelled, I held fast to my new intimation that in the very celebration of the perfect human woman, both humanity and women were subtly denigrated.

A contemporary debate of some vigour is now being conducted in the Catholic communities of the UK and Ireland about what forms of catechetical knowledge and religious education are appropriate in the Catholic education of the twenty-first century. Traditionalists believe that a serious loss of Catholic identity, knowledge of the faith and disposition to practise has followed from the abandonment of the old catechism as a consequence of Vatican II reforms. Catholicity in their view has been weakened by these changes and therefore there is a need to return to the catechetical certainties and the ritual practices of the past.[6] The advocates of the Vatican II spirit of renewal in the Church take the view that new forms of catechetical understanding and new forms of religious education must be found to meet the challenges of a more secular and a more questioning social context for schooling. As later chapters will show, these debates and these tensions are being worked out in the mission of contemporary Catholic schools.

## Encountering the sacred: the sacraments, rituals and devotions

Cardinal Basil Hume (1997, pp. 30–1), speaking of the Catholic Church's mission in education, emphasised the importance of establishing a sense of transcendence in the educational process:

> To acknowledge this transcendence is to recognise that at the heart of our experience of the world and of ourselves, lies a Mystery. In fact to speak of God is to encounter a Mystery.

Traditional Catholic schooling attempted, in various ways, to create conditions in which a sense of transcendence, a sense of the sacred and a sense of the Mystery that is God, might be communicated to, and experienced by, children and young people.

In the protected habitus of the convent school, this dimension of Catholic schooling was at its strongest. Antonia White records Nanda Grey's encounter with the sacred in powerful imagery:

> She really did begin to live all day long in the presence of the court of heaven. God the Father and God the Holy Ghost remained awe-inspiring conceptions, Presences who could only be addressed in set words and with one's mind, as it were, properly gloved and veiled. But to Our Lady and the Holy Child and the saints she spoke as naturally as to her friends.
>
> (White 1999, pp. 45–6)

The rituals of Catholic liturgy and the devotions which marked the encounter with the sacred have had, for some who experienced them, powerful effects, both positive and negative. In Bennett and Forgan's oral history collection (1991, pp. 38–9), Clare Boylan reflects:

> I loved Benediction … That theatrical swinging of the thurible with its clouds of scented smoke. I loved the feast of Corpus Christi when we dressed up in our old Communion dresses for the procession.

In the same collection, Mary Kenny and others have argued that the rich liturgical culture of pre-Vatican II convent schools had a strong aesthetic appeal to many girls and that it was generative not only of a sense of spirituality but also of imagination and creativity:

> all this is excellent for the imagination and I think this is why Catholicism tends to produce writers.
>
> (Bennett and Forgan 1991, p. 127)

In both literary imagery and personal reflective accounts of traditional convent schooling what emerges is a schooling habitus which could at the same time produce experiences of the sacred and the transcendent and feelings of peace and serenity, but also feelings of guilt and personal unworthiness. Above all, what comes through in many accounts of traditional Catholic schooling is a sense of constant struggle with 'the world, the flesh and the Devil'.[7] Outside of the strong boundary insulations of the convent school lay the many corrupting influences of the profane world. Through a strong internal generation of the culture of holiness, the mission of the convent school was to attempt to safeguard its pupils as they set out to pursue their vocations in a fallen world.

For boys and young men, the aesthetics and sensitivities of traditional Catholic schooling were not as finely drawn as in the convent school. However, given that the next generation of priests and male religious and teaching Brothers could be expected to emerge from secondary schools and colleges, the presence of a sacred habitus was a mission imperative for Catholic education. When Stephen Dedalus was asked by the rector of his college if he felt called to the religious life, the question provoked an evocation of the imagery of priesthood which would have been held by many studious and pious boys of that time:

> How often had he seen himself as a priest wielding calmly and humbly the awful power of which angels and saints stood in reverence! His soul had loved to muse in secret on this desire. He had

> seen himself, a young and silent mannered priest, entering a confessional swiftly, ascending the altarsteps, incensing, genuflecting, accomplishing the vague acts of the priesthood which pleased him by reason of their semblance of reality and of their distance from it.
> (Joyce 1985, p. 161)

Traditional Catholic liturgy and an awareness of the possibility of a sacred vocation in life was a central part of Catholic schooling, especially where such schooling was provided by vowed religious or by teaching brothers. The rituals and devotions of the school year could generate a school ethos in which mystery, sacredness, power, symbolism and dramatic theatre could be realised over and against the prosaic routines of everyday life and in the most unpromising settings and locations. For some boys and girls this encounter with the sacred in the process of a Catholic education was compelling. John Walsh, in the Bennett and Forgan collection (1991, p. 162) reflects on the power of such symbolism in these terms:

> What appealed to me was the theatricality of the Church … The Stripping of Christ and The Scourging and The Crowning of Thorns and the Crucifixion … The Exposition of the Blessed Sacrament … was riveting because you were for the first time being brought face to face with the thing itself, the closest you would get to a reified God.

For others, the encounter with the sacred in Catholic education was not inspiring or uplifting but, on the contrary, an oppressive experience. For Hastings (1970, pp. 17–18):

> The round of daily mass and daily prayers in the school chapel was hateful to me. I was never one of the elect … Erratically, I was religious. I parroted the words, I fingered the rosary. But deep down inside, even then, I was wondering what it was all about.

In the recollections of some adult Catholics, the culture of traditional Catholic schooling is associated with some sense of encountering 'the beauty of holiness' in the aesthetic of the Mass and other devotions. For others, the experience was one of mechanical and uncomprehending compliance, which resulted in a final adult status of lapsed Catholic or ex-Catholic.

The liturgical and cultural expression of Catholicity varied according to school category and location. Parish and diocesan schools, as opposed to those run by religious orders, had different forms of the habitus of the sacred in pre-conciliar times. In general, such schools did not possess the same concentrations of spiritual/cultural capital as constituted by school chapels, a vowed religious community living on site and a daily immersion in major liturgical and ritual celebrations. The sense of the sacred was more attenuated in such schools. Following the changes of Vatican II, traditional ritual practices became less frequent in all schools and, in the case of England and Wales, the reorganisation of secondary education resulted in the creation of large, urban comprehensive schools, presenting new challenges. The conditions of large diocesan comprehensive schools, often serving multi-cultural, multi-faith and socially fragmented communities in inner-city areas and large working-class housing estates on the periphery of cities, required new responses if the ethos of the sacred was to be maintained and enhanced in Catholic education.

## Catholic knowledge and Catholic learning

A popular image of traditional Catholic schooling is that it could produce 'good Catholics' characterised by faith, deference and a Church-approved knowledge and understanding of the world and of the world to come. To some extent such an image has validity. Catholic pupils, of a certain disposition, in pedagogic conditions in which the catechism and sanctified knowledge were given high salience, could emerge from Catholic education as exemplars of faithful members of the Church and possessors of true wisdom. The enduring power of phrases like 'give me a child until he is seven' and of 'once a Catholic, always a Catholic' have given to the Catholic schooling mission an image of ideological determinism, cultural conditioning and of virtually guaranteed personal and intellectual outcomes. In short, parents, it was believed, could commit their children to the Catholic schooling system with a high expectation of a 'good' and predictable outcome both in faith terms and in academic achievements. A closer examination of personal accounts of experiencing Catholic schooling shows that this one dominant image is an oversimplification. Traditional Catholic schooling produced its saints and its sinners, its conformists and its rebels, its believers and its atheists, and its conservatives and radicals. In other words, the personal, religious and intellectual outcomes of traditional Catholic schooling were, in practice, and not unsurprisingly, catholic in their nature. Despite the dominance of images of conformity, there exists a rich imagery of rebellion, resistance and of unpredictable personal and intellectual outcomes.

John Walsh (Bennett and Forgan 1991, p. 168) captures this oppositional stance in Catholic schooling in his reflective account:

> But really what a Catholic education gives you is something to fight against. It doesn't set out to, of course, but it gives you something whereby you will have to become a hero unto yourself, or else cave in and become your parents' good little boy or girl. Confronting it makes you a fighter.

In the accounts of three Catholic education oral history projects, i.e. Bennett and Forgan (1991), Tolerton (1994) and Sullivan (1996), themes of rebellion against Catholic knowledge and Catholic learning appear frequently in the reflections of adult professional men and women who experienced the schooling regimes of various religious orders in England, Ireland, Australia and New Zealand. Pre-Vatican II convent education could produce very polarised outcomes, vocations for the religious life, on the one hand, and feminists in the making, on the other. The complex relation between a convent school education and the embracing of an independent, feminist life-style in adulthood is commented on by Carmen Callil, Germaine Greer, Sarah Hogg and Mary Kenny in the 1991 oral history collection. The unintended feminist learning seems to have arisen partly as a result of the role modelling of intelligent, capable and inspiring nuns perceived as being 'in charge' of an educational institution and yet, at the same time, subject to the constraints of larger patriarchal structures and authority. In reflecting upon that contradiction, many intelligent convent-educated young women came to the conclusion that patriarchy in the external world and sexism in the Catholic Church had to be challenged. Thus an unintended consequence of convent school education was the formation of feminist radicals as well as of 'good Catholic mothers' and novices for the religious orders.

A similar unintended consequence of traditional Catholic schooling was the formation of political radicals. The creation of a social conscience as well as an individual conscience was part of Catholic socialisation and with it went a sense of social justice. It could be argued that this social teaching of the Catholic Church expressed in the formal and muted discourse of papal encyclicals was intended to shape the actions of responsible Catholic citizens in the developing democracies of the world. However, once such ideas were presented to intelligent and lively adolescents as part of their Catholic education the outcomes might be unpredictable. Rather than realising such ideas in muted and responsible citizenship some young people could become crusaders for social justice. In short, they might take such ideas seriously as a means of transforming social, economic and political relations *now* and not in some distant utopia. Reactions to church teaching of this type are expressed in the New Zealand Catholic Oral History publications. Hara te Hemara (Tolerton 1994, p. 65), prominent in the Maori liberation movement in New Zealand, records in her account:

> I discovered that a lot of other radical women (and I was branded a radical), like Donna Awetere, Pauline Kingi and Nga-huia Te Awekotuku came from Catholic backgrounds. It seemed that a lot of women who were breaking out came from Catholic backgrounds … The Church teaches you about injustice. It gives you a social conscience and an awareness. I think we break out because of that strong sense of justice and looking for truth. And we go overboard.

The theme of fighting for social justice in ethnic, social and political relations occurs also in the New Zealand accounts of Stephanie Dowrick (founder of the Women's Press), Marian Hobbs (Member of Parliament), Fran Wilde (Labour Cabinet Minister) and Moana Maniopoto-Jackson (campaigner on Maori social issues). As Fran Wilde (Tolerton 1994, p. 106) puts it:

> You knew that you had to serve in some way – *knew*, not thought. You weren't here to look after yourself. You were put on this earth basically to serve others – God included, obviously, but other people as well … If you look at the Labour Party you will find that many people who have been active over the years have been either Catholic or former Catholic.

It would be wrong of course to suggest that traditional Catholic education was radical in content and in pedagogy. On the contrary, it was conservative in content and in pedagogy and traditional in its stances on socialism and communism, the role of women, gender relations, sexual relations, abortion, divorce and social and political order in society.[8] At its most 'effective', pre-Vatican II Catholic schooling formed 'good Catholics' with conservative attitudes on all of these issues. It is this version of Catholic education which has constituted the dominant popular image of what Catholic schooling was in the past. However, as the oral history accounts which have been quoted demonstrate, this schooling culture had unintended outcomes. There was always an internal Catholic education resistance movement among the pupils, which in adulthood flowered into various forms of radical commitment to social justice, while distancing itself from the practice of the Catholic institutional faith.

From an intellectual and academic perspective the quality of Catholic knowledge and Catholic learning varied greatly in pre-Vatican II schooling contexts. At its worst, such knowledge and pedagogy could be classical, formal, arid and oppressive with little space for creativity, dialogue and the enjoyment of learning. At its best, it could be an intellectually stimulating engagement with the classics, with theology and philosophy, with history and literature and with music, art and drama.

In commenting on the historical roots of Catholic education in Europe, Durkheim (1977) observed the central importance of 'bookishness' and of 'dialectic and debate' in the constitution of Catholic knowledge and pedagogy. Catholic medieval learning depended upon these interrelated pedagogical characteristics:

> With the sole exception of mathematical problems, argument inevitably appeared to be the only way in which the human mind could distinguish between truth and falsehood … Disputation in the strict sense of the word was considered as the queen of sciences … At this moment of history, learning how to think consisted of learning how to debate.
>
> (p. 152)

If learning how to think depended so much upon learning how to debate, then this pedagogical mode depended in turn upon the resources available for debate, i.e. bookishness:

> We should be wary of thinking that a bookish education as such is somehow outrageous … On the contrary, it was precisely this concept of education which was … to appear most natural to the human mind … It is in books that the intellectual civilisation of different peoples is to be found preserved and condensed; it was thus quite natural that books were seen as the supreme medium for education.
>
> (p. 153)

Modern forms of Catholic education have been influenced by this pedagogical tradition, as recontextualised and disseminated for instance by the Jesuits from the sixteenth century onwards. In recognising the remarkable significance of the Jesuits in shaping and forming Catholic curricula and pedagogy in Europe, Durkheim (1977) in his classic study

*The Evolution of Educational Thought* devotes two chapters to the analysis of their educational approaches. Important within these was attention to philosophy, theology, rhetoric and dialectic, with the dominant emphasis being 'piety and literature'. Literary culture, i.e. the study of classical language and literature, had a pre-eminent position but the intention of the whole enterprise was to use these cultural forms as means to assist the development of piety.

For those who had the privilege of a Catholic secondary education, mediated by religious orders in the pre-Vatican II period, this particular pedagogic approach had many intellectual benefits, even if the generation of piety was less assured. Germaine Greer (Bennett and Forgan 1991, p. 87) records: 'I realise now I had a terrific education.'

Marina Warner (Bennett and Forgan 1991, p. 176) reflects: 'I owe the nuns an immense amount because they provided me with so much of my subject matter.' Marian Hobbs (Tolerton 1994, p. 99) attributes to her Dominican convent schooling the 'gift of confidence' and an ability to argue a position in public, and Harry Orsman (Sullivan 1996, p. 191) witnesses to the value of Christian doctrine classes from the Marists: 'We were introduced to the thoughts of people like Aristotle and Plato and St Thomas Aquinas. Christian Doctrine was really a very good introduction to general philosophy as well as religious studies and political studies.'

It must be remembered however that these are privileged accounts of a privileged and elite form of Catholic schooling: privileged, in the sense that such evidence comes from published sources and from those who were successful in literary culture and who subsequently became writers, academics and teachers themselves. Privileged also, in the sense that access to these elite forms of Catholic schooling was dependent upon either the possession of middle-class financial resources or the early demonstration of scholarship potential and of intellectual resources.

For the majority of Catholic pupils in parish elementary and primary schools and in Diocesan secondary schools a more comprehensive and varied range of pedagogical environments would have been encountered. Some of them would have involved, as in the experience of Brendan Quigley, an almost total prohibition on asking questions let alone engaging in debate. It also seems unlikely that in Catholic working-class secondary modern schools in many cities there was much opportunity for engagement with the thoughts of Aristotle, Plato and even St Thomas Aquinas. Catholic schooling was as much stratified by distorted geneticist and psychometric assumptions about the abilities of pupils in England and Wales as was the state schooling system in the pre-Vatican II period. The Catholic system tended to subscribe to the 'limited pool of talent' theories dominant in the 1940s, 1950s and early

1960s in the UK. Such theories had real implications for the quality of curriculum experience and pedagogic approaches available for Catholic pupils in non-elite schools. There were those in the Catholic community, such as Terry Eagleton, who were outraged that the Catholic schooling system seemed to reproduce the contours of class and of intellectual advantage. For such critics, a Catholic schooling system could only be comprehensive in nature, comprehensive by class and ethnic intake, comprehensive by ability range and comprehensive in terms of its curriculum and pedagogic provision for all pupils. It is a feature of Catholic schooling in England and Wales, post-Vatican II, that it has become more comprehensive in nature. However, elements of Catholic elite schooling are still present in the form of Catholic independent schools (fee paying) and in some remaining Catholic grammar schools (selective by ability). What forms Catholic knowledge and Catholic learning are taking in the more comprehensive contexts of present-day secondary schooling will be examined in later chapters.

## Purity and danger

When Douglas (1966) wrote her famous text *Purity and Danger: An Analysis of Concepts of Pollution and Taboo* its formal focus was upon concepts of ritual uncleanness in 'primitive' religions. However, as Fardon (1999) has argued, it is possible to see many relational references to the Catholic culture which shaped her own schooling and which gave her a developed sense of the concept of purity and of the sources of danger to it. For traditional Catholic culture, a dominant notion of purity was that of sexual purity, against which were constructed a whole army of sources of danger, pollution and 'sins of the flesh'. A preoccupation of the institutional Roman Catholic Church and of its schooling system was that a habitus should be created in which young people would learn the beauty of purity (most gloriously displayed in the perpetual virginity of Our Lady) and would learn to shun all sexual behaviour before marriage which had illicit and polluting characteristics. In attempting to maintain standards of sexual purity, an important part of Catholic culture was taken up with the regulation of sexual behaviour and the detailed specification of the sexual sins to be avoided, not only by the young but also by married couples. In reviewing Catholic attitudes to sex and family life, Marshall (1999) has argued that Catholic culture has suffered from the puritanical legacy of St Augustine's teaching:

> The Roman Catholic Church has prescribed the sexual behaviour of its members in a way that no other religious group has ever

> attempted. In traditional textbooks of moral theology, for every page dealing with sins against social justice as many as one hundred were devoted to sexual sins.
>
> (p. 67)

The battle against potential sexual sins was a defining feature of pre-Vatican II Catholic schooling and this feature has powerfully constituted some of its enduring images. As Bennett and Forgan (1991, p. 5) remark in the introduction to their oral history collection of convent school accounts:

> It is almost impossible to talk to 'old convent girls' ... without sex coming into the conversation ... The constant admonition 'not to' seems to have worked in reverse, turning it into a major preoccupation.

In the eighteen reflective accounts of convent schooling in England and Ireland (Bennett and Forgan 1991) and in the seventeen accounts in the New Zealand Catholic Oral History collection (Tolerton 1994) this overall conclusion is confirmed. The convent school habitus produced deeply contradictory attitudes to sex among many young women. In Germaine Greer's (Bennett and Forgan 1991, p. 90) account, 'for all convent girls sex is hugely attractive, dark, mysterious and very powerful', and yet, at the same time, this dark mystery is a source of sin, of guilt and of feelings of ritual uncleanness. These contradictions of traditional Catholic schooling on matters related to the body and to sexual relations are, in the view of Mary Kenny (Bennett and Forgan 1991, p. 127), mediations of wider contradictions within Catholic religion and culture:

> There is indeed a worship of the body, if you look at the statues of Bernini and Michelangelo ... 'And the Word was made flesh', at the centre of it all is the Incarnation. However, Catholicism can give contradictory messages in its appreciation of the body: there is the celebration of the body in every church painting and yet there is the mortification of the body's desires both through martyrdom and through chastity and celibacy.

Whether a convent school habitus produced for those who experienced it a 'responsible' and Catholic attitude to sexual relations, or whether it produced wild rebellions or crippling inhibitions and guilt, is difficult to assess. Catholic teaching in this area seems to have resulted in catholic outcomes in practice. Whatever the outcomes, there can be no doubting the social fact that an indelible image of traditional Catholic schooling is of the *attempted* control and regulation of the sexual behaviour of young people. It also seems to be the case that the mode of this attempted control caused significant personal anguish for some who were subject to it. There are qualitative differences in the reflective accounts of women and men on this particular aspect of Catholic schooling. For many young women, an impression was formed that they had a particular responsibility to preserve sexual purity in any encounters with young men. By modesty of dress, deportment and behaviour they were to exorcise the legacy of Eve's temptation of Adam. For Catholic young men their sex education appears to have been either clear cut and functional or virtually non-existent.

In the New Zealand Catholic Oral History research, Geoff Gray's (Sullivan 1996, p. 29) account gives an example of the former mode:

> The message we were getting at school was definitely 'No sex before marriage', and that message was stronger at a Catholic school than anywhere else. Sexual purity was it. Sex was for marriage, for having children and expressing love. That message was given great prominence. Sex was something that married couples did, but fornication before marriage was something that could be forgiven. There was always Confession!

Sam Hunt (Sullivan 1996, p. 42) gives an example of the minimalist position:

> At school, sex education and preparation for relations were totally non-existent … The only sense in which the other sex was put to us was that we had to respect them and open doors for them. That was the extent of sex education … Except for the big, heavy message that sex outside marriage incurs eternal damnation.

While David Lodge's novel, *How Far Can You Go?*, has been able to invest the purity and danger aspects of traditional Catholic education with mordant insight and ironic humour, it does seem clear that the battle to preserve a strong form of sexual purity among the young exacted some heavy personal costs. Whether these are the costs which have to be paid for the maintenance of a Christian conception of sexuality or whether they are the oppressive legacy of Augustinian puritanism[9] is the subject of vigorous contemporary debate in Catholic circles.

## Charity, service and good works

In their authoritative text *The Church and Social Justice*, Calvez and Perrin (1961) present an analysis of the social teachings of the popes of the late nineteenth and early twentieth centuries, in particular those of Leo XIII, Pius XI and Pius XII, as they relate to crucial distinctions between social charity and social justice. Charity, as a concept and as a practice, has a long and honourable history in Catholic culture. Social justice, on the other hand, is a modern concept which only entered the formal discourse of the Catholic Church when it was first used by Pius XI in his much-quoted encyclical, *Quadragesimo Anno* (1931).[10] For the 'modern' popes, the condition of capitalism in the nineteenth and early twentieth centuries made it essential that the Church should clarify distinctions between social charity and social justice. As Calvez and Perrin (1961, p. 164) point out, Pius XI was emphatic about these distinctions:

> A charity which defrauds the worker of his just wage is no true charity but a hollow name and a pretence ... Doles given out of pity will not exempt a man from his obligations of justice ... Pius XI said with some bitterness that the late nineteenth century division of society into two opposing classes 'was quite satisfactory to the wealthy who looked upon it as the consequence of inevitable economic laws and who therefore were content to leave to charity alone the full care of helping the unfortunate; as though it were the task of charity to make amends for the open violation of justice ... True charity, on the contrary, is the virtue which makes men try to improve the distribution of goods as justice requires.'

The habitus of pre-Vatican II Catholic schooling was therefore constituted by a bedrock conception of the need for 'works of charity' for those in unfortunate circumstances and, in its more progressive sectors (where *Quadragesimo Anno* was actually studied), by an awareness that Catholicism entailed working for social justice in the world.

Laurie O'Reilly (Sullivan 1996, p. 145), in his New Zealand account, witnesses to the influence of the social justice dimension of Catholic education:

> My years as a Catholic boy taught me about valuing people and seeing the good in everyone. I've come out of it with a very strong sense of social justice. I'm not surprised that research into a non-religious agency which dealt with street kids ... showed that the key workers were almost always Catholic.

This emphasis on service to others and working for greater social justice is supported by Fran Wilde's (Tolerton 1994) account of the strong associations between Catholics and Labour Party activists and supporters in New Zealand.

The reflective accounts of traditional Catholic schooling in England and Ireland tend to highlight more general 'works of charity' for poor children, orphans, and for the support of missionary activity, especially in Africa. In these contexts, ideas of charity, service and good works were still expressed in traditional forms, rather than in explicit social justice terms. Maeve Binchy expresses well the charity/missionary imperative in her account (Bennett and Forgan 1991, p. 32):

> We gave a lot of money and saw nothing odd in going out to another country and changing its way of life because we thought it was a good thing. If they had no clothes, they must have clothes and then of course they must have faith … so we supported the missions like mad.

Alison Halford (1991, p. 102) remembers the constant efforts to raise funds for the Black Babies in Africa and hopes that this activity was a true act of charity and not some form of unintentional racist learning.

Traditional Catholic schooling had an intention to implant a 'Good Samaritan' ethic in the spiritual and moral formation of its pupils. Involvement in works of charity and mercy were taken to be visible realisations of a lively and active Catholic faith. The great danger with this position is that charity, given out of faith and compassion, can become a substitute for radical social and economic reform. The formation of a modern Catholic social teaching, beginning with the encyclical *Rerum Novarum* (1891) of Leo XIII and Pius XI's *Quadragesimo Anno* (1931), was designed to show that social charity and social justice were two parts of the same impetus to build a better world. Charity was not to be a substitute for social justice, but, on the contrary, the animating spirit and dynamic for social justice reforms.

It seems likely that these social teachings of the modern popes permeated the conservative structures of pre-Vatican II schooling relatively slowly. The commitment to works of charity and mercy remains the dominant image of such schooling but, as the account of Laurie O'Reilly shows, a more explicit commitment to social justice was beginning to emerge in the 1950s and 1960s.

At the centre of modern papal social teaching is the concept of the common good.[11] Given the political and ideological emphases upon competitive individualism by British governments in the 1980s and early 1990s, the status of social justice commitments in contemporary Catholic schools is a matter of considerable research interest. Some examination of this issue will be made in later chapters.

## Catholic identity and a sense of 'the other'

Catholic identity in the pre-Vatican II era was a prime example of what Bernstein (1996, p. 78) has described as retrospective identities, i.e.:

> These identities use as resources narratives of the past which provide exemplars and criteria.

The narratives of the past which provided the exemplars for the identity and character formation of Catholic children and youth in pre-Vatican II schooling were the stories of the saints and martyrs and the history of the struggles of the Church against various forms of persecution, oppression and bigotry. A sense of Catholic identity was therefore constructed within a grand narrative of an endless struggle between the forces of good (all things Catholic) and the forces of evil (all things hostile to Catholicism).

Once again, the formation of a Catholic sense of identity was at its strongest in the schools of the religious orders and the teaching orders where the retrospective habitus was most salient. Reflective accounts of this period of Catholic schooling help to illuminate these socialisation experiences. Hastings (1970) recalls the impact of the stories of the Jesuit martyrs in America, Japan and England, of those prepared to undergo 'prolonged and terrible deaths' for the Catholic faith. Stephanie Dowrick (Tolerton 1994, p. 87) records her experiences in the Sacred Heart Convent School in New Zealand: 'We were taught about the lives of the saints. The virgin martyrs were the favourites – those who died in defence of their virginity.'[12] Warner (1991, p. 181) celebrates the richness of symbolism, structure and tradition in which she was immersed:

> I am glad of being a pre-Vatican II Catholic because of the knowledge of the calendar and of saints' lives. There are so many rules and rituals; I suppose there isn't really another way of incorporating people into the faith. It is a language … The idea of being a member of this very ancient body of the Church gives you a greater historical perspective.

In a very real way, the pre-Vatican II system of Catholic schooling constructed a sense of Catholic identity in its pupils by immersing them in a richness of history, narrative and language – 'Mystical rose, Tower of Ivory, House of Gold, Morning Star'.[13] The Catholic identity of this period was not, however, formed only by the retrospective resources of the Church but also by a lively awareness of the oppositional 'other'. Chief among these were the various manifestations of Protestantism.[14] The Catholic identity of the young had to be forged over and against the potential dangers of Protestant culture in ascendant positions in England, Ireland, the USA, Australia and New Zealand. Mary O'Malley (Bennett and Forgan 1991, p. 149) found the constant emphasis upon the rightness of Catholicism and the wrongness of other religious positions so oppressive that she wrote the play *Once a Catholic* to try to exorcise its legacy:

> I was an expert in bigotry. That was what they taught us although at the time I didn't even know the word. The Catholic Church was all that mattered; anybody else could go to hell – or limbo – literally. I was just full of it. It was coming out of my ears, bigotry, bigotry, bigotry. That's what *Once a Catholic* is about.

Pre-Vatican II Catholic schooling attempted to implant the idea that Catholicism was the repository of absolute religious truth and that all other religious and faith traditions were in error. Where Protestantism was in the ascendant, young Catholics were taught that they would have to be defenders of the faith in a hostile world. As Manuka Herare (Sullivan 1996, p. 157) records of his New Zealand Catholic education:

> It was conveyed to us that being Catholic in a largely non-Catholic country was not going to help our progress and that Catholics were likely to be victimised … If we wanted to get a job, we had to go for good education, and go for success in sport so we would be socially accepted.

After Protestantism, the other great adversary of Catholicism in the narratives of traditional Catholic education was communism. Papal encyclicals from Leo XIII, Pius XI and Pius XII had condemned communist atheism and materialism (as in total opposition to Catholic theology) and the communist doctrine of class warfare and the abolition of private property (as in total opposition to Catholic social teaching). Soviet communism was propagated as the modern form of the anti-Christ and young Catholics were expected to be crusaders against its evil doctrines. In Deane's (1997) autobiographical account, *Reading in the Dark*, some sense of the traditional teaching of 'the other' can be seen:

> McShane then asked if the man was a Catholic priest. Certainly not, answered McAuley, the man was an Anglican or what was called an Anglo-Catholic priest … Although as far as he was concerned there was no kind of Catholic, other than the Roman Catholic … This distinction left us awash. So which was worse, I asked, Communism or the Reformation? Both were bad, but the Reformation was history. Communism was the living threat … There was a family quarrel within the Christian family. It would work itself out. When that had all been resolved, Communism would still be there, threatening anyone who believed in God.
>
> (p. 199)

Catholic social teaching was, in practice, critical of capitalism as well as of communism. In other words, the Catholic Church was announcing a 'third way' in socio-economic relations and organisation long before contemporary social theorists such as Giddens (1998, 2000) had formalised the concept. What made the Catholic critique of communism more salient and more dominant in the messages of traditional Catholic schooling was that communism was not simply an economic ideology but an atheist one. It therefore threatened more directly the very existence of the Catholic Church and of the Catholic schooling system than was the case in capitalist societies. Catholics of this period might be, and frequently were, supporters of the Labour Party and social reformist parties in various societies, and even of Christian socialism, but they could not, in the view of the institutional Church, be Marxists or communists. As Peter Dunne (Sullivan 1996, p. 97) records of his pre-Vatican II education, what young Catholics of the time were learning was a version of international politics in which the key issue 'was a battle between the Catholic Church and the communists'.

If the Catholic identity of the young was shaped at this time by an oppositional relation to Protestantism and to communism, it was also shaped in complex and contradictory ways by a relationship with Irish culture and identity. The Irish diaspora in England, Wales, Scotland, the USA, Australia and New Zealand meant that the culture and practice of Roman Catholicism in all of these countries was strongly influenced by Irish Roman Catholicism as a particular realisation of a universal faith. In England in the 1890s Cardinal Manning estimated that 'eight tenths of the Catholics in England are Irish'[15] and these immigrant communities of Irish Catholics were concentrated in conditions of great squalor in major cities and industrial locations in England and Wales. Meeting the spiritual, cultural, educational and social needs of the Irish diaspora in the UK and elsewhere became the mission of large numbers of Irish priests and nuns, and members of teaching orders such as the Christian Brothers and the Sisters of Mercy. As the Catholic school system developed in the UK and in other countries of the Irish diaspora, its culture was constituted to an important extent by the spiritual, moral and educational dispositions of Irish teaching personnel (of first, second or third generational origin). This habitus was registered by and reacted to in various ways by those who experienced Catholic education at this time. In the three Catholic oral history sources used in this study, twenty-seven out of the fifty reflective accounts make references to the Irishness of a Catholic schooling, pre-Vatican II. In some cases, the Irishness of a Catholic education involved an interweaving of 'imaginative folklore with Catholic dogmas', which produced a rich religious narrative but in other cases it was experienced as having a fixation with purity and a 'bleak and martyred' approach to life. There was also a hidden curriculum and sometimes an explicit curriculum of the wrongs suffered by the Irish at the hands of the English. Francis Pound (Sullivan 1996, p. 79) records his experience of an Irish Catholic education, reconstituted in New Zealand, which involved both home and school influences:

> My father would sing songs like 'Faith of our fathers living still, in spite of dungeon, fire and sword'. There was a memory still alive of the Irish diaspora, a sense of Irish suffering, colonisation and religious persecution at the hands of the English, of English racism, of the Irish as England's 'white negroes'.

The Irishness of a Catholic education produced in some contexts a distinctive habitus which generated the dual identities of Irish-English, Irish-American, Irish-Australian, Irish-New Zealander. Traditional Catholic education of this period was therefore partly about the preservation of a national and ethnic identity as well as about the formation of a religious identity. Tolerton (1994) has argued that a historical and cultural sense of the injustices experienced by Catholics and especially by Irish Catholics provided a dynamic for academic and sporting achievement in Catholic schools. The oppressions of history would be partly exorcised by the demonstration of contemporary achievements in the Catholic school system.

Against these views of a productive relationship between Irishness and Catholicism in the Church's schooling system, Hickman (1995) has argued a contrary case. In the English Catholic school system, she argues, there was a policy from the hierarchy which attempted to mute the expression of Irish culture and Irish identity as detrimental to the acceptance of the Church within civil society.[16] From Hickman's perspective, an English Catholic schooling was intended to be an exercise in cultural assimilation and incorporation of the Irish. Some examination of these ideas will be made in later chapters. The argument of this chapter has been that the images of characteristics of pre-Vatican II Catholic schooling live on, in various ways, and influence contemporary popular consciousness of what a Catholic education is and what it does to young people. Such images also provide an evaluative background for those critics of contemporary Catholic schooling who want to argue that its religious, moral and cultural distinctiveness is weakening over time. Later analysis will suggest that both of these appropriations of images of traditional Catholic schooling can have misleading and oversimplified consequences for the perception and the evaluation of contemporary forms of Catholic education.

This chapter has used as a resource the images of traditional Catholic schooling which have been constructed and projected in literature and in reflective oral history accounts of aspects of pre-Vatican II education as experienced in England, Ireland, Australia and New Zealand.[17] The following chapter will draw upon more systematic empirical research into the characteristics of Catholic schooling in the post-Vatican II period.

# 4 Catholic schools post-Vatican II

## A review of research studies

A challenge in reviewing empirical studies, as every research student knows, is whether to present a historical account, which provides a cumulative record (but which ignores major themes and cultural settings), or, on the other hand, to construct a culturally located and thematic analysis which may obscure the historical sequencing of the work. A further problem arises in making judgements of selectivity, i.e. what are defined to be major and significant research studies in a given field.

What is attempted here is a review of empirical research studies in Catholic schooling, which is culturally located (by country) and thematically focused. Studies are presented in historical sequence within each cultural sector of research. The presentation is selective in terms of a concentration upon major studies,[1] defined as researches which have significantly illuminated the field of Catholic schooling, which have generated debate and discussion and which are known and used in international settings. As such, it follows that the selection made here is open to challenge.

When empirical research studies of Catholic schooling are examined it soon becomes clear that the leading cultural setting for such activity has been the USA. This is hardly surprising given the size of the Catholic population in that country, the number of Catholic universities and colleges[2] and the strong empirical traditions of American social enquiry and intellectual life. Catholic school research generated in the USA has provided not only the largest data source for other researchers but also theoretical concepts and research paradigms which have been used by researchers in other cultural settings. It seems appropriate therefore that any review of empirical research studies in Catholic schooling should begin with some analysis of American work in this field.

## Catholic school research: USA

### *Sectors and controversies*

In his authoritative and comprehensive review of research studies of Catholic schooling in the USA in the period 1965–90, Convey (1992) has identified three major emphases in research enquiry. The first two lines of investigation were research initiatives emanating from the Catholic educational community. These were a focus upon the effects of a Catholic schooling on the religious development and attitudes of young people, i.e. on the extent to which the habitus of Catholicity in the schooling system produced assessable outcomes in terms of faith understanding, faith commitment and religious practice. This sector in Catholic research might be described as *foundational research* since it relates to the basic rationale for the existence of a Catholic schooling system.

A second sector involves a particular focus upon inner-city Catholic schools and upon their service to poor communities and to ethnic minority students. This sector might be described as *preferential option research* since it relates to a renewed commitment in the Vatican II reforms, that Catholic institutions would whenever possible demonstrate a 'preferential option for the poor'.[3] As Convey (1992) argues, these two emphases were Catholic initiatives in research and as such demonstrated a distinctive Catholic perspective in social scientific enquiry, i.e. a fundamental concern with values in action.

The third sector, which became a dominant focus in the 1980s, arose from initiatives of the federal government and from its concern about the quality of publicly provided schooling in the USA. Catholic schools were caught up in larger national research projects designed to probe the relative effectiveness of different forms of schooling. This sector was that of *school effectiveness research*, where effectiveness was largely assessed in terms of the organisational characteristics necessary for high cognitive and academic achievement. In the absence of US government financial support for Catholic schools (unlike the situation in the UK) access to such schools is mediated by a fee-paying policy and the schools are designated as 'private' schools.[4] A number of school effectiveness studies were undertaken in the 1980s, which compared the relative effectiveness of public and 'private' schools. Catholic schools designated as 'private' schools soon became the focus of national attention and of national controversy arising out of such comparisons. Convey (1992, p. 3) notes that this research:

> concluded that, in many areas, Catholic schools produced better outcomes than did public schools and … a storm of controversy ensued concerning the findings.

It is important to point out that at this time the Catholic educational community had not sought to make these public comparative judgements about relative school effectiveness. They were, in general, the outcome of large national research projects and of national education policy concerns. In practice the outcomes of Catholic schooling as revealed by research were being appropriated for political and ideological purposes, especially by critics of the public schooling system in the USA. The argument in effect was that if Catholic schools can achieve good academic results often in difficult circumstances, then why could not the public schools of the USA match these results?

The answer given by many critics of such comparisons was that in all sorts of ways such research failed in the basic rule of comparing like with like. Was it likely that Catholic schools with access mediated by fees (however low) would have the same constituency of students as public schools with free access?

The Catholic educational research community in the USA has sought to distance itself from ideological appropriations of research findings by emphasising the complexities involved in making evaluative comparisons between two schooling systems. Writing with the authority of the National Catholic Educational Association (NCEA), Convey (1992, p. 6) has made a definitive scholarly statement on this subject which serves as a crucial guide to anyone working in this field:

> Self-selection prevents a conclusive answer to whether or not Catholic schools are more effective than public schools. Studies that compare Catholic schools with public schools can never eliminate the possibility that some unmeasured or otherwise uncontrolled attribute of students that is associated with self-selection is responsible for a significant amount of the differences between Catholic schools and public schools … The possibility that the observed differences between Catholic schools and public schools are more a function of the type of students who enroll in each, rather than anything to do with the school, can never be completely eliminated.

### *Themes and major research studies*

In the period 1965–98 the three research sectors – foundational, preferential option and school effectiveness – were advanced by a number of major empirical studies. In the *foundational sector*, the work of Greeley and Rossi (1966) and of Greeley *et al* (1976) was of pioneering significance.

The first study, led by Greeley, *The Education of Catholic Americans*, seemed to confirm all the fears of the Catholic hierarchy that social scientific enquiry in Catholic education would produce disturbing results. Using both interview and survey methods with a large sample of adolescent and adult Catholics, Greeley and Rossi investigated the key issue of the religious impact of a Catholic education. Using constructed indexes of religious behaviour and understanding related to sacramental issues, doctrinal orthodoxy, sexual mores and religious knowledge, Greeley and Rossi attempted to probe the complex question of the extent to which a Catholic schooling impacted upon the religious beliefs and practices of adolescents and adults. Their main findings were dramatic and widely reported:

> We can go so far as to say that for all practical purposes, the religious impact of Catholic education is limited to those who come from highly religious families.
>
> (p. 85)

> Catholic education is virtually wasted on the three-fourths of those in Catholic schools because of the absence of a sufficiently religious family milieu.
>
> (p. 112)

The research theme being argued by Greeley and Rossi at this time was that Catholic schooling had a 'multiplier effect' on Catholicity rather than an originating effect, i.e. it added to an already existing religiosity in the family rather than stimulating faith and practice in those whose homes were religiously dormant.

As might be expected, such research conclusions produced much controversy, debate and criticism of the methodological approaches used. The findings seemed to give social scientific support to those in the Catholic community who were already questioning the need for a separate Catholic schooling system (see Chapter 2). What Greeley and Rossi's research seemed to be saying was that the fundamental mission of Catholic schooling, i.e. the strengthening and enhancement of the Catholic faith among young people, was not being realised in any really significant way.

However, ten years later, a second research study led by Greeley came to different conclusions. In *Catholic Schools in a Declining Church* Greeley, McCready and McCourt attempted a replication of the earlier study but using more advanced forms of statistical analysis and learning from some of the methodological criticisms of the 1966 study. This research with a large national sample of adult Catholics and using religious behaviour scales and factor analysis procedures to generate more reliable 'Catholicity factors' came to a more positive conclusion about the religious impact of Catholic schooling:

> Far from declining in effectiveness in the past decade, Catholic schools seem to have increased their impact. In a time of general decline in religious behaviour, the rate of decline for those who have gone to Catholic schools is much slower. The correlation between Catholic school attendance and religious behaviour is especially strong for those under thirty.
>
> (p. 310)

For Greeley *et al.* (1976) the years of Catholic schooling had now become more important than parental religiosity in predicting adult religious behaviour. In a time of dramatic transformations in the institutional Church arising from the Vatican II reforms and in a larger social context marked by increased secularisation, this 1976 research appeared to show that Catholic schools were crucial to the transmission of the faith in changed circumstances. The research themes illuminated by this study have an interesting and apparently contradictory nature. On the one hand, it can be argued that the Catholic schooling studied by Greeley *et al.* was culturally resistant to external secular influences but, on the other hand, it was showing a capacity to be culturally adaptive to the internal changes within Catholicism and helping young Catholics to make the transitions between pre- and post-Vatican II religious practice. Although subsequent work has raised questions about the validity of the data and of the analysis[5] there can be no doubt that the Greeley *et al.* study produced some important research themes for further investigation. Convey (1992, p. 4) comments that both the 1966 study and the 1976 study were crucial parts of:

> Greeley's extraordinary and enduring research effort to examine in a rigorous and objective manner the effects of Catholic schools on their graduates and the contribution of Catholic schools to the church in the United States.

Reviewing his own research and that of others in the foundational sector of the religious impact of Catholic schools, Greeley (1998, p. 183) concluded:

> The effect of Catholic education on adult religious behaviour has been stronger in the post-conciliar years than before … Catholic schools have an impact independent of parental background.

Such a conclusion challenges the stance of conservative critics of Catholic schools who believe that weaknesses in the religious habitus of these institutions are responsible for the wider decline of the Catholic Church, mass attendances and the number of religious vocations. The work of Greeley and others suggests that, on the contrary, contemporary Catholic schools are significant in keeping the faith alive and in adapting religious practice to meet new circumstances.

*Preferential option research*, with its particular focus upon the service of Catholic schools to inner-city and poor communities, to ethnic groups in difficult conditions and to alienated and troubled youth, received a major impetus when the United States Catholic Conference commissioned in 1977 a review of Catholic schooling in inner-city areas. The study resulting from this, *Catholic Inner-City Schools: The Future* (Vitullo-Martin 1979), was a survey of the changing pattern of Catholic school provision in inner-city areas. It demonstrated that such schools were experiencing severe reductions in enrolments and that this trend had caused a rise in school closures. The research theme illustrated by the Vitullo-Martin study was one of mission renewal and adaptability. As a result of white population migration out of the inner-city, parish schools were now serving larger numbers of black students and students from non-Catholic backgrounds. The study raised questions about the potential of Catholic schools to be valuable spiritual, social and educational resources for poor communities despite the fact that these communities were no longer predominantly Catholic. Vitullo-Martin argued that such schools were making an important contribution to the common good of American society and as such they should receive financial support both from the state and the Church. A form of mission adaptability was required for Catholic inner-city schools faced with the changing demographics and economics of student enrolments. Failure to undertake such mission renewal could only result in Catholic school closures which would not only further impoverish the resources for poor communities but raise serious questions about the Church's commitment to outreach and evangelisation in the wider society. Could the Church be accused of deserting the educational service of the poor, when the poor were no longer Catholic?

Two major empirical studies pursued these themes in 1982. In *Inner-City Private Elementary Schools* James Cibulka and others examined over fifty Catholic elementary schools with ethnic minority enrolments of at least 70 per cent located in Chicago, Detroit, Los Angeles, Milwaukee, Newark, New Orleans, New York and Washington. Data was obtained from almost 4,000 parents and over 300 teachers as well as from school principals. The Cibulka study demonstrated that the families which used the schools were larger and poorer than the average American family and were more likely to be headed by a single parent. More than half of the families were not Catholic.[6] Generally, students in these schools performed at higher achievement levels than students in neighbouring public schools. Cibulka and his colleagues argued that generally these Catholic inner-city elementary schools had highly motivated and dedicated teachers, about 30 per cent of whom were members of religious orders.

The research themes illustrated by this enquiry related to the importance of purposeful leadership, clarity of mission, a sense of community within schools, shared values and purposes and strong school–community links in the local area. These were educational advantages which Catholic inner-city schools possessed more frequently than their public school colleagues. At the same time these Catholic schools faced serious problems about the continuance of their educational missions as critical issues about the financing and staffing of the schools became more pressing.

Further evidence of the 'common good effects' of Catholic schools was provided in Greeley's (1982) study, *Catholic High Schools and Minority Students*. Here the focus was to explore why black and Hispanic students who attended Catholic high schools had higher levels of academic achievement than black and Hispanic students who attended public high schools. Greeley found that part of the explanation for better student performance in Catholic high schools related to home environment factors:

> It is children of the more affluent, better-educated and more successful minority group members who attend Catholic schools. Their families are smaller, their fathers less likely to be absent.
>
> (p. 19)

The success of such students was an outcome of cultural resources in the home, amplified and enhanced by 'superior' academic and disciplinary environments in the schools. Greeley argued that Catholic high schools were particularly successful with those students who had multiple disadvantages arising from home background of low educational achievement.[7]

In these cases the 'Catholic school effect' was the outcome of a focused and demanding academic regime, in a strong disciplinary framework, with significant requirements for homework. In explaining how Catholic schools serving minority ethnic communities came to have these distinctive qualities of academic and disciplinary habitus, Greeley placed great emphasis upon the presence of religious orders:

> Ownership of some Catholic schools by religious communities … seems to have a strong effect on academic and disciplinary environments.
>
> (p. 58)[8]

One of the most interesting research themes articulated by Greeley related to precisely how the presence of a religious order and of its members affected the academic and disciplinary environments of Catholic schools and affected the responses of students within them. In calling for more research into this neglected topic he observed a pressing need to address such questions:

> There is a certain poignancy in the fact that many members of Catholic religious orders have lost confidence in their own work and membership in their religious communities is declining rapidly – precisely when educational research becomes available showing that religious orders apparently make a unique and important contribution to secondary education.
>
> (p. 109)

The changing mission of the religious orders in education and the future of Catholic schools in inner-city communities in the USA and elsewhere are a key issue for contemporary Catholic educational policy, as well as research. As I have argued elsewhere (Grace 1998c), religious orders in inner-city schooling have represented a 'strategic subsidy' in the 'option for the poor' educational mission. Religious orders and teaching orders have provided spiritual, cultural and economic capital for poor communities and a supply of school personnel at both leadership and classroom levels. This strategic subsidy is weakening over time and the urgent question is raised as to what new sources of support are available for Catholic inner-city schools – how will the mission be renewed?

The urgency of these questions has been underlined by the research and scholarly writing of O'Keefe (1996), a Jesuit professor at Boston College. O'Keefe has researched the pattern and pace of Catholic school closings in poor urban communities during the 1990s. This investigation with reference to four major archdioceses – Boston, New York,

Philadelphia and Chicago – has demonstrated a significant closure trend with, for example, eighteen Catholic schools closing in the 1992–3 year in Chicago, the majority located in poor and ethnically diverse communities. The research of O'Keefe has illuminated the disturbing fact that the Catholic Church's preferential option for the poor in education is weakening and that 'at the outset of the 1990s many schools closed precisely in those areas where they were needed most' (p. 193). This finding is also confirmed by Bryk *et al.* (1993).[9]

Here we encounter another irony and contradiction along the lines already indicated by Greeley. Just at the time when educational research has established the particular effectiveness of Catholic schools in urban areas and just at the time when the American Catholic population has experienced its highest levels of social mobility and economic prosperity, the future of Catholic inner-city schooling seems in doubt, largely for financial reasons.

The major research theme which emerges from the work of O'Keefe is that of the practical demonstration of solidarity in educational policy and practice. What reality does it have in contemporary Catholic schooling? The commitment of the Catholic Church to the principle of solidarity is clear, as O'Keefe points out:

> In the *Universal Catechism* one reads that 'socio-economic problems can be solved only with the help of all forms of solidarity: solidarity of the poor among themselves, between rich and poor, of workers among themselves, between employers and employees … among nations and peoples' (p. 424). Solidarity is not simply a pragmatic response to social crisis however, it is an imperative that flows from the Catholic understanding of the nature of God.
>
> (p. 190)

O'Keefe's work challenges the Catholic educational community to research the practice of solidarity in its schooling arrangements and decision making. This challenge applies of course to Catholic schooling systems everywhere and not just in inner-city USA.

Two further major studies in the 'preferential option' sector of Catholic school research need to be examined, i.e. the work of McLaren (1993) and Oldenski (1997). McLaren's study of a tough Catholic junior high school in downtown Toronto is difficult to classify because it has a Renaissance-like comprehensiveness of style and form. It makes important contributions to the study of ritual in Catholic schooling,[10] to school–work relations and to socialisation processes in an inner-city school with a diverse ethnic population.

One of the main research themes which emerges from McLaren's study of 'St Ryan's' is that a Catholic schooling of inner-city youth may be more about social control than about experiences of liberation and empowerment. In the 'making' of good Catholics and good workers at St Ryan's, McLaren argues that Catholic values which are, in part, counter-cultural to the external world are largely in practice integrated with the values of corporate capitalism. The habitus of St Ryan's was heavy with Catholic religious symbolism (for the making of Catholics) but it was also, in the view of McLaren, an environment designed to make good, conforming workers for a capitalist economic system.

McLaren's work highlights the contradictory matrix in which many Catholic schools are located. Parents and students expect from Catholic inner-city schools a form of education and socialisation which will result in much needed employment opportunities. On the other hand, the values of a Catholic education, fully realised, may lead students into a critical and questioning stance about the morality and justice of socio-economic arrangements and of contemporary work relations. The way in which Catholic schools, especially in inner-city areas, seek to resolve or balance these potentially conflicting educational outcomes is of great research interest.

Oldenski's (1997) study of the Vincent Gray Alternative High School, a Catholic school in East St Louis, gives a dramatically different account of what a Catholic schooling for deprived urban youth might look like if informed by the insights of liberation theology and of a critical pedagogy. In Oldenski's view, the VGA High School was an exemplar of what Catholic inner-schooling could be at its best:

> While expressing common elements of the critical discourses of liberation theology and critical pedagogy, all the voices (of students, administrators and teachers) also expressed the qualities and dynamic characteristics of Catholic education … All Catholic educators see their schools as faith communities with a view toward making the world more humane, just and caring. One finds harmony in the common elements of liberation theology, critical pedagogy and the essential identity of the Catholic school. The challenge is to hear and respond to this harmony.
>
> (pp. 219–20)

Oldenski's optimism expresses powerfully the main research theme or hypothesis which emerges from his work, namely that Catholic inner-city schools should be more explicitly informed by a theology of liberation and transformation rather than by a theology of social control and conservative reproduction, such as that demonstrated in McLaren's (1993) study of St Ryan's.

Oldenski's research and advocacy represent a radical strand of writing in the preferential option sector of Catholic school enquiry, as does the work of McLaren. It is significant that both researchers have been strongly influenced by the writings of the Brazilian educator Paulo Freire[11] and particularly by his texts *Pedagogy of the Oppressed* (1973), *Education for Critical Consciousness* (1990), *Pedagogy of the City* (1993) and *Pedagogy of Hope* (1994).

What remains to be investigated in this research sector is just how widespread are models such as the VGA High School in Catholic inner-city schooling and just how aware are most Catholic teachers in such locations of the religious, pedagogical and social insights which arise from a closer engagement with liberation theology and with the writings of critical educators such as Paulo Freire.

### *School effectiveness research*

Convey (1992) points out that two major longitudinal research projects in the 1980s sponsored by the National Center for Education Statistics of the United States Department of Education generated data on school effectiveness, which resourced publications and debates about the issues throughout the decade. The first project, *High School and Beyond*, began in 1980 and involved data collection from over 1,000 schools, 84 of which were Catholic high schools. The second project, *National Education Longitudinal Study* (1988), focused on 24,000 students from a nationally representative sample of public and Catholic schools, 2,578 of which were from Catholic schools.

Using the data generated from the first research project, Coleman *et al.* (1982) published a major book, *High School Achievement: Public, Catholic and Private Schools Compared*. This study appeared to demonstrate that Catholic schools produced better cognitive and academic outcomes for their students than public schools, even after controlling for differences in the family background of the students. The conclusions of this study were destined to provoke an academic and public debate in the USA of some vigour. As Convey (1992, p. 17) reports:

> Coleman and his associates attributed the better performance of students in Catholic schools to the strong discipline, high expectations of the teachers, and structured curriculum that characterised these schools. Catholic schools provided a safer, more disciplined, more orderly environment and Catholic school students had higher

> rates of attendance, did more homework and generally took more rigorous academic subjects than did public school students. Based on their results, Coleman, Hoffer and Kilgore (1982) suggested that public policy should encourage an expanded role for private education in the United States.[12]

In the debates which followed this provocative conclusion much was made of 'selectivity bias' in the analysis. Critics argued that differences in patterns of student intake largely accounted for the differences in academic outcomes and that the controls used in the study to account for this were not rigorous enough. Subsequent analysis by Willms (1984) and by Raudenbush and Bryk (1986) found that the 'Catholic school effect' on academic outcomes was much smaller than the Coleman *et al.* study had suggested. However, achievement differences were largest when comparing lower class Catholic schools with lower class public schools so that the Catholic school effect appeared to be most significant in inner-city areas.

In a second study, using more rigorous research procedures, Coleman and Hoffer (1987) argued in *Public and Private High Schools: The Impact of Communities* that the Catholic school effect did have positive academic outcomes, especially in reading, vocabulary, mathematics and writing and especially for lower class, black and Hispanic students. Catholic schools were also likely to have the lowest drop-out rates and more of their students successfully completed their higher education courses. If these Catholic school effects were evident following the application of more rigorous methods of analysis, how were they to be explained?

In providing their answer to this question, Coleman and Hoffer constructed a significant theoretical concept and a major theme for subsequent research projects, that of *social capital*.[13]

For Coleman and Hoffer (1987) social capital refers to a network of support and trust relations which exist between persons. Social capital is a form of strong functional community. It can exist within families or in agencies beyond the family, such as schools. In a wider context it can exist 'in some isolated small towns and rural areas where adults' social relations are restricted by geographic distance and where residential mobility has not destroyed it' (p. 227).

In short, the argument of the Coleman and Hoffer research is that Catholic schools are able to achieve more academically because they possess, in general, more social capital than do public schools:

> The proximate reason for the Catholic schools' success with less advantaged students and students from deficient families appears to

> be the greater academic demands that Catholic schools place on these students. But the ability to make these demands appears to follow in large part from the greater control that the school, based on a functional community, is able to exercise.
>
> (p. 148)

Catholic schools have an advantage arising from the social capital of being embedded in strong functional communities represented by Church and parish agencies. It is for this reason that the subtitle of Coleman and Hoffer's (1987) book is 'the impact of communities'. The research theme indicated here is that strong community support networks for the educational mission of Catholic schools give most Catholic schools an advantage over most public schools, especially in urban areas. Much less controversy was generated by this second study because of this frank recognition that in social capital terms Catholic schools were relatively advantaged. The enduring power of Catholic community exercised in a close sense of partnership between home and school was highlighted by this research as a key factor in Catholic school effectiveness.

In 1993 a major research study by Bryk *et al.*, *Catholic Schools and the Common Good*, confirmed these findings and extended them to provide what is generally regarded as the definitive study of Catholic school effectiveness in the USA. Using statistical data derived from the *High School and Beyond* project and other related information and extending this by detailed fieldwork in seven Catholic high schools (in Los Angeles, Boston, Baltimore, Cleveland, Louisville and San Antonio), the research team focused upon the search for answers to the questions:

> How do Catholic high schools manage simultaneously to achieve relatively high levels of student learning, distribute this learning more equitably with regard to race and class than in the public sector and sustain high levels of teacher commitment and student engagement?
>
> (p. 297)

Analysis, especially of the fieldwork data and of observations within the seven schools, suggested the importance of four crucial factors in explaining the 'Catholic school effect'. These were academic structure and culture (bookishness), internal community (social capital), devolved governance (autonomy) and inspirational ideology (sense of mission and purpose).

For Bryk *et al.*, Catholic schools achieved relatively good academic outcomes because they insisted upon an academic core of subjects for everyone (with limited option choices), while at the same time proceeding on the pedagogical assumption that all students can learn academic subjects. In other words a strong and traditional culture of bookishness was combined with a modern principle of high expectations and of equal opportunities for all. Commitment to this principle was demonstrated in relatively little use of a tracking (streaming) system for pupil grouping for study purposes. In other words, Catholic schools made academic demands but in a learning culture which was supportive of the students in meeting those demands.

A strong internal sense of community appeared to support the academic structure and culture. This was constituted in the fieldwork schools by the extensive involvement of teachers and students in extra-curricular activities such as athletics, drama, liturgy, debates, charitable work, retreats, concerts, etc., which had a bonding effect on school members. It was also shaped by good levels of collegiality among the teachers which itself was facilitated by the relatively small size of Catholic high schools.[14] The researchers also took the view that the schools which they studied appeared to take seriously the principle in their mission commitments which spoke of the dignity of the person. In the light of these findings Bryk *et al.* argued that Coleman and Hoffer's (1987) concept of social capital should be extended to include the notion of functional community *within* the school as well as around the school.[15]

A relatively high level of school autonomy, with considerable scope for the initiatives of school principals, was noted by the research team. Given the modest salary levels of Catholic school principals compared with their public school colleagues, Bryk *et al.* suggest that the principals (and a significant number of teachers) are in practice pursuing a vocation in the service of Catholic youth. The conditions of school-site autonomy provide greater opportunities for professional fulfilment and creativity than those in more bureaucratically controlled public schools. However, Bryk *et al.* are quick to point out that this is not the free-wheeling autonomy celebrated by the proponents of market forces in education. It is guided by 'the set of fundamental beliefs and values that constitute the spirit of Vatican II' (p. 300).

It is this emphasis upon fundamental beliefs and values which emerges as the fourth key factor in explaining the 'Catholic school effect'. Referred to in the 1993 study as 'an inspirational ideology' it is, in the view of the research team, the animating force which gives shape and purpose to the Catholic educational mission. At the heart of this inspirational ideology is the belief that a Catholic school is in the service of Christ for the salvation and redemption of all and that it has transcendent as well as mundane purposes. If all are made in the image of Christ then all must be treated with respect and in pursuit of this respect Catholic schooling must be part of a struggle against poverty, oppression, racism and injustice wherever these occur. Such religious and transcendent purposes, a sense of mission rather than simply of provision, gives, as Bryk *et al.* (1993, p. 303) argue, 'depth to a schooling process that is otherwise dominated by a rhetoric of test scores, performance standards and professional accountability'.

A main research theme which emerges from *Catholic Schools and the Common Good* is the need for more studies of the inspirational ideology which animates most Catholic schools. The researchers are aware of the scepticism which this idea produces, especially in a research culture strongly influenced by secular and positivistic assumptions, but they make a powerful case for such research:

> Some may question our claim of a causal role for this inspirational ideology … unlike the effects of academic organization or community school structure, which can be largely captured in regression analysis and effect sizes, estimating the influence of ideology is a more complex and less certain endeavour. Ironically, these effects are harder to study and yet also more pervasive … To ignore the importance of ideology because it cannot be easily captured in statistical analysis or summarized with numbers would be a serious mistake. Statistical analysis can help us to see some things but they can also blind us to the influence of factors that are beyond their current horizons.
>
> (pp. 303–4)

In a recent survey of school effectiveness research as a background for encouraging more schools to engage in self-evaluation, MacBeath (2000, p. 104) has argued for the importance of 'an overarching philosophy' in the generation of school effectiveness and improvement. The success of many Catholic schools in academic and other terms seems to be related to their possession of a particularly powerful form of overarching philosophy derived from the theological and social tenets of Catholicism itself.

However, despite the very positive findings on Catholic school effectiveness produced by Bryk *et al.* (1993) a debate has developed within the American Catholic educational and academic community on issues linking 'preferential option' research and 'school effectiveness' research. This debate has been sparked by an article entitled 'The "Eliting" of the Common American Catholic School' by David Baker and Cornelius Riordan which appeared in the journal *Phi Delta Kappan* in September 1998.

The Baker–Riordan thesis, using demographic data as its basis, is that Catholic schools in the USA are undergoing a process of transformation which is making them more elite (wealthier students), less Catholic (more non-Catholic students) and more instrumentally academic rather than religious institutions (as a result of parent pressures). Baker and Riordan (1998, p. 19) have argued that:

> Nothing changes a school more than a large change in the social class make-up of its students. And perhaps nothing changes a religiously oriented school more than the presence of large numbers of non-believers. The American Catholic school is experiencing both of these influences simultaneously and the impact is bound to be considerable.

From this perspective the academic success of Catholic schools is masking the fact that they are moving away from their historical and primary mission, i.e. educational service to the poor and religious service for the Church. Catholic schools in the USA, according to this thesis, are being incorporated into a more middle-class and secular culture of schooling. Andrew Greeley has written a strong critique of the work of Baker and Riordan in the same edition of *Phi Delta Kappan* and in the edition of October 1999, James Youniss and Jeffrey McLellan have replied in more measured terms.

From a research perspective, Youniss and McLellan argue that Baker and Riordan have made too many assumptions and extrapolations from the demographic data which they have used. While it cannot be denied that Catholic schools in the USA are now recruiting a higher proportion of students from homes with higher incomes, Youniss and McLellan point out that given the economic and social mobility of the Catholic population, this is hardly surprising. However, it does not follow from this that Catholic schools are abandoning their historical mission of service to the poor, neither does it follow that less attention is being given to the Catholic and religious purposes of the schools, and they argue that 'it is important not to misjudge the eliting phenomenon as an abandonment of the schools' original reason for being' (p. 110).

The major research theme which emerges from this exchange is the need to investigate in a variety of Catholic school settings precisely what impact the increase in elite students and in non-Catholic students has had on the habitus and the mission of the Catholic schooling system.

Catholic school research undertaken in the USA provides the largest empirical collection of literature available to other scholars. Its contributions to those sectors identified here, i.e. foundational, preferential option and school effectiveness research, have had a major impact on the field both in terms of substantive findings and in the generation of research methodology and research agendas.

The American Catholic research enterprise has stimulated researchers in other English-speaking cultures to investigate aspects of their own schooling systems. In particular, work in Australia has become prominent in recent years and some examination will now be made of major studies undertaken in Australia.

## Catholic school research: Australia

It is widely acknowledged that the scholarly and research work of Brother Marcellin Flynn FMS has had a major impact upon Catholic schooling studies in Australia. Arising from his books, *Some Catholic Schools in Action* (1975), *Catholic Schools and the Communication of Faith*(1979), *The Effectiveness of Catholic Schools* (1985) and *The Culture of Catholic Schools* (1993), Flynn, along with Andrew Greeley in the USA, can be regarded as one of the 'founding fathers' of Catholic educational enquiry. His major study of Catholic school effectiveness, a ten-year examination of Year 12 (18 year old) students in Catholic high schools in New South Wales and the Australian Capital Territory has had an international impact. With the cooperation of 2,041 senior students, 1,377 parents and 717 staff drawn from twenty-five Catholic high schools, Flynn sought to answer some of the fundamental questions of Catholic school research, i.e. do Catholic schools have a religious and educational effect upon their students and, if so, is this in any sense independent of factors in their home backgrounds?

In terms of the three research sectors identified earlier in this chapter, Flynn's (1985) study incorporates two of them, the foundational sector and the school effectiveness sector. Flynn's operative concept of schools' 'effectiveness' is that which promotes 'the full development of their students' (p. 10) and in this he subsumes both religious and faith development as well as academic development. Data collection was undertaken largely by the use of questionnaires to students, parents and teachers and the results were subject to factor analysis. From such an evidence base Flynn (1985, pp. 312–13) concluded that:

> The Catholic school appears to be having an effect on students' personal faith development which does not depend … on the prior religious socialisation of the home. Through its RE Curriculum the school is having a strong independent effect on the personal faith of its students.

However, in terms of formal religious practice and especially of Mass attendance, the evidence demonstrated that the example of parents was prime, leading Flynn to conclude that:

> Parents cannot place this duty on the Catholic school or expect schools to take over this responsibility when they do not practise the faith themselves.
>
> (p. 320)

Further analysis also confirmed the view that there is a 'Catholic school effect' on academic achievement and that this is mediated through the social climate and ethos of the school.

The major research theme which emerges from Flynn's (1985) study is the crucial importance of school climate and ethos on the development of young people in a comprehensive sense:

> One of the most distinctive features of an effective Catholic school is its outstanding social climate which gives it a special ethos or spirit. This climate has a religious as well as educational character and is generated in an intensely relational environment in which persons are respected and ultimate questions such as life, love, death, faith and God are confronted.
>
> (p. 342)

While Flynn's (1985) study was a major empirical contribution to the systematic understanding of Catholic schooling, questions have been raised about the relationship between his research methodology and his conclusions, especially on the issue of school climate and ethos. In essence, the issue arising from Flynn's early work was: is it possible to make strong claims about school climate and ethos from a research methodology using largely questionnaire responses? Does the systematic study of ethos not require, in addition to questionnaire responses, the use of qualitative methods involving focused interviews and participant observations within schools?

Flynn's (1993) study, while acknowledging the importance of qualitative methods and of ethnographic studies in Catholic school research, continued to employ large-scale empirical survey methods to collect data. With the research cooperation of 50 Catholic high schools, 6,000 Year 12 students, 2,200 parents and 728 teachers, and using questionnaires for data collection, Flynn sought answers to a number of research questions. Probably the most significant question under investigation was that which concerned important changes in the culture of Catholic schools in Australia in the period 1972–90. Notwithstanding some positive findings about the independent 'Catholic school effect' on young people's development and also the fact that Flynn's students expressed a warm regard for their Catholic schools, his overall conclusions sounded a note of warning for all Catholic educators. In particular, the conclusions that 'there has been a marked decline in the level of their religious beliefs, values and practice over the past two decades' and 'the perceived religious influence of teachers had declined … over the period' (pp. 426 and 428) suggested that in the face of growing secularisation in society and of lack of religious practice in families, Catholic schools in Australia and elsewhere would have to find new sources for spiritual empowerment. At a substantive level, Flynn's (1993) study suggests that a major research theme for Catholic schools must be to examine in detail the challenges of a more secular culture in society and in home life and the religious and educational responses which contemporary Catholic schools must develop to meet these challenges. At a methodological level Catholic school research clearly needs to draw more intensively upon a range of qualitative modes of enquiry if concepts such as school culture, ethos, habitus are to be fully appreciated and also if the in-depth understanding of students' attitudes, values and beliefs on religious and moral issues is to be illuminated.[16] As Treston (1997, p. 15), in a reflection upon Flynn's work, puts it:

> The dissonance between the official rhetoric about Catholic schools and the world views of students and parents (and some staff) is a very serious issue confronting the movement to authenticate Catholic schools.

The understanding of these world views seems likely to require greater use of qualitative methods of enquiry.

In a refinement of the research directions suggested by Flynn (1993), an empirical study of twenty-three Marist secondary schools by Fahy (1992) suggested that researchers should focus more closely upon the dynamics and climate of individual classrooms and not simply upon notions of whole-school culture. Arising from his study of 103 classrooms in Catholic schools, Fahy (1992, p. 220) argued that:

> For faith development, classrooms are an important grouping that must be considered in all subsequent research. Classrooms have a unique character or climate, some more fully supportive of religious values than others.

It seems likely, however, that if a deeper understanding of the climate or culture of Catholic school classrooms is to be obtained then the concept of the self-researching school will have to be given much greater prominence in Catholic school systems. In-depth understanding of the transactions and relationships of classroom life will clearly call for greater use of participant observation methods over an extended period. This seems to be a paradigm case where suitably prepared teacher–researchers acting in partnership with external researchers could significantly advance our understanding of the impact of Catholic classrooms on both faith and academic development.

O'Keefe (1999b), in an overview of research on Australian Catholic schools, has suggested that more empirical as opposed to theoretical research is required, with special reference to the socio-economic status of students in the schools and in relation to questions of Catholic identity. The founding of the Australian Catholic University in 1991 suggests that there will be a significant expansion in Catholic school empirical research in the near future. The implication of O'Keefe's review is that *preferential option research* needs more attention from Australian Catholic school researchers. To what extent, for instance, are academically successful Catholic schools in the service of the poor and of ethnic communities which may be disadvantaged in Australian society?[17] These questions await detailed contemporary examination.

## Catholic school research: UK

In reviewing the state of Catholic education research in England and Wales, Arthur (1995, p. 255) observed that:

> The main difficulty for any study of Catholic education is to overcome the paucity of scholarly critical literature in the area.

The undeveloped state of research into the culture and effectiveness of Catholic schools in this context is the outcome of a number of historical factors, but the crucial one appears to be the absence of a Catholic higher education system with an active research culture in England and Wales. Whereas Catholic school research in the USA and Australia has benefited from the presence of Catholic universities and from significant numbers of Catholic academics working in secular universities, in England and Wales the fifteen Catholic Colleges of Education (now reduced to five) have been historically preoccupied with the supply of Catholic teachers for Catholic schools and not with research activity or advanced graduate study.[18]

With the exception of early studies, such as Brothers' *Church and School* (1964), systematic sociological analysis of Catholic culture and schooling in England and Wales has been found largely in the work of Hornsby-Smith (1978, 1987, 1991, 2000). This work has sought to illuminate social structural and cultural changes within the Catholic community in England and within the schooling system. In his most recent contribution to the field, Hornsby-Smith (2000, pp. 204–5) has summarised his findings in this form:

> The task of Catholic schools as we enter the third millennium is very much more complex and difficult and replete with ambiguity and moral dilemmas than was the case 50 years ago. With general social and religious mobility and the dissolution of the distinctive Catholic subculture of the embattled fortress church there has emerged a general pluralism of belief and practice within the church. With this has come a radical transformation of accepted notions of religious authority.

In the *foundational sector* of Catholic school research in England, Arthur (1995) took up some of these themes in his provocative book, *The Ebbing Tide: Policy and Principles of Catholic Education*. After sustained engagement with historical and contemporary documentation on Catholic education policy, some small-scale fieldwork enquiry and the creation of theoretical modelling of types of Catholic school, Arthur concluded that despite external academic indicators of success, Catholic schools were losing their distinctive sense of mission. In the changed educational and policy contexts of the 1980s and 1990s in England, Arthur claimed that the Catholic bishops were failing to give clear leadership on the distinctive values of Catholic education;[19] that the Catholic community in England and Wales was no longer united on purposes and objectives; and that in the face of growing state intervention in educational policy and practice, Catholic schools were becoming 'institutions practically indistinguishable from those under LEA control' (p. 253).

The argument of *The Ebbing Tide* is that Catholic schools in England and Wales were originally founded on a 'holistic' model, with a priority concern for the transmission of the Catholic faith and with an ethos in which awareness of the faith permeated all aspects of school life, its pedagogy and its curriculum. In Arthur's view, Catholic schooling of the holistic type is giving ground, especially at secondary school level, to 'dualistic' and 'pluralistic' models of schooling. The dualistic Catholic school separates the secular and religious aims of schooling and the pluralistic school involves an inclusive stance of accepting other faiths into Catholic institutions. With the suggested decline of the holistic school and the increase in dualistic and pluralistic Catholic schools, Arthur's thesis is that Catholicity as a distinctive ethos is ebbing out of Catholic secondary schools in particular. A main research theme which emerges from the text is that Catholic secondary schools in England are undergoing a process of educational, cultural and religious incorporation with a dominant external schooling culture. A distinctive Catholic habitus of the sacred, it is argued, is weakening in the face of contemporary pluralism and utilitarianism in schooling.

This research has provoked a lively debate within the Catholic educational community in England and Wales. For some, it has given expression to their deepest fears that Catholic schools are undergoing a process of incorporation which will extinguish the rich distinctiveness of the Catholic faith in the education of young people. Those taking this position could point to an earlier research study undertaken by Egan (1988) in the Catholic comprehensive schools of Wales which suggested cause for concern. From a survey of the attitudes and practice of 1,642 (15 year old) pupils in 15 comprehensive schools in Wales, Egan found that less than half of the pupils were practising Catholics and many had negative attitudes to the religious education provided in the schools. Furthermore, in the view of the pupils:

> The over-riding concern of the schools … is with examinations at the expense of all other aspects of school life.
>
> (p. 142)[20]

For others, however, Arthur's argument was based upon a spurious 'golden-age' construct of the Catholic schools of the past and a too pessimistic reading of the different forms which Catholicity could take in contemporary schooling. In a critical review of *The Ebbing Tide*, Peter Boylan, an experienced Catholic headteacher and prominent member of the Catholic Association of Teachers, Schools and Colleges in England and Wales, wrote:

> There are many Catholic schools in many parts of the country which shine like beacons in witness of their work for the young Church.
>
> (1996, p. 14)

The whole debate on the current integrity and vitality of Catholicity in the Catholic schools of England and Wales has been restricted by the limited amount of empirical research in this foundational sector. Arthur's (1995) work which stimulated the current debate was based upon small-scale fieldwork with Catholic schools in only one English county, Oxfordshire. In the absence of more extensive fieldwork research in the foundational sector of Catholic schooling in England and Wales, the whole question of the integrity of the Catholic distinctiveness of the schools remains at the level of claim and counter-claim.

A major empirical contribution to the preferential option sector of Catholic schooling research in the UK was produced in 1995 by Mary Hickman under the title *Religion, Class and Identity: the state, the Catholic Church and the education of the Irish in Britain*. Hickman's research, which has a strong historical component as well as a report of contemporary fieldwork in Catholic schools, cannot be classified as precisely in the same genre as the work of Cibulka *et al.* (1982), Greeley (1982) and O'Keefe (1996) in the USA. While these researchers have been concerned to monitor relationships between Catholic schooling and communities disadvantaged by class and ethnic locations in contemporary settings, Hickman has sought to illuminate the deeper historical relations between the Catholic Church, its schooling system and the large population of working-class Irish immigrants living in the UK. What this research demonstrates is the complex and contradictory relations which have existed between Catholicism and nationalism[21] and between education for liberation and education for domestication in the specific case of the Irish in the UK. As Hickman (1995, p. 16) expresses it:

> State-assisted Catholic elementary schooling came to be viewed as the principal long-term means of resolving the 'problem' posed by the Irish Catholic working class. The State and the Catholic Church both had their own rationale for drawing the Irish into any arrangements agreed for elementary education. Catholic schools were to have a dual role: they 'dealt' with the Irish by attempting to incorporate them into the British national collectivity whilst simultaneously segregating and differentiating them from the rest of the working class.

Hickman's historical analysis makes a powerful case that the Catholic schooling system in the UK was, on the one hand, a provider of educational opportunities necessary for the social and occupational mobility of the Irish community and a context within which its Catholic faith could be preserved, but, on the other hand, a cultural system with incorporating tendencies to mute the expression of a distinct Irish nationalist identity. From this perspective Irish immigrants were seen to constitute a social and political threat to the British state and therefore the expectation was that Catholic elementary education in the nineteenth and early twentieth centuries would:

> incorporate the children of Irish migrants by strengthening their Catholic identity at the expense of weakening their Irish identity.
> (p. 17)

In effect, Hickman's (1995) thesis is that British state agencies were prepared to give state support for the expansion of the Catholic schooling system because it was viewed as an effective means of social and political control of the Irish working-class community.

In a later paper, 'The Religio-Ethnic Identities of Teenagers of Irish Descent', Hickman (1999), drawing on her contemporary fieldwork in four Catholic secondary schools in London and Liverpool, has focused upon the responses of 100 pupils. Using structured interviews as her research approach, Hickman concluded that a significant number of Catholic pupils wanted to know more about Irish identity and Irish history and, in particular, to have more understanding about the situation in Northern Ireland. She has also argued that Catholic schools in the UK do not engage seriously with the issues involved in Northern Ireland because of fears about the potential divisiveness of this subject, both within the schools and within the wider communities in which the schools are located. A major research theme which Hickman's work illuminates is the politics of Church–state relations in the provision and practice of faith-based schooling. The Catholic Church and its schooling system represent a relatively autonomous cultural space in which a critique of state policies on various issues is possible. However, the Church and the Catholic schooling system have to come to some accommodation with the state if the system's resourcing and future are to be assured. Achieving a balance of principled integrity and of pragmatic survival is therefore a constant challenge for Catholic schooling. Hickman's study of the specific case of the Irish in the UK illustrates the complexities of that process very well.

An important research focus on Church–state relations in Northern Ireland and on the relations between Protestants and Catholics in schooling can be found in the work of Chadwick (1994). In *Schools of Reconciliation: Issues in Joint Roman Catholic-Anglican Education*, Chadwick has documented the 'cool' approach of the Catholic hierarchy in Northern Ireland to the idea of interdenominational or integrated schools as one way forward to healing the divisions of that community. In the 1970s, the position of the Catholic hierarchy was that:

> the replacement of Catholic by interdenominational schools in Ireland would not contribute to overcoming the divisions in our midst … We must point out that in such schools the full Catholic witness is inevitably diluted.[22]

By the 1980s, Cardinal O'Fiaich was giving reluctant agreement to the idea that some integrated schools could be recognised on an 'experimental' basis.

In taking this stance of cool detachment from the movement for integrated denominational schools in Northern Ireland, the Catholic bishops were pursuing a complex and historically formulated educational policy. In a province in which the Catholic faith had for centuries been oppressed, the symbolic value of cultural spaces, such as schools, in which the faith might be 'fully expressed', was very great. Interdenominational or integrated schools therefore could be represented as a form of dilution of authentic Catholic religious culture. The Catholic hierarchy was also wary of the idea that the troubles of Northern Ireland had their origins in a religiously segregated system of schooling and could therefore be overcome or greatly alleviated by the introduction of integrated schools. This was regarded as a simplistic analysis of a socio-cultural context formed by centuries of political and economic oppression and injustice. It is within this complex context that Chadwick's research case study of Lagan College, an integrated Protestant–Catholic school in Belfast, has great significance.[23]

Chadwick's work provides an important agenda of research questions for future investigation. Is it the case that integrated schools will involve a dilution of Catholic faith culture? To what extent can integrated schools through their ethos and hidden curriculum overcome external bigotry, prejudice and social divisions in the wider society? Will ecumenical Christian schools receive more parental support in the future than segregated denominational schools?

In many ways the work of O'Keeffe (1986, 1988, 1992, 1997, 1999) has involved a sustained engagement with these sorts of questions and with the stance of Catholic schooling in relation to inner-city areas[24] and ethnic minority communities in England. Reviewing her own research and that of others in the UK, O'Keeffe (1992, pp. 42–3) noted:

> The demographic changes which have taken place in British society are manifested in all aspects of British life including the pupil population of Catholic schools … Catholic schools face the need for development of good practice in multicultural education, the adoption of anti-racist stances and the demands of a multi-faith intake.

It is clear from O'Keeffe's scholarly writing that she believes that the Catholic Church in the UK and the Catholic schooling system have been very slow in coming to terms with the implications of pluralism in its various forms – pluralism of Christian denominations, pluralism of religious faiths in society and ethnic pluralism in urban areas.[25] From this perspective Catholic schools have not in practice shown the degree of openness to other Christian faith communities or to communities of other religious faiths which might have been expected in the new spirit of Vatican II. Neither have they been at the forefront of development in multi-cultural and anti-racist education when this might have been expected of them as Christian schools.

Of all the research themes emerging from the work of Bernadette O'Keeffe, perhaps the most disturbing has been the implication that Catholic schools in the UK have not been prominent in the educational struggle against all forms of racism. In modern times the institutional Catholic Church has declared its opposition to racism, as, for instance, when Pope Pius XI stated in 1938:

> Catholic means universal, not racist, not nationalistic in the separatist meaning of these two attributes … We do not wish to separate anything in the human family … There is only one human, universal, 'catholic' race … and with it and in it different variations … This is the Church's response.[26]

O'Keeffe's research provokes questions about the relation between official pronouncements of the Church authorities on issues such as racism, ecumenism and multi-faith dialogue and the actual practice of the Catholic schooling system.

In another sector of Catholic school research in England, that of *school effectiveness*, the work of Andrew Morris has been prominent. Morris (1997) has investigated the possibility that different models of Catholic schooling may produce different academic and religious outcomes. In a case study research of two Catholic secondary schools, one which could be described as traditional/holistic and the other as progressive/pluralist, Morris argued that a traditional Catholic school ethos seemed to produce more positive academic and religious outcomes than was the case with the progressive/pluralist school. Although this research is based upon a very small sample of schools, it does appear to support the findings of Bryk *et al.* (1993) on the effectiveness of a particular form of Catholic school habitus. However, some caution has to be expressed in interpreting this work. The teaching approach at St Peter's (a traditional school) was 'geared towards examination success' (p. 383) whereas that at St Paul's (a progressive school) was designed to encourage individual intellectual exploration. The assessment of the religious outcomes of both schools was a problematic exercise. What Morris's work points to is the complexity involved in making judgements about the relative effectiveness of different models of Catholic school. Just as there are different models of a school, there are also different models of educational, social and religious 'effectiveness'. Morris has acknowledged this complexity in a later paper. Reviewing the educational outcomes of Catholic schools in England, when compared with those of county (state) schools, he has concluded:

> The superiority of Catholic schools, in respect of measures adopted by OFSTED [Office for Standards in Education] is very noticeable.
> (1998a, p. 189)

This makes clear that the judgement of 'effectiveness' is based upon the criteria of an official inspection agency and is open to question on both conceptual and methodological grounds by other researchers.

Research on Catholic school effectiveness in Scotland has been stimulated by the work of Paterson (1991) and Willms (1992). In a major quantitative survey of 345 secondary schools in Scotland, 61 of which were Catholic, Paterson (1991, p. 95) concluded that:

> We can propose that the large change in the ranking of the Catholic sector indicates some especially effective school practices, good enough to overcome the disadvantage of whole communities.

However, this conclusion is qualified by the possibility that the effective academic performance of Catholic secondary schools in Scotland might arise as much from a wider community context factor (what Coleman (1988) would call social capital) as from any internal school factors.

Developing this theme, Paterson (2000a) has argued that the crucial relationship between Catholic schooling and a concept of social capital could have a major role to play in the future in the strengthening of Scottish democracy, 'as a source of ideas for how civic culture and democracy could be renewed' (p. 46). This is a provocative and radical thesis given the long association of Catholic culture with hierarchy and authoritarianism rather than with democratic practice, but perhaps we have here a perceptive insight into the future role of the post-Vatican II school. On less speculative grounds, Paterson's (2000b, p. 154) conclusion on the crucial role of Scottish Catholic schools in the social mobility of the Catholic population confirms similar findings from the USA and Australia:

> Education was of enormous benefit to Scottish Catholics in the twentieth century, especially in the last three or four decades. The Catholic schools have been consistently more effective than non-denominational schools in enabling their working class pupils to gain good qualifications. In a classic instance of education's role in fostering social mobility, these formerly working-class young people have been able to use their credentials to compete successfully for good jobs.

While the work of Paterson and others demonstrates the academic and social utility of Catholic schooling in Scotland, no major research study appears to exist in relation to its spiritual utility. John Haldane of St Andrew's University has written an important paper on 'The Need of Spirituality in Catholic Education' (1999) and has reminded Scottish Catholics and others that the ultimate purpose of a Catholic education 'should be to lay down the foundations of a good life and of a good death' (p. 191). This is an implicit challenge to Catholic school researchers in Scotland and elsewhere to focus their enquiries in the foundational sector of Catholic 'effectiveness' and not only in its utilitarian sectors.

## Catholic school research: Ireland

Reviewing schooling in the Republic of Ireland, Drudy and Lynch (1993, pp. 6–7) point out that:

> Church ownership and control is found at both primary and second level. At primary level, church ownership is practically universal … Of the 476 Church secondary schools, 253 are owned by female religious orders and 136 by male religious orders … Since 1986

> non-fee paying secondary schools receive 90 per cent of approved capital expenditure from the state.

In short, the Catholic Church in Ireland exercises a degree of control and influence in educational policy and practice which is probably unprecedented in contemporary Europe. Writing from a standpoint of critical sociology, Drudy and Lynch (1993) make some sharp observations of contemporary contradictions in Catholic schooling in Ireland, particularly of those relating to the 'preferential option for the poor' as a principled commitment of Catholic education:

> The churches themselves are key institutions in the up-holding of fee-paying secondary schools, which fits uneasily with their claim that their primary concern is for the poor and underprivileged.
> (p. 86)

However, an OECD Report (1991) on education in Ireland has pointed out that the majority of Catholic schools are non-fee paying and that the Catholic schooling enterprise in Ireland has radical elements within it (often associated with religious orders) as well as conservative elements. In other words, the Irish Catholic school system is not monolithic but is characterised by internal differentiation and by internal ideological struggles.[27]

This theme has been developed in the work of O'Sullivan (1996) who has highlighted three major changes in the culture and practice of Catholic schooling in Ireland, i.e. the secularisation of teaching and educational roles, the weakening of Catholic Church hegemony in the control of education and the radicalisation of the social and educational policies of many church agencies. As O'Sullivan (1996, p. 43) concludes:

> Specifically in relation to education … The Conference of Major Religious Superiors has increasingly emerged as the most radical agency involved in policy analysis … Within no more than a decade the ideological leanings of church bodies have changed dramatically.

Evidence in support of this claim can be found in a series of publications sponsored by the Conference of Major Religious Superiors in the 1980s and 1990s. While these have essentially been reviews of existing research studies rather than commissioned investigations, they have nevertheless provided an important research agenda for Catholic education in Ireland. Publications such as *Inequality in Schooling in Ireland*

(1988), *Education and Poverty* (1992) and *Women For Leadership in Education* (Conference of Religious of Ireland 1994) have been designed to stimulate some radical forms of research into the present operation of Catholic schooling in Ireland. The relatively undeveloped state of systematic research into the evaluation of Catholic schools in Ireland has been recognised in a review undertaken by McDonagh (1991, p. 72) for the Conference of Religious:

> Relatively little has been done in Ireland to evaluate our schools from the perspective of Catholic education ... The overwhelming reality is that the Irish Church has not to date responded to the invitation to evaluate schools under its authority.

However, there are now signs that this situation is changing. The Christian Leadership in Education Centre at Cork, under the direction of Brother Matthew Feheney FPM, has become a focus for research studies and scholarly reviews of Catholic education in Ireland and elsewhere. In two recent major collections, *From Ideal to Action* (1998) and *Beyond the Race for Points* (1999), Feheney has focused research attention upon the impact of social and educational change upon Catholic schooling and upon the foundational concern of spiritual and pastoral care in Irish schools. In addition to this, the Centre has provided resources to encourage more research activity among Irish teachers and school principals.[28] It seems likely that the Republic of Ireland will be in the future a major source of research studies in the three sectors of Catholic education enquiry: foundational, preferential option and school effectiveness.

## Overview and conclusion

This chapter has attempted to review and critically comment upon some main themes in Catholic schooling research in a number of English-speaking contexts: the USA, Australia, England and Wales, Scotland and Ireland. These contexts have been chosen largely because systematic empirical research studies of Catholic schooling have been undertaken or are emergent in these countries. For a more comprehensive and indeed catholic view of the research field it would be necessary to engage with the scholarship of Europe, Latin America[29] and other international contexts in which Catholic schooling is significant. Constraints of space and time have prevented this in the present study.

What emerges from this review overall is that apart from a substantial body of scholarship in the USA, the systematic investigation of post-Vatican II Catholic schooling is remarkably undeveloped, considering the scale of the Catholic educational mission. However, there are now many signs that serious research enquiry in this field is developing in Australia, England, Scotland and Ireland. The following chapters which report an empirical research enquiry with sixty Catholic secondary schools and colleges in England are intended to be a contribution to what might be called the *Catholic school research movement* which is emerging in each of these countries.

# Part III

# Catholic schools in three English cities

## Fieldwork studies

# 5 Research approaches and fieldwork

The present enquiry is an attempt to understand the challenges which contemporary Catholic secondary schools face in their mission, as expressed through research interview accounts arising from the collaborative involvement of sixty headteachers in London, Liverpool and Birmingham and of fifty Year 10 pupils in five London schools. In addition to these central participants, research accounts were also obtained from ten other professionals with extensive experience of Catholic education.

From a review of research into contemporary Catholic schooling in a number of countries (see Chapter 4) a range of significant research questions had become apparent, questions such as:

- Was the integrity and the distinctiveness of the Catholic school mission being compromised by the influence of market values in education and by a secular 'academic success' culture?
- To what extent were Catholic schools actually showing a 'preferential option for the poor' in ethnically mixed and poor urban communities?
- What effects were Catholic schools having upon the spiritual, moral and social development of their pupils?
- Were Catholic conceptions of community and of the common good in education being eroded by contemporary emphases upon the individualistic, 'winning' school?
- Was Catholicity as a distinctive realisation of a religious and moral culture weakening in modern Catholic schools?
- How were Catholic headteachers responding to mission challenges, market challenges and moral challenges in their work?
- What were the sources of support for Catholic headteachers in meeting these challenges and were they sufficient?
- How did pupils in Catholic schools evaluate their own experience of Catholic schooling?

It was recognised that it would be impossible for any one research project to find definitive answers to these questions but it was hoped that a small-scale qualitative enquiry could provide some illumination and some indicative findings which would be of value both to the field of Catholic education and to other researchers of it.

Denzin and Lincoln (1998), in their important text *Collecting and Interpreting Qualitative Materials*, point out that:

> Qualitative researchers are more likely than quantitative researchers to confront the constraints of the everyday social world. They see this world in action and embed their findings in it.
>
> (p. 10)

In so far as the present research involved observational visits to the sixty participating schools and the communities they served, and on-site interviews with headteachers and pupils, some claims to seeing this world in action can be made. It is also the case that the intention of the following chapters is to 'embed' the analysis within this context of action. However, as I have argued elsewhere (Grace, 1995), a policy scholarship approach to educational research requires a larger sense of embeddedness, i.e. the location of contemporary fieldwork data within a developed theoretical, historical and cultural analysis of the phenomenon under investigation. The previous chapters have attempted to construct this larger framework within which the fieldwork material can be interpreted. Contemporary fieldwork material cannot simply be read in the 'vivid present' or it becomes another form of Wright Mills' (1973) 'abstracted empiricism'. It has to be read and interpreted against a theoretical framework, a historical set of relations and a cultural configuration of which it is a part.

## Collecting qualitative material, Phase 1: the London headteacher enquiry (1997–2000)

In 1997 a semi-structured interview schedule was designed to focus discussion with Catholic headteachers in twelve areas relating to their own leadership conceptions and experiences and their perceptions of contemporary challenges for Catholic secondary schools especially in difficult urban locations. The schedule covered most of the research questions indicated earlier but the rubric stated: 'The topics indicated are a suggested agenda and can be added to or deleted from as appropriate. The interview is intended to be a dialogue based upon these topics.' (See Appendix 2 for the interview schedule.)

The intention throughout the research was to stress the collaborative nature of the enquiry and headteachers, pupils, administrators and others involved in Catholic education were encouraged to add to the agenda of issues under investigation. With the approval of the diocesan education authorities for the archdioceses of Westminster and of Southwark, letters inviting participation in the project were sent to all the headteachers of Catholic secondary schools in inner London and, for comparative purposes, to some in outer-London areas. Of thirty Catholic inner-city secondary schools approached, twenty-seven agreed to assist with the enquiry, as did the three outer-London schools which were also approached. In forming the participating sample of headteachers and schools, advice was sought from diocesan education officers to ensure a high representation of schools serving ethnically diverse and relatively poor urban locations in London.

The participating schools ranged in size from 250 (an inner-city school in the process of closure) to a large outer-London school of 1,150 pupils. The range of free school meals entitlement in the schools (as an approximate poverty indicator) included a low of 7 per cent in an outer-London school to 64 per cent in an inner-city school facing many challenges. Compared with a national average figure for free school meals entitlement in 1997 of 18 per cent, the average for the participating schools was 37 per cent.

Academic indicators (GCSE passes A*–C) ranged from an inner-city school achieving 9 per cent to a remarkable 85 per cent achieved in an inner-city boys' school. In general, the Catholic secondary schools in inner London were achieving higher levels of academic performance than comparable state schools in the local area. (See Appendix 1 for school details.).

Twenty-seven of the thirty Catholic schools in London recorded the proportion of Catholic pupils as in excess of 60 per cent, with eight of these claiming a 100 per cent pupil profile. The representation of Catholic teachers in the schools was lower, with sixteen of the schools recording below 60 per cent and two as low as 33 per cent. All the headteachers were Catholics.

Against this contextual background, thirty secondary school headteachers were interviewed in the period 1997–2000. Using the schedule described, interviews lasting one and a half hours were tape-recorded in on-site locations. The tapes were transcribed and returned to the participants for further reflection and additional comments. The final agreed interview accounts were then submitted to a process of content analysis in terms of central meanings and categories of discourse.

## Collecting qualitative material, Phase 2: the Liverpool headteacher enquiry (1998–2000)

With the approval of the Schools Commission of the Archdiocese of Liverpool, the enquiry was extended to include Catholic secondary schools in the City of Liverpool and adjacent urban areas in Merseyside. Of the twenty-one schools approached, twenty agreed to assist with the enquiry. The participating schools in Liverpool and Merseyside ranged in size from 278 (a school in the process of closure) to an outer-metropolitan school of 1,466 pupils.

It became apparent that poverty levels in the Liverpool area were higher than those in London when judged by the free school meals entitlements of Catholic secondary schools. None of the schools had a free school meals (FSM) entitlement below 20 per cent of the pupils and eleven had entitlements above 40 per cent of the pupils, with three of the schools recording figures above 70 per cent.

Academic indicators (GCSE passes A*–C) were in general lower than those for Catholic schools in London. Four of the schools had examination passes of 10 per cent or lower and the highest figures of 54 per cent were achieved by pupils at two girls' comprehensive schools under the jurisdiction of religious orders. (See Appendix 1.)

As was to be expected from the history and demography of the area, the Liverpool schools were more comprehensively Catholic than their London counterparts. Of the twenty schools involved in the research, only three schools had Catholic school populations below 90 per cent. The representation of Catholic teachers in the schools was also higher with fifteen of the schools recording 60 per cent or more. All the headteachers were Catholics.

Against this contextual background, twenty secondary school headteachers were interviewed in the period 1998–2000 in the manner already described. In addition to one-to-one interviews, the researcher was invited to be a participant in the Diocesan Headteachers Residential Conference in 1998 and this provided further opportunities for dialogue on the issues being raised in the research.

## Collecting qualitative material, Phase 3: the Birmingham headteacher enquiry (1999)

In 1999 the researcher received an invitation from the Birmingham Catholic School Partnership to include the ten Catholic secondary schools in the city as part of the research investigation. This was an unexpected and welcome opportunity to extend the enquiry geographically by the inclusion of the Midlands but, much more important, to focus the enquiry on two innovative aspects of Catholic schooling in England, i.e. the nature of the Partnership itself and of the Zacchaeus (Pre-exclusion) Centre in Birmingham supported by the ten Catholic schools. In a larger political and ideological climate in which English schools had been officially encouraged to become more individualistic and competitive in orientation, the Catholic secondary schools of Birmingham had acted in a counter-cultural way in establishing a partnership arrangement to assist each other's operations and development in various ways. In a larger policy context in which the permanent exclusion of 'disruptive' pupils from secondary schools in England was increasing, the Catholic schools had combined to support the establishment of a Centre designed to try to prevent pupils from being permanently excluded from their schools. Both of these important developments were added to the Birmingham schedule of interview questions so that the headteachers' interpretations of these innovations could be assessed.

The ten Catholic secondary schools in Birmingham ranged in size from 460 to 1,300 pupils and most of the schools were co-educational. FSM entitlements varied from 10 per cent in an outer-metropolitan school to 60 per cent in two inner-city schools.

Academic indicators (GCSE passes A*–C) varied from 10 per cent in one inner-city school to 70 per cent in a girls' comprehensive school in a suburban area. (See Appendix 1.)

Against this contextual background, ten secondary school headteachers were interviewed in 1999. In addition to these, interviews were also conducted with five other professionals having detailed knowledge of the Catholic school system in Birmingham (see below). Two of the schools had proportions of Catholic pupils below 40 per cent (both inner-city schools), whereas four of the schools had over 90 per cent Catholic pupils. Most of the schools had proportions of Catholic teachers above 50 per cent of the staff. All the headteachers were Catholics.

## Collecting qualitative material, Phase 4: other professionals 1997–2000

In order to extend the enquiry beyond perspectives internal to the schools, interviews were conducted with ten other professionals involved in the work of Catholic education. These included four diocesan education officers (all former headteachers of Catholic secondary schools), two support workers for the Birmingham Catholic

School Partnership, two heads of pre-exclusion centres in Birmingham and Liverpool (both former teachers), a retired former Director of the Catholic Education Service in England and Wales and a former Principal of a Catholic Sixth Form College. A modified form of the interview schedule for headteachers was used with these participants and interviews were recorded, transcribed and returned for further reflection and comment from these professionals. The intention of these interviews was to widen the perspectives on Catholic schooling in England to include national policy issues and relations with local education authorities and to obtain a more in-depth understanding of the actual operation of the Birmingham Partnership. In addition it was hoped that certain questions relating to the nature of Catholicity in contemporary education practice would be clarified by these discussions.

## Collecting qualitative material, Phase 5: pupil perspectives 1999

Any research project which is attempting to provide a deeper understanding of school ethos and culture as part of a movement to improve the quality of schooling for children and young people can hardly ignore the perspectives of those young people. This position has been convincingly argued by Rudduck *et al.* (1996) in their pioneering book *School Improvement: what can pupils tell us?*.

A small-scale attempt to implement this research strategy was used in the present enquiry. With the cooperation of five inner-London Catholic secondary schools, focus-group discussions were held with two groups of five pupils in each school. Headteachers were asked (in consultation with other senior teachers) to select for these discussions five Year 10 pupils (14–15 years) who were model pupils and strong school identifiers (informally called 'the saints') and five who were regarded as troublesome school resistors ('the sinners'). Confidential focus-group discussions took place in the schools with the separate groups of 'saints' and 'sinners'. The conduct of these groups followed Wilson's (1997) suggestion that focus groups should be characterised by a high degree of interaction between the participants, and between the participants and the researcher. At the same time the basis for this interaction derived from some preliminary written comments which the participants were asked to make about their own Catholic school experiences. In particular they were asked to reflect upon the extent to which the schools, in their opinion, lived up to the principles proclaimed in their mission statements (photocopies of the mission statements were provided). These focus-group discussions were undertaken in one boys' school, two girls' schools and two co-educational schools and involved the participation of twenty boys and thirty girls.

Rudduck and Flutter (2000, p. 86) argue that both educational research and school improvement projects have been impoverished by lack of serious attention to the perspectives of pupils:

> This traditional exclusion of young people from the consultation process, this bracketing out of their voice, is founded upon an outdated view of childhood which fails to acknowledge children's capacity to reflect on issues affecting their lives.

In Chapter 9, the voice of the fifty Year 10 pupils will be represented as they report their experiences and reflections upon their own Catholic schooling.

## Interpreting qualitative material: the interview accounts

Usher and Scott (1996, p. 177) remind all educational researchers of the problematics of interpretation:

> Interpretation is not simply a matter of 'reading out' a meaning which is already there. Rather, meaning is read *into* the data and this is not simply a matter of elucidating it by applying neutral techniques. Interpretation is a social act and the meaning that is read into the data is dependent on the paradigms and research traditions within which the researcher is located. It is this which makes the researcher the 'great interpreter' with privileged access to meaning.

The implication of this observation is that all acts of interpretation of research data are open to challenge from other researchers and, in the case of educational and social scientific research, from the participants in the research enterprise. This implication is accepted in the present study.

In analysing and interpreting the seventy research accounts derived from headteachers and other education professionals in Catholic education and the fifty focus-group discussions conducted with pupils in Catholic schools, the present writer has been guided by principles and procedures derived from what Habermas (1978, p. 309) has called 'the historical-hermeneutic sciences' and what Denzin and Lincoln (1998, p. 6) indicate as a central feature of the qualitative paradigm, 'the interpretive understanding of human experience'.

Specifically, the interpretive strategies suggested by Glaser and Strauss (1967) as modified in the writer's previous research (Grace 1978, 1995) were utilised. The accounts were subjected to a process of content analysis. This analysis was based upon a procedure of initial discourse 'saturation', followed by the identification of the central meanings and categories of discourse used by the participants. Close and repeated readings of the accounts were undertaken in order to achieve some in-depth understanding of the content and texture of the participant discourse.

On the basis of this close knowledge of the accounts, central meanings and discourse categories were derived for each participant. These were defined as those aspects of their discourse to which they devoted most time and to which they returned as a point of reference in the interview/discussion. Also important in the definition of central meanings and categories was the degree of engagement, animation and, in some cases, obvious emotion which participants demonstrated in relation to particular issues.

In the elucidation of central meanings and categories of discourse every attempt was made by the researcher to respect the *integrity of the account*, i.e. that edited versions to be used in direct quotation should be faithful to, and representative of, the overall stance of the participant on a given question.

By these procedures, central meanings and categories of discourse on the challenges of Catholic schooling in England were derived from the sixty research accounts of the headteachers differentiated in the following ways:

| | |
|---|---|
| 36 male headteachers | 24 female headteachers |
| 48 lay headteachers | 12 religious or teaching orders |
| 24 less than 5 years' experience in present school | 36 more than 5 years' experience in present school |
| | (See Appendix 3.) |

O'Keeffe (1999, p. 246) has shown that the number of priests and members of religious and teaching orders in Catholic secondary schools in England and Wales dropped from 975 in 1980 to 155 in 1996. However, the influence of clerics and religious may not have declined in the Catholic school system to the extent that these national figures suggest. It is noteworthy that in this research sample of secondary school headteachers in three major cities, 20 per cent of the school leaders were still vowed religious, and among the forty-eight lay headteachers, three were former members of religious orders. It could also be argued that a mediated form of the influence of religious orders was still present in many of these schools as a result of the formative educational experiences of the headteachers themselves. Of the sixty headteachers involved in this project, forty had received their secondary education in schools run by religious orders in England and Ireland and twenty-one had subsequently attended Catholic teacher education colleges for their professional formation. Many of these colleges were also under the jurisdiction of religious orders.

In the analysis of the central meanings and categories of discourse used by these Catholic headteachers it was possible to discern mediated forms of the habitus of the religious orders which had shaped, in various ways, the formation of the headteachers and of their views of Catholic education.

## Interview accounts and patterns of discourse

A preliminary overall analysis of the interview transcripts revealed that these Catholic headteachers drew upon five forms of discourse in explaining their conceptions of Catholic schooling, of Catholic leadership and of the challenges facing contemporary Catholic schools in urban areas. These forms of discourse are presented, for the purpose of analysis, in ideal-type form but in practice they did not occur in entirely discrete categories. In the interview situation headteachers drew eclectically upon different forms of discourse in responding to questions, in some cases using the complete range of forms indicated and in other cases only a limited selection. In practice, forms of discourse were frequently interrelated in answers to specific questions.

The forms of Catholic headteacher discourse may be characterised as follows:

- *A discourse of the sacred and of faith leadership*: here the central meanings in use made reference to the transcendental purposes of Catholic schooling and to its religious and spiritual aims. A discourse of the sacred incorporated, in a naturalistic way, reference to God, Jesus Christ, Our Lady and to the charisms of saints and founders of religious and teaching orders. These references were integrated into explanations of the work of the school, the state of its Catholicity and of the responses being made to current challenges in schooling.
- *A discourse of morality*: here the central meanings in use drew upon moral categories expressing conceptions of the good life, the good

person and the good community as realised within Catholic religious culture. The discourse of morality incorporated references to a range of individual virtues such as love and compassion, charity and forgiveness, and to social virtues such as good citizenship, community involvement and actions in pursuit of the common good. Moral discourse also included references to various aspects of human behaviour including personal and sexual conduct.

- *A discourse of the option for the poor*: although this discourse did not, in general, use a formal language derived from the social teachings of the Church, it was realised in a distinct sense of solidarity with poor communities, with those in difficult personal and social circumstances and with the powerless and socially excluded. In some cases a discourse of the option for the poor was related to a headteacher's own social origins in poor communities. In other cases it arose from the historical commitments of particular religious and teaching orders to the service of the poor in education.
- *A discourse of school effectiveness*: this discourse drew upon concepts derived from a strongly disseminated literature and reporting of school effectiveness research and of related studies in school improvement. It was especially salient where headteachers had undertaken advanced studies for MA or EdD degrees. However, the discourse of school effectiveness was more pervasively influenced by the universal experience of OFSTED school inspections. All of the headteachers used an evaluative discourse about their school which was derived from the categories, assumptions and language of the formal inspection process of OFSTED. While reactions to the OFSTED inspection experience varied, the discourse of OFSTED was in the process of becoming a hegemonic category in the professional lives of the headteachers.
- *A discourse of management and markets:* here the central meanings in use were derived from a literature of educational managerialism which many of the headteachers had encountered on training courses related to local management of schools (LMS) or in courses of advanced study related to management. This discourse was concerned with logistics, financial management, action plans and 'human resource' deployment. The concept of a 'senior management team' was part of this discourse.

Interrelated with managerial perspectives were perspectives derived from market values in education and a heightened sense of competitive market relations among schools about pupil numbers and an attractive image for the parent/customer of the 1990s.

> This discourse was, in general, secular, pragmatic, calculative and taken to be a language functional and necessary for the survival of any school in contemporary conditions.

More detailed analysis of the interview accounts as reported in later chapters will show the complexities, nuances and internal contradictions of these discourses in use.

## Triangulating the data

Ideally this study of Catholic secondary schools would have involved a process of triangulation of the data whereby perspectives and evaluations from positions external to the Catholic educational community would have been obtained. It would be fascinating to know, for instance, what interviews with local state school headteachers would have produced in terms of their evaluations of, and comments about, the Catholic schools studied here. Apart from time and resource constraints, a major obstacle to the implementation of such a research strategy is the existence of a professional ethics culture which inhibits the expression of such inter-institutional judgements, at least in the public realm.

Some form of triangulation of data was, however, available to the researcher in the form of the OFSTED inspection report for each school. These reports, produced by a secular, external and largely non-Catholic group of inspectors, were read in all cases.

In the following chapters a detailed analysis is presented of the responses of the headteachers, the pupils and the 'other professionals' to the contemporary challenges of Catholic schooling in England, supplemented where appropriate by insights derived from other forms of documentation.

# 6 Mission and leadership

## Concepts and challenges

As a result of educational, social and ideological changes in England during the 1980s and 1990s, more emphasis was placed upon an individual competitive ethic in education. This was apparent in the application of market values and market culture to educational institutions and stronger forms of accountability to education 'consumers' in the form of published league tables of school test scores and external examination results. At the same time a policy and research focus upon 'successful', 'effective' and 'winning' schools was accompanied by a 'naming and shaming' official policy towards schools labelled as 'failing'.

New responsibilities for English headteachers arising from the introduction of local management of schools (LMS) led to a significant increase in the growth of education management studies as a professional resource for headteachers and to the rise of a new culture and discourse of managerialism in educational practice.

At the socio-cultural and political level English society, especially during the 1980s, became more secularised, materialist and consumerist in orientation and ideas of the welfare state and of the common good weakened in political culture and discourse.

These changes taken together marked a profound transformation in the educational, cultural and political environment in which the sixty Catholic headteachers participating in this study had to pursue their conceptions of educational mission and of educational leadership. In this changed environment Catholic schools faced sharper challenges to the integrity of their religious, educational and social mission. Catholic school leaders could find themselves in situations of fundamental conflict between the commitments of their distinctive educational mission (as expressed in school mission statements) and the current requirements and imperatives for institutional 'success' and 'effectiveness' and even of basic institutional survival.

One of the first focal points of this research enquiry was to investigate how these sixty Catholic headteachers interpreted concepts of mission and leadership in contemporary circumstances and what challenges they encountered in trying to realise these concepts in practice.

## The mission statements of Catholic schools

The Vatican, through the agency of the Congregations for Catholic Education, has published a series of statements (1977, 1982, 1988, 1998) designed to give guidance about what should be the distinctive features of the Catholic educational mission internationally. In summary form these may be stated as five regulative principles, i.e.:

1 education in the faith (as part of the saving mission of the Church);
2 preferential option for the poor (to provide educational services to those most in need);
3 formation in solidarity and community (to live in community with others);
4 education for the common good (to encourage common effort for the common good);
5 academic education for service (knowledge and skills: a means, not an end).

These principles may be called the *formal Church mission* for contemporary Catholic schooling. But some necessary questions for research investigation and discussion are 'to what extent do Catholic school leaders actually endorse these principles?' and 'what impediments do they face in trying to realise them in practice?' In other words, what is the *lived mission* in particular Catholic schooling contexts?

The mission statements of contemporary Catholic schools are not simply reproductions of the formal mission as articulated by the Vatican. Local mission statements tend in practice to be adaptations of the formal mission mediated by a whole variety of agencies in the local context. These can include the local hierarchy, religious orders, school board members and school governors, local priests, parents, teachers and students, as well as the designated school principal or headteacher. The process whereby mission statements for schools are shaped and formed is itself of great research interest and of considerable institutional significance in understanding the culture and effectiveness of a particular school.

As I have argued elsewhere (Grace, 1998a), mission statements were being used in Catholic educational culture long before the concept was appropriated and generalised in modern institutional practice. Mission statements have many Catholic virtues. They constitute a principled and comprehensive charter of what a school claims to be its distinctive educational, spiritual, moral and social purposes. Such statements characteristically specify a range of desired educational outcomes. They are published to the community as a statement saying 'this is what the school is about' and implicitly saying 'this is the basis upon which you can judge us'.

The mission statements of the sixty Catholic secondary schools[1] in this enquiry were analysed in order to elucidate stated mission priorities. While many Catholic schools include a wide range of principles and aspirations in their institutional statements, some principles appear to be given more emphasis than others in terms of priority ranking or public presentation.

## The discourse of the faith mission

As might be expected, all the mission statements of the sixty schools were explicit about the faith mission of Catholic education. However, variations in the discourse used to describe the mission (especially for parents of prospective students) suggested different priorities about this mission and about its purposes. Some institutional statements were very clear that a serious engagement with the religious culture of the Roman Catholic Church was a prime aim of the school:

> The main aim of the school is to educate the pupils in accordance with the principles of the Catholic Faith. The spirit of Christ's teaching should be seen in all areas of school life.
>
> (Corpus Christi)

> Students of all ages take part in religious retreats and visits … we aim to bring students to an understanding of the teachings of Christ in the context of the Roman Catholic Church today.
>
> (Holy Angels)

> The ethos of this school is based firmly on the Roman Catholic faith.
>
> (St Bernard's)

> This is a Roman Catholic comprehensive school and the teaching is according to the doctrines of the church.
>
> (St Flannan's)

> The school is part of a network of Roman Catholic schools provided by the Archdiocese … and it exists to educate children within a Roman Catholic ethos.
>
> (St Dominic's)

As parents and other community members read such statements of intent in the school's prospectus, it seems likely that they would come to the conclusion that the distinctive culture of Roman Catholicism was being maintained and enhanced in these schools and was central to the ethos.

In other schools, however, while the Catholic identity of the school was clearly acknowledged, the aims of the mission statements tended to be expressed in more open and comprehensive terms. These mission statements characteristically used a discourse of Christian religious commitment and of adherence to Gospel values as a major theme in presenting the school to the external world. While some mission statements made reference to 'Gospel values' (as implicitly understood), others were more explicit both about the nature of these values and about the implications of taking them seriously:

> We will provide a Christian Education for all pupils based on the teachings of Jesus and the Spirit of the Gospels. The whole life of the school will be determined by the Gospel Values of Love and Justice.
>
> (St Brendan's)

> We strive to be a community in which the Christian values of love, reconciliation, justice, peace and equality are the basis of all relationships.
>
> (St Patrick's)

> We set out to promote Gospel values such as service to others, tolerance, prayer, spirituality and forgiveness.
>
> (St Mark's)

> We believe that the Gospel message of love of the Lord and one another should permeate all aspects of school life.
>
> (St John of the Cross)

> Our task is to interpret for today's generation the meaning of the gospel in their lives, sharing with them eternal values, opening up

> to them a vision of a wider, better world … and to understand more fully their role in working to establish a new order in the world.
>
> (Holy Cross)

While the commitment of these schools to the particular realisation of Catholic religious practice was not in question, the discourse of these mission statements showed a sensitivity towards the values of a wider Christian culture and could be endorsed by a larger constituency of Christian parents and citizens beyond the Catholic community.

Those schools located in multi-ethnic and multi-faith inner-city communities sought in their mission statements to extend this sensitivity to relations with other faiths:

> We aim to enrich pupils' understanding of the Roman Catholic faith and to cultivate respect and understanding for other religious traditions.
>
> (St Francis)

> To maintain our own Christian tradition and practice while recognising the importance of fostering understanding and respect for other cultures, traditions and faiths.
>
> (St Eugene)

> We aim to support pupils in their faith and to build bridges between people of different faiths.
>
> (Ascension)

> Our aim is that each student will know about and respect the richness and variety of other races, cultures and religions so as to develop the ability to act with justice and take a stand against everything that undermines her own dignity and that of others.
>
> (Holy Rosary)

The interpretation of the discourse of the faith mission of these Catholic schools as expressed in these examples is not a straightforward exercise. At one level, they can be taken to be sincere professional and religious statements of intent formulated by school leaders and teachers (and sometimes students). In this sense they constitute an important part of what Bryk *et al.* (1993) referred to as the 'inspirational ideology' of Catholic education. More cynically (or perhaps realistically) they could be interpreted as part of a contemporary public relations emphasis in all

English schools designed to attract greater student numbers in a competitive situation. In this sense, and in the eyes of external critics of Catholic schooling, they could be seen as calculative marketing of spiritual assets. A later section of this chapter will report on the responses of the headteachers to these different interpretations of their faith mission.

## The inspiration of the charism

Twenty of the sixty Catholic secondary schools in this research had been founded by religious or teaching orders and although only twelve of them currently had headteachers belonging to these orders, all of them continued to receive spiritual, cultural and economic support from their respective religious communities. These orders were the Brothers of Christian Instruction, The Christian Brothers, De La Salle Brothers, Faithful Companions of Jesus, the Franciscans, the Jesuits, La Retraite Sisters, La Sainte Union Sisters, Society of the Sacred Heart, Salesians of Don Bosco, Servite Sisters, Sisters of Mercy, Sisters of Notre Dame, Sisters of St Paul and the Ursuline sisters.

The mission statements of fifteen of these schools made explicit references to the influence of the charism of the founder of the order upon the present-day work of the school.

Max Weber, who elaborated the classic sociological understanding of charismatic leadership, referred to it as an 'extraordinary quality' possessed by some leaders which gave them a unique power and influence over others.[2] In Catholic culture this notion has been recontextualised in the concept of *charism* whereby the extraordinary qualities of certain religious leaders are seen to be a special inspiration of the Holy Spirit demonstrated, for instance, by the founders of religious orders. Thus in his Apostolic Exhortation on the Renewal of Religious Life (1971) Pope Paul VI reminded religious orders of their obligation 'to be faithful to the spirit of their founders, to their evangelical intentions and to the example of their sanctity'.[3]

In this sense, the charism of the founder and the spirit of the order is intended to be a significant influence upon the culture and work of those Catholic schools derived from these traditions and origins. If mission statements can be taken as some evidence that particular charisms were still active in some schools, then the influence of charism must be taken into account in any analysis of Catholic schooling. In this study some examples of charism influence were expressed as follows:

> Jesuit education is inspired by the vision of St Ignatius Loyola in which God reveals his love for us in all things. The aim of Jesuit

education is the formation of people of competence, conscience and compassion, who are men and women for others.

(Pope Paul III)

We who work in [this school] state our belief in our young people. We recognise that they come from differing backgrounds but that they are of equal value to God and to us. In the spirit of St John Bosco we turn our efforts to those who stand in special need because of the lack of material or emotional security.

(St Robert Bellarmine)

Despite the turbulent educational world in which we find ourselves at this time, we, the staff and students [of this school] maintain a stance of optimism, hope and good humour. Inspired by St Julie's words, 'Ah! Qu'il est bon, le bon Dieu', we believe that … we will experience a determination to achieve and be blessed with success.

(Our Lady of Lourdes)

In our methods and practices of management and teaching we follow the example of St John Baptist De La Salle.

(St Richard's)

The Society of the Sacred Heart has always sought to promote the education of women and academic excellence … We seek to constantly improve everything we do so that we can make a difference for the young women who will shape the society of the future.

(Holy Rosary)

As might be expected, explicit references to particular charisms as guiding the educational mission of Catholic schools came from those schools where the headteacher was a member of a religious order or a lay headteacher strongly influenced by the traditions of an order. As such they represented a tradition of charism influence which appeared to be in decline in Catholic schooling, although much attention is being given in the Catholic educational world to find ways of 'handing on the charism'.[4]

## The academic mission

In their analysis of secondary school prospectuses and the impact of educational markets, Hesketh and Knight (1998) have shown that in comparisons made between 1991 and 1996 school prospectuses had become more detailed, more glossy and more image conscious. In particular, more space and emphasis was given, in the most recent prospectuses, to the reporting of academic achievements (by high scoring schools) or of academic improvement (by lower scoring schools). This greater attention to a school's academic profile was partly the result of government legislation requiring such publication and partly a response by schools to a more competitive market environment for student recruitment.

Similar research has been undertaken by Maguire *et al.* (1999) in an analysis of 129 brochures used by Post-16 providing institutions in South-East England as they seek to attract more students in a competitive market situation for post-compulsory education.

Catholic schools and colleges are caught up in the market dynamics of their particular locations and therefore an analytical focus of this research was to probe the ways in which this had affected the expression of their academic mission in their public documents.

The classic Catholic position that academic achievement finds its full meaning in the service of higher ends was still a strong feature of the expressed missions of many of the schools in this research. Mission statements might now be printed in larger and glossier prospectus packages than in the past, but they continued to use a traditional discourse of 'holiness and learning':

> The school seeks to enable its pupils to reach their maximum potential in all areas of the curriculum, using their talents to the greater glory of God.
>
> (St Margaret Mary)

> We strive to affirm, develop and challenge the abilities of each pupil … While recognising that national standards have a part to play … our main criterion will be personal worth. In doing this we prepare young people to be a positive influence in the places where they live and work with others.
>
> (St Robert Bellarmine)

> Each pupil is challenged and sustained in his or her efforts to be someone who is aware of their many talents … and realises that talents are gifts to be developed for the good of the human community.
>
> (St Rita's)

> To teach pupils through Christ's own teaching and through the advancement of knowledge, to understand God and humanity better.
>
> (St John Fisher)

> The Congregation … has always placed a high priority on the education of women, particularly of those in inner-city areas. It strives to educate women to reach their full potential, to be confident, to be successful and to become mature and responsible Christians.
>
> (Sacred Heart of Mary)

While the majority of the sixty Catholic schools continued to use a traditional discourse of 'holiness and learning' and of 'service and learning' to describe their academic missions, there was some evidence that a more utilitarian discourse was beginning to emerge, albeit in a minority of the schools. This new discourse was constituted in various ways. It could take the form of a much stronger emphasis upon academic achievement and standards *per se*, not explicitly connected to the religious and social purposes of a Catholic school. In other cases greater use was made of a discourse of 'excellence', often associated with statistical tables or academic results showing the relative achievements of the school compared with borough, city or national averages. This strategy was used, not unsurprisingly, by those schools with high levels of academic achievement or by schools which could demonstrate significant improvements over a given period of time.

Viewed overall, however, the expression of the academic mission of these Catholic secondary schools had not changed dramatically as a result of the impact of more competitive market conditions in education. Presentations of the mission both in principle and in outcomes were more detailed than in the past, but much of the discourse had remained in a distinctive Catholic form. What Catholic schools were doing in response to market culture was to set the statements of their academic missions in the context of glossy school prospectuses which utilised, wherever possible, references to a scholarly heritage, with the use of crests and other symbols, and references to contemporary academic excellence.

What still remains unanswered in this analysis is whether the unchanging discourse of the academic mission represents its unchanging nature in practice or whether it is a formal discourse and an historical residue which do not equate to what actually goes on in Catholic schools. Any satisfactory answer to this question would require a considerable number of in-depth ethnographic case studies of Catholic schools in action, and this remains a major challenge for Catholic educational researchers in the future.[5]

## The community and social mission

Aspects of the expressed community and social missions of these Catholic schools have been touched upon in the earlier sections. Such references naturally occur in relation to the faith mission, the influence of particular charisms and the principles of the academic mission. Some schools, however, made strong and particular references in their mission statements to community and social commitments:

> to provide a school environment where justice is a key value in all our learning and relationships … encouraging the sharing of resources, material goods and personal talents, working on racist attitudes as they manifest themselves.
>
> (Mary, Mother of God)

> We recognise that … there are many social and educational tensions that stretch our staff, at times, to breaking point. In our school, we undertake to affirm and support each other.
>
> (St Robert Bellarmine)

> Since we are part of a multicultural, multi-racial society all pupils should be educated towards an understanding of, and commitment to, that society and every effort should be made to secure the elimination of racism.
>
> (Carthusian Martyrs)

> We put a high value on the idea of cooperation because we know just how much can be achieved in partnership and with trust. We do our best work when we work together.
>
> (Cardinal Hume)

> To encourage awareness of, and promote, the position of women in society.
>
> (Our Lady of Lourdes)

It could be argued that there is nothing distinctively Catholic about these expressions of community and social principles in the mission statements and it seems likely that entirely comparable statements would be found in any analysis of similar documents in state schools. A qualitative distinction nevertheless is to be found in many cases in what may be called the *legitimation context.* The community and social aspirations of these Catholic school mission statements were frequently related to the teachings of Christ, to Gospel values, to direct biblical quotations, to papal statements or other Church pronouncements and to the charisms of religious orders. In this way, Catholic schools could invest their community and social aims not only with a secular legitimation (arising from national and local policies) but also with a religious and sacred legitimation. The ultimate source of the community and social values advanced by the schools was represented as the will of God. Racism, for example, in Catholic schooling culture was not only a violation of concepts of respect for persons and a violation of equal opportunities, but also a violation of the teaching that all persons had equal value in the sight of God.

## Catholic headteachers: articulating a personal mission

The mission statements of schools are not simply the expression of the headteacher's mission. Most mission statements are the outcome of various processes of consultation and participation and they represent an agreed public statement to the external world as well as to the school community.

In addition to the messages conveyed by these institutional statements, this research was also interested in the personal constructs of mission held by the sixty Catholic headteachers. These personal constructs might be regarded as important in sustaining and directing the leadership dynamic of individual headteachers. As part of the research enquiry every headteacher was asked, during the interviews, to articulate their personal conceptions of the distinctive mission of the schools. Analysis of these statements was undertaken using constructs of 'central meanings' and 'patterns of discourse' as indicated in Chapter 5. Three dominant patterns of discourse (in ideal-type form) could be said to exist when headteachers spoke about their own conceptions of school mission. These were (1) a discourse of the sacred and of faith leadership, (2) particular service to inner-city and poor communities and (3) a discourse of school effectiveness and academic achievements. In many instances headteachers would draw upon all three forms of discourse in describing their mission concepts. However, within these comprehensive statements of purpose, detailed examination often indicated particular emphases or priorities among their aims.

## The priority of the sacred and of faith leadership

Virtually all of the headteachers made some reference to their responsibilities for the renewal and development of the Catholic faith among the students in their schools. In some cases it appeared that this aspect of the mission was given a nominal or ritual acknowledgement rather than a committed endorsement.[6] In just over half of the interview accounts (thirty-three) strong and explicit references to faith leadership were made and a sense of committed endorsement to this as a personal mission was conveyed. The discourse of those who might be called the committed faith leaders conveyed a sense of personal spiritual vocation as central to their conceptions of the role of a Catholic school leader. Of the thirty-three whose interview accounts contained this sense of personal, spiritual engagement, six were consecrated religious and twenty-seven were lay headteachers. The priority of the sacred and of faith leadership in these Catholic schools was expressed in various ways:

> The question is what have you personally got to bring and the answer is … one's own relationship with Christ … to be a role model where it is quite clear that one's own beliefs and practices are firmly rooted in the teachings of Christ and built on a prayer life, not neglected because of the 'busyness'.
>
> (Woman lay headteacher, St Genevieve)

> When I communicate with governors, when I communicate with parents eg in the newsletter … I always give priority to some spiritual aspect of the life of the school. I try to do that to remind myself and the community at large that the purpose of the mission of this place is to further the Christian ethos.
>
> (Woman religious headteacher, St Joan of Arc)

> The importance of regular attendance at spiritual retreats … I think that's allowed me to focus … It is not well behaved boys, it is not school uniform, it is not academic results … At the end of the day [the mission is achieved] through spirituality.
>
> (Male lay headteacher, Pope Paul III)

> We have got to try our very best to be a sacrament in the world.
>
> (Male lay headteacher, St Lawrence)

> I saw teaching as a vocation. It was on a par, believe it or not, with going into the priesthood … I have always taught in Catholic

> schools ... I think it's an enormous challenge to actually spread the Faith in a community like this.
>
> (Male lay headteacher, St Dominic's)

Given the insistence of the Catholic school system in England and Wales that only active and practising Catholics can be appointed to school headships, it might, at first sight, seem surprising that only thirty-three of the sixty secondary headteachers made extensive or committed expressions of faith leadership as central to their roles. However, this runs the risk of oversimplifying the responses of other headteachers. In other words, in clarifying their personal conceptions of the mission of Catholic school leaders, some headteachers might draw extensively upon the discourse of faith (as in the examples above) while others would draw upon a discourse of 'good works' as exemplars of faith in action.

While therefore, for analytical purposes, a separation may be made between clear expressions of faith leadership, on the one hand, and emphasis upon a leadership in 'good works' on the other, in practice it seems likely that these two features of Catholic headship are closely interrelated. What is at stake here turns upon differing interpretations of this personal discourse of mission. Some Catholics will be alarmed that only about half of the headteachers utilised an explicit discourse of faith leadership and they are likely to conclude that this indicates a progressive weakening or erosion of a distinctive language of Catholic school headship. Other Catholics will see in the discourse of good works a working out of the new spirit of Vatican II with more emphasis upon faith in action in the wider world.

## Service to inner-city and deprived urban communities

Of the sixty Catholic secondary schools participating in this study fifty-six were located in inner-city or deprived urban communities and served student populations which were substantially working class and poor (as judged by FSM entitlements). In London, FSM entitlements of over 40 per cent of the students were recorded in half of the schools. In Liverpool, thirteen of the twenty schools served populations with FSM entitlements of over 40 per cent, and, of these, six schools had FSM entitlements in excess of 60 per cent of students. In Birmingham four of the ten schools had FSM entitlements in excess of 40 per cent of the students.

If the words of the Sacred Congregation for Catholic Education (1977, p. 44) still define a key priority for Catholic schools, i.e. that 'first and foremost the Church offers its educational service to the poor', then these schools were front-line agencies of this mission. A significant number of the headteachers had themselves originated from Catholic working-class families and in some cases from the local communities in which they now worked. While therefore in Gramsci's (1971) terms they might be labelled as 'traditional intellectuals' since they had entered the service of the Church, they were also 'organic intellectuals' by virtue of their strong consciousness of service to the class and communities from which they had derived.

Seventeen of the headteachers expressed as part of their personal mission in Catholic schooling an explicit commitment to the education of the poor, e.g.:

> I was brought up in a Catholic parish which is in the area of this school – a working class community … I feel a particular affinity for the Catholic system in general and I support the Catholic community in this area.
>
> (Male lay headteacher, Corpus Christi)

> I wanted to teach in an inner-city. This was my mission and I asked the Order if I could teach in an inner-city school … I saw this as an area where staffing would always be a problem. I said 'We as Sisters should be teaching in an area where lay people don't want to go'.
>
> (Female religious headteacher, St Mark)

> Our charism is particularly to, in the words of our foundress, 'educate the poor in the most abandoned places'. Our basic philosophy is to educate, particularly people from deprived areas and especially girls.
>
> (Female religious headteacher, Sacred Heart of Mary)

> The drive of the Irish Christian Brothers was a service to the poor and I still feel quite strongly that sense of vocation, not being lived out as a Brother but being lived out in terms of the job I'm doing. It has a big influence on me. This is what I'm here to do.
>
> (Male lay headteacher, former Christian Brother, Holy Redeemer)

> My personal vision for this school is service. I see that the school is here to serve the young people of this area … To make them feel important and valued as members of society … And then to give them values, to give them a sense of what is right and of what is wrong … this is one of the most deprived areas in Europe.
>
> (Male lay headteacher, St Flannan's)

In the shaping of these Catholic school leaders' personal sense of an education mission to the poor, two influences appeared to be powerful. The first was a socialisation and formation experience in a particular religious culture, either as a member (or former member) of a religious or teaching order or as a student in institutions run by such orders. These experiences had engendered what might be called a distinctive urban mission for some headteachers. The second was a personal biography of Catholic working-class upbringing and schooling which had produced an 'organic intellectual' professional commitment to the service of that class.

The Catholic school system in inner-city and deprived urban areas has clearly benefited from the presence of these two forms of professional vocation among its headteachers and leaders. This sense of vocation has motivated individuals to accept appointments in schools and districts which are educationally and socially challenging and even, in some cases, dangerous. It is a matter of some importance to the future of Catholic schooling in these challenging areas to know whether or not these forms of professional vocation are being renewed among contemporary or potential school leaders. Given the declining influence of the religious and teaching orders in Catholic education and given the cultural and ideological effects of sustained social mobility in the Catholic community, the renewal of a distinctive urban mission may become problematic in the future.

## The mission of school effectiveness and of academic success

In a strong critique of 'the current dominance of school effectiveness research and school improvement discourses in education policy-making', Slee *et al.* (1998, p. 2) have argued that notwithstanding good intentions, their influence upon schooling in England and elsewhere has been narrowing and reductionist. Despite the progressive origins of school effectiveness research (SER) in attempts to improve the schooling of the urban poor and despite some positive and impressive achievements in the last twenty years (Sammons *et al.* 1995), an unintended consequence of SER is that constructs of school 'effectiveness' have often been reduced to quantitative assessments of test scores and examination results. Even when school effectiveness researchers have qualified their findings in various ways or have included assessments of personal, social and moral developments in schools, such work has been appropriated by political, media and policy agencies to keep the focus sharply upon measurable academic outcomes. The recontextualising of what it means to be an effective school was shaped not only by this partial use of SER studies but also by the public reporting processes of OFSTED and in particular by the personal ideological crusade of the Chief Inspector for Schools in England on standards and effectiveness.[7] All schools in England were subject to an intensified surveillance and accountability regime driven by narrow academic criteria and constructs of effectiveness during the 1980s and 1990s. The 'results' of OFSTED inspections, categorised in hierarchical league tables of results for each area, were amplified in both national and local media. By these means, some schools were publicly acclaimed as successful and 'effective' and others were publicly named and shamed as failing and 'ineffective'. These publicly amplified judgements of schools in terms of their relative effectiveness became critical to their academic reputations, their position in an intensified competitive marketplace for students and critical to their own institutional survival. For school leaders this meant in practice that those high in the league tables of effectiveness had to maintain that position over time. Those low in the league table ranking had to be able to demonstrate school improvement in results and thereby gain a place in media listings of 'most improved schools' in the country.

A key question for this research was, therefore, to what extent had the discourse of school effectiveness and of school improvement become a major part of the personal schooling mission of these Catholic headteachers?

In its 1998 publication *The Catholic School on the Threshold of the Third Millennium*, the Congregation for Catholic Education had noted what it perceived to be a changed relation between many parents and pupils and Catholic schooling. It perceived the emergence of a secular and utilitarian attitude to such schooling in contemporary settings:

> What is in fact required of the Catholic school is a certificate of studies or ... quality instruction and training for employment.
>
> (pp. 37–8)

If many parents and pupils were now expressing a fundamentally utilitarian attitude to Catholic schooling, to what extent could these developments be seen in the attitudes and discourse of the sixty Catholic headteachers participating in this study?

All of the headteachers spoke seriously about their personal and professional commitment to achieve the best possible academic results for their students and they spoke at length about the current academic status of their schools, characteristically quoting GCSE A*–C examination statistics and comments from OFSTED inspection reports. The language of school effectiveness and of school improvement was very evident in the interview accounts. However, this was not, in the main, an abstracted utilitarian and technical discourse of 'results' alone. Characteristically commitments to the academic mission of the schools were linked to other religious, social and moral aims of Catholic schooling:

> Inevitably the achievement aspect is very important. I mean that's the whole national political scene isn't it ... We've got to do the best for these kids because really we are talking about a lot of educational and social disadvantage.
>
> (Male lay headteacher, Carthusian Martyrs)

> In this school, which is in one of the most deprived areas in Western Europe ... I see that education is breaking into the cycle of deprivation ... When I do education, it's a bit for God and a bit for Mammon. The education is for 5 A-Cs, the certificates they get, but I don't think you can have a healthy mental attitude unless you have something more spiritual.
>
> (Female lay headteacher, Bishop Anselm)

> My first and most important principle is, no concession to anything to do with inner-city location problems. I think that it's part of the mission that we are seeking to do the best we can for all of the children here ... We're a Catholic school ... I feel that the children have a great advantage in having some kind of moral framework to equip them to lead the rest of their lives.
>
> (Female lay headteacher, St Margaret Mary)

> Lots of our children come from very disadvantaged homes. My vision is to ensure that we raise achievement levels so that our youngsters can find their way out of the poverty trap and experience a better life. I was fortunate to go to a good school. I came from a poor family myself and it was through the education process that I did better ... I believe that Catholic education, Catholic schools can make a profound difference because our vision is very clear ... it points to the twin philosophies of raising achievement and promoting Gospel values.
>
> (Male lay headteacher, St Francis)

In a minority of cases a more abstracted and utilitarian discourse of academic results could be discerned. Such interview accounts tended to make limited or passing references to a Catholic matrix of achievement or purposes, concentrating their focus upon the academic or institutional profile of the school *per se*. In other words, when these headteachers spoke about their personal missions for the school, academic outcomes appeared to have a dominant place in their consciousness:

> When I came here I promised them all the things that my grammar school had given me. If their children were bright I promised them all the good things – and if their children were less bright. As a result the school has doubled in size ... The problem is that this city is tainted with under achievement – many parents settle for their children being safe and happy before they think about league tables.
>
> (Male lay headteacher, St Anthony of Padua)

> We aim to provide excellence – not just academic excellence because we obviously have a tradition of excellence in achieving results but we're also focussed on obtaining excellence in other areas too. We are a strong sports school and a strong music school ... We have a strong tradition of providing Oxbridge with Classicists and we have a tradition in the sixth form of pushing people for academic results.
>
> (Male religious headteacher, St Pius X)

> I want this particular school to be 1000 pupils strong in about five years from now ... I want them to be getting examinations in the order of 30% getting GCSE A-Cs.
>
> (Male lay headteacher, St James)

As might be expected, a major preoccupation with academic results, institutional size and OFSTED evaluations could arise in a variety of school circumstances. Schools which could have been labelled as 'underachieving' were necessarily concentrating their attention about school improvement in this sector. Headteachers of schools in highly competitive urban situations could not afford to ignore the academic ranking of their schools in the local league table of results. The leaders of Catholic schools with high academic success profiles wanted to elaborate the nature of that success and the reasons for it.

With all these pressures towards a culture of 'performativity'[8] and measurement in English schooling, the attention given by these Catholic headteachers to the academic mission of Catholic schooling has undoubtedly increased. Despite these pressures, the majority in this study appeared to be holding issues of school effectiveness and of measurable outcomes in a *Catholic synthesis* with issues of spirituality, morality and social and community service in schooling. This resistance to the domination of technical performativity in education may be an outcome of the religious and professional formation of this particular sample of school leaders. A question which is inevitably raised is: will the next generation of Catholic school leaders be able to resist similar pressures in the future? Whereas most of the Catholic headteachers in this study still used a discourse which related concepts of school effectiveness, school improvement and academic results to religious, social and moral purposes, it is possible that they represented a leadership culture of the past. As more newly appointed Catholic headteachers are socialised and professionally formed in secular teacher education institutions and secular headteacher preparation programmes such as the National Professional Qualification for Headteachers (NPQH), will what has been called here a *Catholic synthesis* of educational objectives be maintained?

## Conceptions of leadership in Catholic schools

Catholic culture and institutional life have been profoundly influenced by historical forms of hierarchy, authority and authoritarianism[9] which have manifested themselves in the development of the institutional Church. For modern analysts of Catholic culture such as Collins (1997) many of these features have been distortions of the authentic characteristics of Christian living and leadership.

In a powerful critique, Groome (1998, pp. 43–4) has suggested that these historical distortions of Catholic Christian culture have had negative effects upon the Church's mission in education:

> Contrary to its own tenets … Catholicism has shown itself capable of making people feel like hopeless sinners instead of affirming their essential goodness … of controlling their experience of God's presence … of practising authoritarianism and blind obedience.

For Collins, the greatest 'sin' of the institutional Church has been to create and project a model of leadership, represented by the papacy, which has been characterised by a form of papal monarchism, absolute and infallible. Any reform of the Catholic Church in the third millennium must involve, from Collins' perspective, a new conception of leadership, with a Pope who is:

> Focused outward toward the stimulation and support of the abilities and gifts of others, rather than inward through a conviction of a

> 'messianic' mission to dominate the Church ... This does not mean that the Pope should not make decisions but they need to be made collegially with others who are sensitive to the complexities involved.
>
> (p. 150)

In the light of this larger cultural and historical context it is not surprising that leadership in many Catholic schools has, in the past, reproduced the sense of hierarchy and of authoritarianism characterising the institutional Church. Catholic education and schooling has, in this way, operated in the mode which Bernstein (1990) describes as 'a cultural relay' for the renewal of the legitimacy of autocratic leadership.

It was therefore a matter of some interest in the present research to probe the extent to which the concepts of school leadership held by contemporary Catholic headteachers either reproduced or departed from traditional models.

Extensive media attention to inner-city schools at the time of the research had amplified the notion that what such schools required was 'strong leadership' from exceptional headteachers. These media constructs tended to project an image of dominant, executive school leaders (generally male) who would be able to 'turn around' a difficult school by personal dynamism, competitive skill and market intelligence and by the ability to give strong leadership and to take tough decisions. This was, in some ways, a recontextualisation of the traditional 'headmaster' model of strong leadership in English education by a new executive 'trouble-shooter' model for the contemporary market conditions of urban education.[10] The headteachers in this research were asked to respond to both traditional and contemporary models of strong school leadership in reflecting upon their own conceptions of leadership.

Analysis of the interview transcripts[11] demonstrated a variety of interpretations of what strong school leadership could or should mean. As a broad categorisation, thirty-three of the headteachers used a discourse of strong leadership although this was qualified in important ways; twenty-seven emphasised a discourse of collegiality in talking about modern school leadership.

## Varieties of 'strong leadership'

For some headteachers, who had experienced autocratic leadership in their own careers, it was important to distinguish leadership strength from autocracy:

> Strong in the sense that you've got to have a vision for the school and strong in the sense that you've got to be able to make decisions ultimately, but I don't perceive a strong head as being an autocrat and I don't believe in autocratic leadership. I won't say that it can't work in certain circumstances but I do believe that autocratic leaders will have people working with them who are immature in their concept of authority … The only mature way of leadership is to work with people to recognise the gifts of people and to always be able to consult where it is appropriate and to delegate.
>
> (Female religious headteacher, Sacred Heart of Mary)

Under the dual influences of an emphasis on collegiality in Vatican II culture and an emphasis on collegiality in modern management literature, none of the headteachers defended the traditional strong leadership models of Catholic education in the past. However, there was a view that particular situations might require particular forms of strong and decisive leadership. These situations might relate to taking over a school in difficulty (or operating at a low level) or to specific challenges of urban schooling. In such contexts some headteachers believed that high-profile leadership had to be demonstrated:

> I think that in a school such as this, the leadership has to be strong. I see strong leadership as almost the social cement which the girls and the staff look to me to provide in a way that is too dependent but necessary. They know that I can make this a better place for them … The kids that come here are tough. They are very street-wise … They want to look at somebody and think, 'she knows what to do and she'll do it right'.
>
> (Female lay headteacher, Holy Angels)

> I don't know about leadership in general but I was brought in with a mandate to change things … some of the leadership which I have to give is leadership that goes against the grain of the staff involved. It has meant being prepared to tackle things straight off. It has, in the end, meant having to give people instructions rather than asking … I had to make some unpopular decisions … I knew that it would not be an easy school to take over.
>
> (Male lay headteacher, St Peter Damian)

> I think you do need strong leadership and I think that it needs to come across as strong to all the different constituencies in the school … So far as the boys are concerned, I think leadership is

> important … you have to have that very clear with boys from an urban setting.
>
> (Male religious headteacher, Pope Pius VII)

Many of the references to the 'need' to demonstrate strong, high-profile leadership came from headteachers who were trying to change the cultures of 'failing' or underachieving urban schools or from those who claimed that this is what was expected of headteachers by parents and students (especially boys) in inner-city communities. It will be noted later that those headteachers who wanted to move from a tradition of strong school leadership to more consultative and collegial forms frequently encountered a conservative resistance to this among sections of the school staff and among parents and students. In some cases headteachers adopted in these situations a leadership strategy which could be called *strong/collegial*. This involved using first-phase strong leadership to make significant changes in the culture of the school and second-phase collegiality to consolidate the changed environment. Those who took this position argued that leadership styles have to be responsive to changing conditions in a school:

> I recognise in my own leadership style that things change over time. I inherited a school that … needed rapid change in a short time. That necessitates therefore a very directive, up-front, hands-on kind of style … Now, six years on, it will be a more measured approach and through other people … There are specific situations in which it is absolutely critical that action is rapid. There isn't time for debate or a lot of philosophical arguments about what we should do.
>
> (Male lay headteacher, St Basil's)

The discourses of leadership which have been discussed so far might be described by the generic category *context-specific strong leadership*. In these cases a claim is made that the particular features of a school's situation require high-profile, decisive and rapid leadership responses, at least as a first-phase strategy for change. It is seen to be the responsibility of the headteacher to give such leadership. Such discourses and concepts of leadership are generally premised on the assertion that a previous regime of weak or inappropriate style of leadership played an important part in creating a school's current difficulties.

Many of those who endorsed a more *context-independent* discourse of leadership sought to redefine in various ways what it means to be a strong school leader. In doing so they appeared to be distancing themselves from concepts of leadership where 'strong' implied dominance and executive direction. This group of headteachers interpreted strong leadership to mean commitment of purpose, clarity of vision and strength of character. A generic category of *mission-focused leadership*[12] was strongly represented among these headteachers. The responsibility of a Catholic school leader in their view was to be strong and clear about mission priorities amid the many pressures of day-to-day school life. The challenge of leadership from this perspective was not to allow the ultimate purposes of a Catholic education to be buried by bureaucratic, academic and managerial 'busyness':

> I think leadership has to be strong. But what I'm really saying is that the person who is prepared to stand up and be counted on certain religious and moral issues has to be first of all a strong person. And has to be quite clear about how they see the school moving forward.
>
> (Female lay headteacher, St Genevieve)

> You have to clearly articulate the principles on which the school was founded, for staff, for the community, for parents … There has to be a very clear sense of mission or vision about the school. You have to communicate that this institution has what I call unity of purpose.
>
> (Male lay headteacher, St Gabriel's)

> One of the important factors in leadership is to keep the vision of the school to the fore and that colleagues must see what your vision is and the direction in which you are going.
>
> (Male religious headteacher, St Pius X)

> The use of language by OFSTED gives an implication that to be effective as a leader you need to be almost tough or macho. I don't actually think that's the case. I think leadership is essentially about having a vision of where you are going and having the ability to communicate that vision.
>
> (Male lay headteacher, St Alphonsus)

These concepts of leadership were frequently elaborated and extended by references to qualities of purposefulness, clarity, resilience, optimism and moral courage. Those who utilised a discourse of strong school leadership in any of the previous forms tended to present an image of leadership which was individual in emphasis and in some senses heroic in nature. These constructs of leadership, without celebrating traditional modes of hierarchy, recontextualised hierarchy in new forms as change agent, mission guardian and institutional animator. While this was probably unintentional in many cases, the overall effect of these forms of discourse was to invest the position of school leader with very special qualities and with very heavy responsibilities. From this perspective the question arose that if so much in Catholic urban education depended upon 'strong' school leaders (however defined), could enough of them be found to maintain and develop the school system in the future? In research undertaken on Catholic school leadership in urban elementary schools in the USA, O'Keefe (2000, p. 240) had located among his respondents a similar reaction:

> I don't know where they'll come from.

One possible answer to the question was provided by those headteachers in this study (twenty-seven in number) who argued that shared and collegial modes of leadership had to replace the model of the individual 'hero headteacher' or, in Catholic terms, of the headteacher saints and martyrs.

## The leadership of collegiality

The reformed culture of Catholicity which the Second Vatican Council hoped to inaugurate called for a larger place for dialogue and collegiality in all forms of Catholic institutional life. Daniels (2000), in a recent review of these developments, has come to the conclusion that much less progress has been made in establishing practices of dialogue and collegiality in Catholic institutions than had been hoped for. This has partly been accounted for by the sheer durability of a long historical tradition of hierarchical leadership and partly by a revisionist reaction against some of the more liberal principles commended by the Council. In short, a tradition of strong hierarchical leadership does not give way easily to new forms of shared, consultative and collegial leadership.

It is in the light of this larger Catholic context and of internal struggles about the proper nature of leadership within the Church that the responses of the sixty Catholic headteachers in this study have to be interpreted. From one perspective, the fact that less than half (twenty-seven) of these school leaders gave explicit endorsement to concepts of shared leadership in schools might be seen as surprising and disappointing. However, viewed against a centuries-old tradition of Catholic leadership in another mode, it could be interpreted as significant evidence of the emergence of a more liberal form of contemporary Catholic school leadership.

Analysis of the interview transcripts revealed that headteachers adopted collegial modes of leadership for a variety of reasons. Just as it had been possible to identify context-specific forms of strong leadership, where strong leadership was thought to be required because of difficulties experienced by a school, it also became evident that *context-specific forms of collegial leadership* were being articulated by some headteachers:

> They had previously a strong dominating leader … I joined the school when it had just been named and shamed and the staff morale was exceedingly low. It was my purpose to lead the school forward but I could not do it on my own, I had to bring the staff with me. My leadership style is cooperative and collegial. We are all leaders within our own sphere of responsibility within the school … There's no way that improvement could have been brought about just by me telling people what to do. It was about developing them as people.
>
> (Male lay headteacher, St Rita's)

> The previous regime was a bit autocratic … I wanted to create a culture where it was more open … it became obvious to me that people had not been used to expressing their views openly as they do now in open professional debate … A more collegiate approach.
>
> (Male lay headteacher, Carthusian Martyrs)

In situations such as these, headteachers were attempting to change the cultures of strongly hierarchical schools which appeared to be underperforming academically, perhaps because the full range of talents of the teachers had been unduly constrained by a dominating mode of leadership.

A variant of what has been called context-specific collegiality was expressed by those headteachers who believed that the leadership of challenging urban schools had to be a shared responsibility because this was the only way in which the pressures of inner-city schooling could be coped with successfully:

> I think there is a strength of character required to lead schools in urban areas. You have got to be able to take the knocks but I don't think that means an authoritarian style … You have to work as a team, especially in a school where you've got problems of chal-

> lenging behaviour, low achievement and deprivation. Unless you work together as a team you are going to sink completely.
>
> (Male lay headteacher, St Ciaran's)

In addition to context-specific forms of legitimation for shared and collegial leadership, other headteachers argued that in personal and institutional terms, collegiality simply made sense as a form of leadership and management strategy which would actualise and liberate the reserves of talent and innovation in the school:

> I think the head has to be inspirational but not in an autocratic sort of way. I think the whole idea of a collegiate approach helps people grow. It isn't one person's vision. You make sure the vision permeates all the leadership roles within the school.
>
> (Female lay headteacher, St John Fisher's)

> I think a head is a leader, not a manager … A leader should be a listener, not a teller … It is a question of sharing values; it is something that the leaders in the school form together … All have leadership roles and it is important that people with leadership roles do share values and do have a common sense of purpose.
>
> (Male lay headteacher, St Matthew)

An impediment to changing to more open, collegial and shared school leadership models was mentioned by a number of headteachers. Resistance to such change appeared to arise from those constituencies of teachers, parents and students who believed that the 'proper' role of a Catholic urban school leader was to be visibly strong and dominating and clearly in charge. From these more conservative social constituencies, which could also include priests and school governors, expectations for school leadership style were traditional. These included the idea that consultation was a form of weakness or that headteachers were the legitimated sole agents of decision making. As one headteacher put it, 'they almost refuse to be consulted at times on many things' (St Patrick's).

Changing to collegial school leadership was not therefore an easy option. It frequently required professional and moral courage on the part of some headteachers and no small measure of leadership skill and diplomacy to inaugurate it. As many of the schools were located in difficult communities and served frequently challenging students, there had been a pervasive notion that the leadership of such schools would necessarily have to be 'strong' in a dominating sense. Those headteachers who opposed this view argued that, on the contrary, the authentic sign of leadership strength was the ability to share leadership responsibilities and to be consultative and collegial. They also tended to believe that this was the way that Catholic institutional culture in general ought to be moving.

## Catholic women headteachers

There were twenty-four women headteachers in this research enquiry, fourteen of whom were located in London inner-city schools. Of the twenty-four women headteachers, fifteen were in charge of Catholic girls' secondary schools, eight in charge of co-educational schools and one newly appointed as headteacher of a boys' school. Nine of these women school leaders were religious sisters and one was a former sister.[13]

Hall (1994, p. 1), in reviewing empirical work on educational leadership in the UK, has argued that:

> Theories of educational management and administration continue to be based largely on research into men as school leaders … Such studies have tended to use 'no differences' as a rationale for not focusing on gender as a potentially significant factor in understanding educational leadership.

The interview transcripts of the twenty-four women involved in this study were therefore scrutinised to see if the 'no differences' hypothesis mentioned by Valerie Hall would be substantiated or rejected in terms of the concepts and discourse used about educational leadership by these women.

This analysis showed that women headteachers were marginally more likely to use a discourse of shared leadership than was the case with male headteachers.[14] While the numerical differences with men were not great in terms of endorsement of collegial styles of leadership, a qualitative difference was apparent in the nature of the discourse used about collegial leadership. Women headteachers were more likely to refer to themselves as enablers or facilitators of the talents of others and more likely to refer to the importance of changing school cultures through the leadership of teams and the acknowledgement of leadership qualities in their colleagues than was the case with men headteachers.

In an earlier research involving women headteachers (Grace 1995) it was found that relatively few of these school leaders made explicit references to feminist perspectives on educational leadership as informing their actions. This pattern was repeated in the present study. On equal opportunity issues, the strongest endorsement of the importance of education for girls came from four headteachers of girls' schools. Three of these headteachers were religious sisters and the other was a former religious sister. They articulated a view of educational leadership where a special commitment to the educational progress of young women was given as a particular priority:[15]

> We want to develop Christian women who are confident – that's a big thing in this school. Women able to take their place in society – to be able to be leaders in society.
>
> (Female religious headteacher, Sacred Heart of Mary)

> I think being a head is the most exciting thing I can do because you can have a vision of education for these girls and you're actually in a key place to make it happen … I feel very passionate, especially for women, that education is about change, it's about making things better and it's about being involved.
>
> (Female ex-religious headteacher, Holy Rosary)

A special commitment to the education of girls among the headteachers appeared to be counter-cultural to perceived forms of patriarchy in the environment of these young women. One form of patriarchy was seen to be related to traditional working-class cultures of the inner city and, in some cases, to particular ethnic cultures. These cultures were believed to give the education of girls a lower status than that assigned to the education of boys. In addition to these sociological forms of patriarchy some of the women headteachers had an awareness of ecclesiastical forms of patriarchy as represented in the Catholic Church and in Catholic culture generally. Catholic girls' schools therefore were seen to have a special significance as potential cultural sanctuaries against the influences of external patriarchy in the community and in the Church.

It must be noted, however, that this was a minority perspective among the total sample of headteachers and even a minority among the fifteen headteachers of Catholic girls' schools.[16]

## Mission and leadership: an overview

This chapter has demonstrated that stereotyped views of Catholic schooling as monolithic and uniform cannot be sustained. There is significant internal differentiation in the formal and personal constitution of the Catholic educational mission and in constructs and articulation of appropriate forms of educational leadership. In the following chapter this differentiation will be explored further with particular reference to constructs of school effectiveness and to accounts of the academic 'success' (or otherwise) of these sixty Catholic schools.

# 7 The use of talents

## Catholic theories of academic 'success' or 'failure'

Catholic schools in many societies have established an ever growing reputation for achieving relatively high levels of academic success for their students. This academic success profile has been demonstrated in the USA in the research studies of Coleman and Hoffer (1987) and Bryk *et al.* (1993), in the UK in the research of Rutter *et al.* (1979), Mortimore *et al.* (1988), Goldstein *et al.* (1993), Morris (1998a, 1998b), Paterson (2000a, 2000b), the reports of OFSTED and in Australia in Flynn's (1993) study among other work (see Chapter 4). This general international association of Catholic schools with constructs of effective use of talents and achievement of good academic outcomes has tended to increase the popularity of Catholic schools in recent times with a wider constituency of parents, not all of whom are Catholics. Overall, Catholic schools seem to be relatively successful in their academic mission, at least as judged by conventional performance indicators. Such visible success has generated a debate about why this should be so. Is there a distinctively 'Catholic' factor which accounts for this successful use of talents or does it relate to more generic features of faith-based schools as contexts for learning? Why should Catholic schools, as the research of Greeley (1982) and others has demonstrated, be particularly effective with students from disadvantaged backgrounds?

Harvey Goldstein, one of the leading researchers and critical scholars* in the field of school effectiveness studies, is deeply sceptical about the existence of a distinctive Catholic factor in educational achievement. For Goldstein the most likely explanation for Catholic school academic success will be found in evidence that Catholic secondary schools receive more students with higher levels of prior achievement than their competitors: 'I don't really think that a "Catholic matrix" should take much credit from having the effect of attracting high achievers, in a zero-sum situation where someone else inevitably gets the low achievers'.[1] From this perspective a Catholic school 'image' may operate as an informal selective mechanism in the recruitment of students at the secondary stage.

Among other answers given to these sorts of questions, those provided by Greeley (1982), Bryk *et al.* (1993) and Morris (1997) have a particular relevance for this study.

## Greeley: effective socialisation and quality of instruction

Greeley's (1982) research, which showed that black and Hispanic students from deprived backgrounds had better levels of academic achievement in Catholic schools in comparison with their peers who attended public high schools, had two major explanations for these results. The first suggested that the disciplinary environments of the Catholic schools were, in general, more defined and structured than those in public high schools. These disciplined environments were, in Greeley's view, related to the disciplined cultures of the religious orders who were largely responsible for the schools. Such school cultures, it was suggested, provided effective socialisation settings for academic learning especially for those students who might lack structured environments in their home backgrounds.[2]

The second explanation related to 'quality of instruction' in the Catholic schools. Convey (1992, p. 19), summarising this research, concluded: 'academic instruction in Catholic schools was superior to that in the public schools. The quality of instruction was the strongest correlate of academic outcomes.' Quality of instruction remained a significant factor even when all background variables were taken into account.

In interpreting Greeley's explanations for the academic effectiveness of Catholic schools when dealing with disadvantaged students, critical attention needs to be given to his central construct of 'quality instruction'. As a pedagogic process, 'instruction' suggests a transmission mode of teaching closely related to the mastery and reproduction of a given text. It is, in Bernstein's (1997) terms, a 'visible pedagogy' marked by hierarchical relations between teacher and learner, by explicit rules for sequencing and pacing and by explicit criteria for evaluation and graded performance. Bernstein also implies that the visible pedagogy of instruction may be particularly effective with students from certain class and ethnic backgrounds, at least for first-level schooling. It may, however, be less effective as a mode of teaching and learning at higher levels of the educational process. Nevertheless Greeley's research gives support to the theory that a particular form of Catholic visible pedagogy (or 'instruction') mediated by teachers with a strong sense of vocation about the mission of education can have significant effects upon the academic achievement of inner-city students.

## Bryk *et al.*: a Catholic matrix for achievement

Bryk *et al.* (1993), in a major research study into the academic effectiveness of Catholic schools in the USA, have generated a more comprehensive explanation for their successful profile. This explanation is referred to here as *a Catholic matrix for achievement.*[3] For Bryk *et al.*, the academic effectiveness of Catholic schools with a wide range of students, including those who are disadvantaged in various ways, arises from the conjunction of four cultural and organisational features.

The first element of the matrix relates to curriculum and pedagogy. Bryk *et al.* found that the curricula programmes of the Catholic schools which they studied required all students to take a significant core of traditional academic subjects and elective options were very limited. In addition to the focused nature of the curriculum there were demanding requirements for the amount of study undertaken and for homework assignments.[4] The operative principle of the curriculum was that difficult subjects could be mastered by diligent application and this was urged upon all students. Unlike Greeley, the researchers did not find 'quality instruction' a particular feature of the schools, in the sense of dynamic or innovative teaching. In fact most of the observed teaching was described as 'ordinary' (p. 99) and traditional in format. However, the context of human relations within the classrooms observed appeared to be a crucial factor in helping this ordinary pedagogy to be effective in learning outcomes. This human relations dimension had to do with a sense of shared purpose and of community which characterised most of the schools. Expressed as 'social capital', this was the second element in the Catholic matrix of achievement.

As outlined in Chapter 4, social capital refers to a network of support and trust relations which exist between persons in certain social settings. It is a form of strong functional community. Coleman and Hoffer (1987) related the academic success of Catholic schools in the USA to the strong community support networks which acted in partnership with the schools to maximise educational effectiveness. Bryk *et al.* extended this concept to include a strong sense of internal community and shared values within Catholic schools. Thus with the benefits of these forms of social capital, both external and internal, Catholic schools were seen to possess considerable advantages over neighbouring public high schools.

The third element in the Catholic matrix for achievement was identified by Bryk *et al.* as a relatively high level of school autonomy for Catholic schools in comparison with the more constrained bureaucratic contexts of public high schools. Such relative freedom from bureaucratic demands ('paperwork') allowed Catholic principals and teachers to devote more time and thought to front-line teaching and to student relations.

The 'inspirational ideology' of Catholic schooling was suggested as the final element of the achievement matrix. This ideology was constituted, for Bryk *et al.*, by a sense of transcendent purpose in Catholic schooling, by a sense of the commitment of an educational mission rather than simply an educational programme, and by the existence to a large degree of a view of teaching and of educational leadership as a vocational calling and not simply as a job. This larger ideological/theological climate in Catholic schools provided, it was claimed, an animating spirit which gave shape and purpose to the whole school culture.[5]

Bryk *et al.*'s analysis of the academic effectiveness of Catholic schools in the USA has argued that it is the *conjunction* of the four elements outlined in what is called here *a Catholic matrix for achievement*, which accounts for the visible scholastic effectiveness of the schools even with disadvantaged students.

## Morris: variation in Catholic school achievements: 'holistic' models and 'pluralistic' models

In a series of analytical papers in the UK (1994, 1995, 1998a, 1998b) Morris has examined the academic effectiveness of Catholic schools in England in comparison with county (or state) schools. These papers have demonstrated, according to Morris (1998a, p. 186):

> the superiority of Catholic secondary schools over others in the maintained sector, at least on measures used by OFSTED.

However, in a parallel analysis Morris has also been investigating intra-school achievement differences within the Catholic sector. While it is the case that many Catholic secondary schools in England achieve academic results well above local authority and national averages, it is also the case that some Catholic schools have been designated as 'underachieving' or even 'failing' and some have been closed down as a result of a 'naming and shaming' policy for academically underachieving schools.

In a preliminary and small-scale analysis of this phenomenon, Morris (1997) has suggested that differences in the academic and religious outcomes of Catholic secondary schools may be related to differences in the internal ethos of the schools. From Morris's perspective those Catholic schools which conformed to the 'traditional confessional' or 'holistic' model of Catholic schooling were likely to be more successful than 'pluralistic' Catholic schools. In other words, Catholic schools which had a strong internal Catholic ethos (constituted by a high proportion of Catholic students and teachers) were more likely to be effective than pluralistic Catholic schools (constituted by a more differentiated student and teacher population).

The theory advanced by Morris amounts to an argument that the internal culture of pluralistic Catholic schools is, in effect, weakened by the presence of students and teachers from non-Catholic backgrounds. This reduction in Catholic social capital and shared values has, it is claimed, an impact upon the ethos of the school and in the longer term upon its achievements both academic and religious. Thus the argument is made:

> The clear, agreed and focussed mission of the traditional model would seem to help facilitate high levels of academic effectiveness to be achieved precisely because it provides the social cement which holds organisations and communities together.
>
> (p. 390)

It has to be noted here that large theoretical claims are being made on a small empirical research base[6] but nevertheless Morris's work provides a provocative hypothesis for the investigation of internal differences in academic achievement within the Catholic school sector.

In addition to the theories of published researchers on Catholic school academic achievement, there exists also another body of theory constituted by the explanations given by Catholic school leaders for the relative academic 'success' or 'failure' of the schools for which they are responsible. It is to some examination of these theories[7] that we now turn. Headteacher explanations for academic achievement will be cross-referenced, where appropriate, to the insights of Goldstein, Greeley, Bryk *et al.* and Morris.

## The academic and social profiles of the research schools

Media and parental judgements about the academic effectiveness of English secondary schools are in practice strongly influenced by the published results of the GCSE examination taken at the end of the secondary school phase. While educationalists and headteachers point to the importance of a school's record across the full grade range of A*–G results, media and parental evaluation tends to focus upon the 'good grade' band of A*–C results.[8] A school's academic reputation is greatly affected by its performance in this 'winning' band. By adapting Bernstein's concepts of visible and invisible pedagogy, it is also possible to say that there are visible and invisible academic outcomes. GCSE A*–C passes have high visibility (and influence on status) whereas

A*–G passes, despite being a more comprehensive and balanced profile of a school's achievements, have relatively low visibility.

Of the Catholic secondary schools participating in this research, fifty-eight entered students for the GCSE examinations at the end of their secondary school career.[9] An analysis of the GCSE results across the period 1997–9, with special reference to A*–C outcomes, was undertaken in relation to three categories:

| | |
|---|---|
| High visible success (HVS) | schools with A*–C passes achieved by 60 per cent or more of the students |
| Above-average visible success (AAVS) | schools with an A*–C pass rate greater than the local education authority average |
| Below-average visible success (BAVS) | schools with an A*–C pass rate lower than the local education authority average |

Of the fifty-eight schools, nine had HVS status according to this classification and the academic and social profiles are given in Table 7.1.

The majority of these HVS schools were in inner-city or deprived urban locations[10] and all were comprehensive schools (i.e. with no formal academic selection criteria). What is apparent from the profile of these schools is the strong representation of girls' schools (all of which were 'convent' comprehensives), the high proportions of Catholic students and, for the areas in which they were located, the relatively low levels of FSM entitlements (as an approximate poverty indicator). The

*Table 7.1* Catholic HVS schools in urban areas

| *School* | *Gender* | *A*–C (%)* | *FSM* (%)* | *Catholic students (%)* |
|---|---|---|---|---|
| Pope Pius XII | Boys | 85 | 13 | 100 |
| St Scholastica | Girls | 70 | 20 | 99 |
| Holy Rosary | Girls | 69 | 23 | 100 |
| St Joan of Arc | Girls | 67 | 20 | 100 |
| Holy Family | Girls | 64 | 28 | 100 |
| St Francis | Boys | 63 | 22 | 85 |
| St Clement | Mixed | 61 | 10 | 95 |
| Pope Paul III | Boys | 60 | 10 | 100 |
| Mary, Mother of God | Girls | 60 | 47 | 99 |

FSM* Free school meals entitlement (an approximate poverty indicator)

significance of these characteristics will be discussed later. It must be noted at this point, however, that the headteachers of neighbouring Catholic secondary schools believed that these schools had become unofficial 'magnet' schools. The 'magnet' effect might have arisen from historical causes (i.e. former grammar school or convent school status) strengthened by contemporary publicity for high academic achievement. This led some headteachers to suggest that covert academic and social selection might be taking place in the competitive struggle to gain access to such schools.

Of the remaining schools, twenty-four had AAVS status in that their A★–C results were above the average for the local education authority (LEA) in which they were situated. Table 7.2 indicates the details of these schools.

*Table 7.2* Catholic AAVS schools in urban areas

| *School* | *Gender* | *A★–C (%)* | *FSM★ (%)* | *Catholic students (%)* |
|---|---|---|---|---|
| St Monica | Girls | 54 | 32 | 100 |
| St Colette | Girls | 54 | 25 | 100 |
| St Margaret Mary | Girls | 53 | 30 | 98 |
| St Matthew | Boys | 53 | 50 | 85 |
| Pope Pius VII | Boys | 50 | 7 | 95 |
| St Patrick | Mixed | 49 | 35 | 95 |
| Holy Angels | Girls | 49 | 51 | 90 |
| St Gabriel | Mixed | 48 | 33 | 94 |
| Sacred Heart of Mary | Girls | 47 | 27 | 100 |
| St John Fisher | Mixed | 46 | 40 | 100 |
| St Pius X | Boys | 46 | 21 | 100 |
| St Basil | Mixed | 44 | 25 | 88 |
| Bishop Anselm | Girls | 43 | 54 | 75 |
| Holy Cross | Mixed | 42 | 22 | 99 |
| St Mark | Mixed | 40 | 47 | 100 |
| Holy Disciples | Girls | 39 | 60 | 85 |
| St Helena | Girls | 39 | 48 | 95 |
| St Cyril | Mixed | 38 | 35 | 50 |
| St Genevieve | Girls | 36 | 36 | 82 |
| St Bede | Mixed | 36 | 46 | 50 |
| St Eugene | Girls | 32 | 57 | 56 |
| Corpus Christi | Mixed | 32 | 50 | 90 |
| Carthusian Martyrs | Mixed | 32 | 44 | 85 |
| St Brendan | Boys | 26 | 58 | 90 |

*Note*: These schools were located in fifteen different local education authorities and this accounts for the variation in the percentage of passes qualifying for AAVS status.

FSM★ Free school meals entitlement

With the exception of Pope Pius VII School, which was in an outer city location, all of these Catholic comprehensive schools served inner-city or deprived urban communities. However, despite this location, some of the schools, e.g. St Colette, Sacred Heart of Mary, St Pius X, St Basil and Holy Cross, recorded lower than average FSM entitlements for the area. This led to further suggestions from other headteachers that unofficial 'magnet' school factors might be operating in favour of these schools. These explanations were rejected by the headteachers of the schools concerned, as will be shown later. If Pope Pius VII School is excluded (because of its relatively privileged setting), the table shows that only two inner-city Catholic boys' schools achieved AAVS status and of these only St Matthew's School achieved notable academic results against a background of high FSM entitlements. The success of this school had been reported and amplified publicly by OFSTED not only for its academic achievements for inner-city boys but also for above-average successes with boys from a range of ethnic backgrounds[11] However, it must be noted that in the year following the completion of the fieldwork enquiry, the academic results for this school declined sharply. This demonstrates something of the vulnerability of inner-city schooling, the conditions of which can change rapidly in terms of population movements, teacher retention and teacher supply.

Viewed in international perspective, one of the great assets of the Catholic schooling system in the past was that its inner-city schools could count upon teaching staff and leadership stability related to the presence of members of religious orders. Contemporary Catholic inner-city schools now largely staffed and led by lay teachers can be subject to high levels of staff mobility.

Of the fifty-eight Catholic secondary schools involved in this analysis, twenty-five had GCSE A*–C pass records below the LEA average for the areas in which they were located. These schools are designated here as BAVS schools and are described in Table 7.3.

The schools with less than 10 per cent GCSE A*–C passes, i.e. St Stephen Martyr, St Rita, St Jude and St Flannan, had all been subject to adverse publicity and to 'naming and shaming' policies arising from critical OFSTED inspection reports. Two of them, St Stephen and St Jude, were subsequently closed down as 'failing' schools. As will be seen later, the majority of the headteachers of Catholic schools in difficulty took the view that the schools, the teachers and the students had not received justice from the state and media agencies which had judged them. In some cases it was also felt that the agencies of the Catholic Church had failed to give the necessary support for schools under pressure. From this perspective a school might enter a cycle of decline arising from radical

*Table 7.3* Catholic BAVS schools in urban areas

| *School* | *Gender* | *A*–C (%)* | *FSM* (%)* | *Catholic students (%)* |
|---|---|---|---|---|
| St Vincent | Boys | 34 | 36 | 90 |
| Epiphany | Mixed | 33 | 33 | 100 |
| Ascension | Mixed | 33 | 60 | 51 |
| St Finbarr | Mixed | 29 | 36 | 87 |
| St Peter Damian | Boys | 28 | 35 | 90 |
| Cardinal Hume | Boys | 28 | 38 | 99 |
| St Claire | Mixed | 27 | 43 | 90 |
| Our Lady of Lourdes | Girls | 26 | 62 | 98 |
| St Robert Bellarmine | Mixed | 26 | 55 | 98 |
| St Alphonsus | Boys | 25 | 43 | 90 |
| St Martin de Porres | Mixed | 25 | 50 | 33 |
| St Ciaran | Mixed | 24 | 34 | 99 |
| St Dominic | Mixed | 23 | 67 | 90 |
| St Lawrence | Boys | 21 | 55 | 55 |
| St Anthony of Padua | Mixed | 21 | 35 | 99 |
| St Richard | Boys | 20 | 47 | 99 |
| St Sebastian | Boys | 18 | 45 | 70 |
| St Lazarus | Mixed | 18 | 64 | 80 |
| St James | Mixed | 16 | 51 | 90 |
| English Martyrs | Mixed | 10 | 42 | 90 |
| St John of the Cross | Mixed | 10 | 60 | 35 |
| St Stephen, Martyr | Mixed | 9 | 45 | 33 |
| St Rita | Mixed | 6 | 71 | 92 |
| St Jude | Mixed | 6 | 71 | 95 |
| St Flannan | Boys | 3 | 76 | 85 |

FSM* Free school meals entitlement

changes in local community conditions involving population mobility, the effects of large-scale unemployment and the social consequences of increased poverty upon the young people of an area. While internal problems within these schools were not denied (e.g. past poor leadership, low expectations, etc.) the headteachers of the BAVS schools in general, and especially of those deemed to be 'failing', took the view that contemporary education policy in England had unreasonable expectations for inner-city schools in challenging circumstances. Such schools could not, single-handedly, overcome all of the psychological, motivational and social effects arising from various forms of distress and disorganisation in their local communities. In other words, they endorsed the continuing validity of Bernstein's (1970) observation that 'education (alone) cannot compensate for society'.[12]

Thirteen of the BAVS schools were located in one Catholic archdiocese which had experienced some of the highest levels of unemployment and poverty in England. The resulting effects of these conditions upon motivation, aspiration, morale and family life had been disastrous in the view of the Catholic headteachers of that region.

In explaining the achievement of high or low levels of academic success in Catholic secondary schools, two bodies of theory are available to the student. The first may be called *research theory* since it is based upon the outcomes of empirical enquiry. Such theory derives from the work of Greeley (1982), Bryk *et al* (1993), Flynn (1993), Morris (1998a, 1998b) and Paterson (2000a, 2000b) among others. The second may be called *professional theory* because it derives from the explanations given by professionals, such as headteachers, who have immediate responsibility for monitoring and improving the academic profiles of particular schools. Some examples of this form of theorising from the headteachers of the three categories of Catholic schools identified will be given below.

## High academic success in Catholic urban schools: headteachers' accounts

In reviewing research about the academic success of Catholic schools in the USA, especially with disadvantaged students, Lauder and Hughes (1999, p. 16) argue a thesis similar to that of Goldstein at the start of this chapter – that caution must be exercised about their growing reputation as highly effective schools because:

> the prior achievements of students on entering [Catholic] high school, which is a key predictor of their future performance, was significantly absent from the research design.[13]

This is an important observation because it raises the possibility that the visible academic success of Catholic secondary schools in the USA, the UK and elsewhere is in fact simply a function of receiving (or selecting) a more talented student intake than that of neighbouring schools.

In the present research enquiry similar claims had been made about the academic success levels of the HVS Catholic schools by neighbouring Catholic and state school headteachers. Of these nine high-scoring schools, seven were located in the inner city (St Francis, Pope Pius XII, St Scholastica, Holy Rosary, St Joan of Arc, Holy Family, Mary Mother of God) and two were located in outer-ring areas (St Clement, Pope Paul III). Prima facie their academic profiles of 60 to 85 per cent GCSE A*–C passes were remarkable and all of the schools had received public praise, highly positive OFSTED inspection reports and media attention for their achievements. They were all over-subscribed schools with more first-choice applications for entry than the places available and five of the headteachers interviewed applicants before entry. With the exception of St Scholastica the top-scoring schools used interviews as part of the admissions process and this raised certain critical questions about the purposes of the interview given that all of the schools were formally non-selective comprehensive organisations. The key issue raised by Goldstein and by Lauder and Hughes (1999) about the prior achievement of pupils entering Catholic schools was raised with each of the headteachers of the HVS schools and especially with those using interviews in the admissions procedure. The issue was presented during the course of the interviews in these terms:

> Some observers of the academic successes of Catholic secondary schools have asserted that interviews (apparently about faith questions) are in fact being used for covert selection on academic, social and even racial grounds. What would be your response if such a charge was made about this school?

In answer to this question the five 'interviewing' headteachers all claimed that interviews related only to the faith practice and commitment of the students and of their families. The 'faith selection' system was particularly well organised at the highest achieving school, Pope Pius XII:

> The purpose of the interview is really to establish the degree of Catholicity of the application.[14] … We send them a form to fill in relating to Catholic practice, eg regularity of attendance at Mass on the part of the parents and child; degree of involvement in the parish and parish activities by parents and applicant.
>
> (Headteacher, Pope Pius XII School)

Copies of the forms were then sent to the appropriate priests to confirm or to comment upon what the parents had recorded. This headteacher rejected the suggestion that such procedures might have an unintended bias towards middle-class families by asserting that 'the majority of the boys are of working class origin and Irish working class at that'. However, in his explanation of the outstanding academic success of the school there was an indication that 'faith selection' might also encode other desirable qualities in the students and their parents:

> It is a matter of being able to attract parents who are very keen to get their boys in here and who are therefore disposed to cooperate and support the school in terms of discipline but more importantly in terms of their children's education – supervising their homework for instance. The boys themselves are overwhelmingly cooperative and the staff have high expectations. It is a very hard-working staff. We have a very tight and demanding homework schedule and they've got to do it.

In terms of his own academic leadership, the headteacher identified as his prime role the monitoring of the homework programme in the school.

While 'faith selection' was identified as the major factor in controlling entry to Pope Pius XII School, there were indications that other processes relating to the prior achievement of students were being utilised. The headteacher was open about these processes:

> We already know before the interview what the applicant's ability is. We might get a slightly more finely tuned idea at the interview because they are asked to bring their latest reports from the primary school.

The outstanding academic results of Pope Pius XII School appear to be a dramatic realisation of the Catholic matrix for achievement identified by Bryk *et al.* (1993). There is no doubt that such academic excellence in an urban working-class school for boys was partly the outcome of a disciplined environment, a focused and demanding academic programme and considerable application on the part of both teachers and students. The focused academic leadership of a series of headteachers (clerical in the past, lay in the present) had given to the school an academic reputation arising from its past as a selective grammar school, confirmed and amplified by its public success as a comprehensive school in the present. However, in their sophisticated school process model analysing the academic outcomes of Catholic schooling in the USA, Bryk *et al.* (1993) have demonstrated the complexity of the variables involved.[15] Important among these variables are student background (personal, family and academic) and student engagement (identification with the aims of the school) in accounting for the academic profile of any school. It should be noted that among the Catholic schools of the inner city, Pope Pius XII School had a low poverty indicator for its student population (13 per cent FSM) and the fortunate possession of 'cooperative' students and 'supportive' parents. In these senses it was not typical of the other urban

Catholic schools involved in this study. There was some evidence among other Catholic headteachers of annoyance with government, inspection and media agencies which suggested that if Pope Pius XII School could achieve such results in the inner city, so could any other Catholic (or state) school in a similar location.[16]

The headteachers of the other 'interviewing' HVS schools were emphatic that this admission procedure was entirely an assessment of the Catholicity of the student and the family and had no covert academic or social selective function. 'Faith selection' by interview had been necessary, it was claimed, because these schools were over-subscribed and some criterion other than academic ability had to be used to regulate the entry. This was explained in various ways:

> We're not going to interview those who come from the Catholic primary schools who can produce a reference from the parish priest and baptismal and first communion certificates. We will interview those however where there may be some question about their Catholicity.
>
> (Headteacher, St Francis School)

> The more evidence (about Catholicity) they can produce, the better, because it is coming down now to who produces most evidence of commitment.
>
> (Headteacher, Holy Family School)

> We are selecting Catholics; sadly I think that some other Catholic schools do covertly select on other grounds.
>
> (Headteacher, Holy Rosary School)

External critics of Catholic schooling are likely to regard these explanations with some scepticism. All that can be reported[17] here is that of the five HVS headteachers who interviewed for admission, four categorically denied the existence of covert selection on academic grounds. However, as has already been noted, there were suggestions arising from this research that 'Catholicity' (constituted by strong religious practice and parish identification) was in itself an indicator of cultural, social and organisational qualities that would facilitate the schooling process. In other words Catholicity, while indicating a religious/spiritual status, was also a form of cultural capital. The possible association between degree of Catholicity and the relative academic success of some of the HVS schools seems to give support to Morris's (1997) hypothesis, but the relationship is not a simple one.[18]

Of the nine HVS Catholic schools, six had an historical record of consistent high academic achievement. Three of the schools (St Francis, Holy Rosary and Mary Mother of God) had achieved HVS status from a relatively low baseline in the past and were now publicly praised as examples of 'highly improved' schools.

St Francis School for Boys, which had been a 'failing' school in the mid-1980s with a falling enrolment, was now a school with over 1,000 students and a GCSE A*–C pass rate at 63 per cent which was virtually double the average for the LEA in which it was located. The reasons for the school's previous decline, according to the present headteacher, were weak school leadership and the inability of a formerly grammar staff to change the teaching and learning environment of the school to meet the new needs of a comprehensive and multi-ethnic student population.

The transformation of the school from 'failing' to HVS status was accounted for by the present headteacher (fifteen years in post) as partly the result of 'old' staff leaving and new staff recruited in innovative ways,[19] partly by the creation of systems and structures appropriate for a comprehensive intake and partly by his own adoption of a high-profile monitoring role in relation to the academic outcomes of each subject department in the school. As a result of his success in transforming the performance of St Francis School the headteacher had been invited to take temporary charge of a nearby 'failing' state secondary school. This had given him the unusual opportunity to compare his student intake with that of the 'failing' state school. While both schools had a comprehensive and multi-ethnic student intake, socio-cultural characteristics were significantly different:

> The fact of the matter is that practically all of our youngsters come from 'concerned' homes and the fact that they come from religious backgrounds helps – in that sense we have a better intake in terms of background support.
>
> (Headteacher, St Francis School)

A similar account of contemporary HVS status was given by the headteacher of Holy Rosary School. This school had experienced a decline in its reputation and examination results, partly as a result of diocesan school reorganisation and partly as a result of ineffective leadership in new circumstances. The present headteacher (eight years in post) had implemented a policy of staff restructuring and a policy of close monitoring of teaching in classrooms and of the academic outcomes of individual subject departments. Those staff who were not prepared to cooperate with a new teaching and learning culture of high expectations and accountability were encouraged to leave the school. This was, in the account of the headteacher, a difficult and painful process of transformation but she believed that such robust action was justified as being 'in the best interests of the children'.[20] During this period of cultural and organisational transformation the school's GCSE A★–C passes had risen from 35 per cent in 1992 to 69 per cent in 1998. As a result of this rising profile the school was over-subscribed and it was beginning to attract more students from middle-class backgrounds. While the school was predominantly working class in composition, its FSM entitlement at 23 per cent suggested that the majority of the girls were recruited from families that were in employment. This contrasted quite sharply with the FSM entitlement of the girls at Mary Mother of God School which at 47 per cent indicated considerable poverty in the areas served by this school. Despite these characteristics, a GCSE A★–C pass rate of 60 per cent had been achieved. This was accounted for by the headteacher as arising from the quality of the teaching in the school, the commitment of the teachers, the particularly strong partnership existing between the school and the parents, and the fact of its being a girls' school:

> They are girls and girls do better than boys. They are here because their parents have made a very positive effort to get them here and that gives us parental support … The turnout to parents' evenings is good and if a parent isn't there we are on the phone to them saying 'you have got to come'. We are very demanding about the support we expect.
>
> (Headteacher, Mary Mother of God School)

This headteacher, perhaps reflecting her status as a religious sister, was particularly proud of her students' results in GCSE A★–C passes in religious education which at over 60 per cent were one of the highest results in the city for that subject.[21]

## Accounting for the Catholic matrix of high academic achievement

The previous pages have given some support to Bryk *et al.*'s (1993) observation that successful academic outcomes in Catholic schools cannot be explained in any one-dimensional way. The accounts presented have demonstrated the relevance of a whole series of variables including the prior achievement of students; the academic leadership of headteachers; the quality and commitment of teachers; the influence of strong community and parental support (social capital); the influence of Catholicity (as a form of cultural capital); demanding and largely traditional academic programmes; the importance of a structured environment and of a clear sense of mission.

In keeping with the findings of Bryk *et al.* (1993), the present enquiry would argue that the conjunction of these variables in a given school situation creates a context and culture for achievement which can overcome *some* of the external impediments to scholastic progress arising from poverty and disorganisation in local communities. While this study cannot assign numerical values to the influence of individual variables, it seems likely from the evidence examined that Bryk *et al.*'s emphases upon student background (including prior achievement) and upon student engagement (identification with the school) are crucial elements in the story of these successful schools. That said, it is significant that all of these nine HVS Catholic comprehensive schools had certain historical, status and resource advantages when compared with other Catholic and state schools in their localities. These advantages might be the 'image' asset of convent status (five schools), the resources of a religious order (six schools), a grammar school heritage (eight schools), an impressive site and location (six schools). In a contemporary competitive situation for student recruitment intensified by the influence of market forces in English secondary schooling, such schools, given appropriate educational leadership, were likely to be academic 'winners'.

## Above-average academic success in Catholic urban schools: headteacher accounts

Twenty-four of the Catholic comprehensive schools involved in this study had AAVS status in that their GCSE A*–C results were above the average for the LEA in which they were located. In practice this meant a considerable variation in their academic results given the range of averages for the LEAs concerned. Thus a school such as St Brendan qualified for AAVS status with results as low as 26 per cent which was still above average for its particular LEA. However, the majority of these schools had academic results in the range of 30 to 40+ per cent and five of them had a 50+ per cent 'success' rate. With the exception of Pope Pius VII School (in a privileged setting), all the AAVS schools served inner-city or deprived urban communities and seventeen of them served student populations with FSM entitlements in excess of 30 per cent. Against the grain of significant levels of unemployment and poverty in the local communities, these Catholic secondary schools were achieving above-average academic results.

Within the AAVS schools, a subset had been designated as 'highly improving schools' and had received public praise and recognition (sometimes at national level) for these achievements in academic performance. Leading examples of schools with dramatic improvement in their GCSE A*–C examination passes included St Basil (from 22 per cent to 44 per cent in six years), St Bede (from 5 per cent to 36 per cent in five years), St Brendan (from 5 per cent to 26 per cent in ten years), St Gabriel (from 20 per cent to 48 per cent in seven years), Holy Angels (from 27 per cent to 49 per cent in three years), Holy Disciples (from 14 per cent to 29 per cent in four years), St Mark (from 20 per cent to 40 per cent in three years) and St Matthew (from 21 per cent to 53 per cent in seven years). Such improvement profiles had been amplified by media attention and they had contributed powerfully to a growing public perception of Catholic schools in urban areas in England as academically successful. Such success has also generated a whole range of theoretical explanations for these academic 'star performers'[22] in difficult settings. These have included the suggested beneficial effects of a more competitive environment, of OFSTED inspections, of the publication of league tables and of management and staff development courses for headteachers and teachers. Government representatives have claimed that such improvements have resulted from robust and focused government education policies on academic achievement including the use of 'naming and shaming' strategies. It is therefore of some interest to scrutinise the explanations given by the headteachers of these highly improving Catholic schools.

In their text *No Quick Fixes: Perspectives on Schools in Difficulty*, Stoll and Myers (1998, p. 9) argue that attempting to change the internal culture of a school:

> takes the greatest time because it involves intensive staff development, new learning and frequently the need for a fundamental shift in beliefs about ways of working with pupils and their ability to learn.

This was the experience of the headteacher of St Matthew's School:

> I think for about 10 years we worked on changing the culture into some sort of a learning culture … The harder change of course is the staff … Those that have been there for a long time still think in terms of 'what do you expect from boys like ours?'

In changing the internal culture of St Matthew's, the headteacher pointed out that a falling school enrolment from 1,000 down to 400 students helped to concentrate the minds of all teachers on the need for change. The headteacher's own involvement in advanced staff development stimulated the application of staff development principles within the school and particularly the systematic use of total quality management (TQM) procedures. With focused attention upon literacy and academic results and with continued staff development led by the headteacher, the culture of expectations at St Matthew's gradually changed. As there was no significant change in the nature of the student intake during the period of transformation, the headteacher of St Matthew's was convinced that a greater use of talents had resulted from the changed culture of teaching, learning and expectation.

At St Bede School, which recorded the greatest improvements of any of the participating schools (i.e. from 5 per cent to 36 per cent in five years), the transformation of the profile of the school was explained by the headteacher as arising from two factors. The first was changing the experience of urban teaching from 'individual battleground' to that of supportive team enterprise. The second was a decisive policy of staff restructuring and renewal.[23] In the case of St Bede, the newly appointed headteacher inherited a school with strong internal staff conflicts and demarcations between 'senior management' and 'teaching staff'. Central to the transformation of St Bede was the headteacher's determination to overcome these divisions by making commitment to teaching (as a shared enterprise) the dominant feature of a new culture. A targeted policy of promoting good teaching involved the headteacher in significant classroom teaching himself – in partnership with other teachers and a policy of encouraging teachers in the school to share good pedagogic practice. Unlike his predecessors, who did no classroom teaching, this headteacher publicly demonstrated that commitment to quality teaching was his first priority. A minority of the staff (three teachers) who resisted this new culture of shared teaching experience were encouraged to find employment elsewhere and new appointments committed to this pedagogic approach were made.

What the experience of St Bede School demonstrates is that once the social capital of a Catholic school, i.e. its sense of internal community, is weakened or fragmented by organisational dissension, the teaching and learning culture suffers and the academic outcomes of students are adversely affected. St Bede School appears to be a case study of the potentially divisive effects of the 'new managerialism' in education, where polarisation between 'senior management' and 'teacher workers' can undermine the sense of teaching as a shared enterprise of the whole staff and indeed their most important activity. Ironically, in this case, the arrival of a new headteacher was not the arrival of 'management man' or of 'superhead', but of a Catholic professional committed to restoring a sense of Catholic community among the teachers and between teachers and pupils about the importance of educational outcomes.

This is not to suggest, however, that Catholic AAVS schools owed their success simply to remaining faithful to traditional forms of association (although this helped). There was much evidence in the headteacher accounts of new forms of school leader behaviour and of new developments in stimulating the learning cultures of their schools. In particular, almost all the accounts of school improvement referred to academic monitoring, mentoring (of staff and students) and target setting (for staff and students):

> I've set them targets and set them targets and set them targets and if staff don't meet them the third time, I ask them what is to be done? I give them any in-service courses they want and I give them resources within the limits I have.
>
> (Headteacher, Bishop Anselm School)

> If it's improved exam results for the children it's got to be good so it's made us do things like individual mentoring of the children ... We now have most of the staff mentoring groups of children. What you tend to do is to focus on the children who are on the borderline of five A*–Cs.
>
> (Headteacher, Sacred Heart of Mary School)

> Achievement is the number one aim in this school. We target pupils and track them by means of various tests so that it becomes a more precise science. We don't say to a parent 'he could do better'; we say 'last year he was Level 5 and we expect him to be Level 6 this year.' I didn't realise how unfocussed we were before ... Our teachers give extra classes after school. The school is buzzing – extra classes for the SATs, extra classes for GCSE.
>
> (Headteacher, Corpus Christi School)[24]

It was clear from the interview accounts of the twenty-four headteachers of AAVS schools that the headteachers were enacting a school leadership role which was more interventionist and demanding than that of many of their predecessors. Academic leadership was much more salient, as was a targeted and focused monitoring of the achievement profiles of subject departments, of individual teachers and of individual students. At the same time fourteen of the AAVS headteachers emphasised that the title of 'headteacher' was not just symbolic but functionally important in demarcating a prime responsibility for the quality of teaching and learning in a school. While the managerial and marketing demands of modern headship had reduced the amount of time these headteachers could spend in direct classroom teaching, they believed that direct classroom experience was crucial for relations with their teachers and for in-depth understanding of the learning environment. This view of the headteacher as necessarily a current classroom practitioner[25] was expressed in various ways:

> Headteachers are very good at talking. This is partly how we get the jobs in the first place. I think that to lead is to put into practice. It is not just articulating the vision. It is actually translating that vision into action. To me it is very important that I am part of the whole school endeavour for education. I think that part of that for me is still to be in the classroom. That gives me a basis in reality. It keeps my feet on the ground.
>
> (Headteacher, St Cyril School)

> The main purpose and work of the school is to teach youngsters to create a learning environment and a headteacher who cuts themselves off and sees themselves as an administrator or manager has lost it. They really need to keep their feet on the ground, to relate to youngsters, to try out different teaching methods, to write their schemes of work – all the things they expect of their teachers in creating a learning environment … I can't see how a headteacher can do their job well without teaching.
>
> (Headteacher, St Bede School)

> I have always taught 6 periods a week. I teach Religious Education and I deliberately teach the bottom group, the most difficult. I believe that if I do that I have a certain credibility within the staffroom. My job is not about finance (we have others to do that). It is about the teaching and learning and the vision.
>
> (Headteacher, Corpus Christi School)

Overall these Catholic AAVS schools and especially the eight 'highly improved' schools were characterised by strong academic leadership strategies implemented by their headteachers. In some cases headteachers indicated that possibly too much attention had been given in the past to the Christian impulse to care for disadvantaged students (the Good Samaritan parable) to the detriment of making achievement demands upon them (the parable of the use of talents). What had now been constructed in these schools was a balanced relationship between pastoral care *and* academic achievement – as one of the school documents expressed it, 'caring to achieve'.

This Catholic synthesis of caring and effective use of talents characterised all of these schools but the conditions in which they realised their academic outcomes varied greatly. Schools such as St Eugene, Holy Angels, Bishop Anselm, St Brendan and Holy Disciples produced their above-average results against the grain of a significant poverty profile among their students (FSM entitlements above 50 per cent) whereas other schools had FSM entitlements below 30 per cent. Ten of the AAVS schools were supported by the cultural and economic resources of religious orders and by personnel from these orders. Among the schools now over-subscribed by students, partly because of their academic results, nine had introduced admission interviews for the assessment of Catholicity. In other words, the improved academic results of these Catholic secondary schools were a simple outcome not of a changed internal culture of teaching and learning (important though that was) but rather of an interaction of this with other contextual factors relating to each individual school.

## Below-average academic success in Catholic urban schools: headteacher accounts

Twenty-five of the Catholic comprehensive schools in inner-city and deprived urban areas had BAVS status in that their GCSE A*–C results were below the average for the LEA in which they were located. During the course of the fieldwork two of the schools, i.e. St Stephen Martyr and St Jude, were closed down as 'failing' schools. In addition to these, seven other schools were identified as having serious weaknesses in their academic profiles. These schools included St Flannan (3 per cent A*–C passes), St Rita (6 per cent), St John of the Cross (10 per cent), St Lazarus (18 per cent) and St Sebastian (18 per cent).

In the parable of the talents (Matthew 25: 14–30) the servant who had failed to use his talent is dealt with sternly and is called 'slothful' and 'worthless'. For a number of the headteachers of the BAVS schools, this parable and its harsh judgements had been recontextualised in secular form in a government education policy of 'naming and shaming' underachieving schools. In other words, public judgements had been made about the low academic achievements of their schools which suggested that these outcomes were the result of pedagogic slothfulness on the part of teachers and headteachers and which implied that the schools as learning institutions were virtually worthless. The headteachers of the BAVS schools and especially of the 'serious weakness' schools wished to place on record that the causes of underachievement in their schools were far more complex than the one-dimensional judgements being used against them:

> On all the statistics from the Census this is one of the most deprived areas in Europe … I could show you the intake scores which show that only one other school has a lower profile than ours … It used to be said that anyone with a score of 115 was predicted five A*–Cs. Well, in our school we would have only one person in each year group with a score of 115 … We are not really a comprehensive school, we are not socially comprehensive and we are not academically comprehensive … We don't have that range of social mix which would provide different role models.
>
> (Headteacher, St Flannan School)

St Flannan Boys' School with its 76 per cent student entitlement for FSM and its 3 per cent score for academic achievement was a school of the front-line Catholic urban education mission. Despite the obvious commitment of its headteacher and of the majority of the teachers, it faced massive problems arising from central city decay, high levels of unemployment and the personal costs of this in community and family breakdown, irregular school attendance and alcohol and drug abuse. The headteacher's account stressed the significance of very low levels of prior achievement among its students, poor school attendance patterns and a school culture lacking in a balanced social and academic mix. While critical of a public policy which named and shamed the school (and added to its problems), the headteacher felt that the institutional Catholic Church needed to give more support to front-line urban schools such as St Flannan. In other words, if the Church proclaimed a special education mission for the poor, then it must demonstrate resource policies and support policies to sustain Catholic schools in the most challenging urban areas.[26] Part of the difficulty at St Flannan School had been caused, according to the headteacher, by an individualistic ideology which largely left the school to fight its educational battles alone. For this headteacher, a distinctive Catholic approach to schools in difficulty ought to involve strong positive action from the hierarchy and a collective and community network of support from other Catholic schools in the area.

Accounts from the headteachers of other BAVS schools such as St Rita, St Lazarus, St Stephen and St Jude documented the complex network of locational impediments and challenges which had to be overcome or at least ameliorated if academic progress among the students was to be improved. These factors included numbers of refugee children (often with no English), population mobility and poor school attendance, and the stress encountered by teachers in inner-city and deprived urban school classrooms. These were not presented as 'excuses' for poor academic achievement in such schools but as objective features of their working environment which had to be taken into account in any evaluation of academic outcomes.

Unlike the headteacher of St Flannan, who believed that the Catholic Church authorities were strong on inspirational rhetoric but weak on practical support, many of these headteachers reported that their diocesan officials had given them support in the front-line educational mission. However, a number of them pointed out that the staffing and resourcing of Catholic diocesan education agencies made sustained support difficult because of the limited number of personnel available:

> I think that the Diocesan Authority needs to be as efficient and effective as a local education authority, so that they can look not only at the spiritual being of its schools but also the physical and mental being of a school. The first question they should ask of a school in difficulty is 'what can we do to make it better?' I think they'd like to say that but I don't think they've got the backup. The Catholic Church needs to look at its infrastructure, its educational infrastructure in large conurbations, and say 'what do we need to do to make it better?'.
>
> (Headteacher, St Jude School)

In an earlier study of Catholic urban secondary schools in England, Bishop David Konstant (Catholic Bishops' Conference of England and Wales 1997a) argued that such schools needed many sources of support in their struggles to improve academic achievement in deprived communities. The research report, *A Struggle for Excellence: Catholic Secondary Schools in Urban Poverty Areas*, recommended that:

> in local areas an effective framework should be established for cooperation between schools in order to share good practice, identify areas for cooperation and mitigate the worst effects of market competition on schools which serve disadvantaged communities.
>
> (p. 51)

There were many signs of informal support networks among the Catholic urban schools in the present enquiry and there was evidence of a distinct sense of professional community and collegiality at the level of the headteachers. However, in only one of the three cities studied, i.e. Birmingham, was there evidence of an established and formal supportive framework among Catholic secondary schools which could act collectively to help a particular school in difficulty. This important development will be examined in Chapter 8.

Myers and Goldstein (1998, p. 176) have argued that:

> most schools currently identified by OFSTED as 'failing' serve deprived and disadvantaged students. This is not, of course, to argue for complacency or low expectations in disadvantaged environments but it does emphasize the need to contextualize judgements properly. Naming schools as 'failing' often has the effect of lowering morale and obscuring positive aspects. Public humiliation is not the best way to improve matters.

The validity of this argument is confirmed by the present study. Two of the schools which had received the greatest public humiliation from media and official agencies, i.e. St Stephen Martyr and St Jude, had spiralled down to final closure partly as a result of such treatment. In both cases newly appointed headteachers had found their plans for reform and renewal undermined by a 'naming and shaming' policy.

As mentioned earlier, thirteen of the BAVS schools were located in one Catholic archdiocese which had experienced some of the highest levels of unemployment and poverty in England. The headteachers of these schools claimed that their struggles to improve academic achievement had to be accomplished against the grain of a local culture where large-scale unemployment had eroded confidence in education, motivation to succeed and family stability and organisation to provide the home conditions that would be supportive of learning. The headteacher of English Martyrs, with a GCSE achievement record of only 10 per cent, contextualised any judgement of the school in these terms:

> A major factor in the poor performance this year was the non-attendance of that particular year group – it was only 73 per cent … A lot of parents round here have no jobs, no future, no expectation. So what you have here is an area where the people have lost faith in themselves, in education and in anything to do with the establishment. We have a large number of parents who think 'well, I did my best at school – but what did it do for me, I'm on the dole

> – and he (the student) will be on the dole …'. It's a society where people have been crushed, the spirit has been driven out of them.

As practising Catholics, the headteachers of these thirteen secondary schools understand that they, their teachers and their schools had to be agencies of hope in communities assailed by despair. They sought in various ways to generate conditions for hope and for student achievement in their schools and this depended crucially upon the professional commitment of the teachers and, even better, upon a sense of vocation among such teachers. Here was one of the major challenges for Catholic urban education. Could enough teachers of quality and of vocational commitment be found to serve in schools whose reputations had already been publicly tarnished?[27] However, despite the many impediments faced by the thirteen schools in this archdiocese, a Catholic synthesis of faith, hope and pedagogic strategy appeared to be having some success. In the GCSE A*–C results for summer 2000, eight of the schools in the archdiocese recorded improvements. These included St Flannan (from 3 per cent to 8 per cent), St Rita (from 6 per cent to 12 per cent) and English Martyrs (from 10 per cent to 30 per cent). However, given the rates of population mobility in many inner-city areas, of students, of teachers and of headteachers, no simple linear improvement can be expected of these schools.

## Catholic schools and academic effectiveness: some reflections

Reviewing the evidence presented in this chapter, it is argued that a Catholic matrix for academic achievement does exist and that it has beneficial effects for students in inner-city and deprived urban locations. This matrix is constituted by a host of variables including the prior achievement of students (the effectiveness of Catholic primary schools),[28] the academic leadership of headteachers, the quality and vocational commitment of teachers, the influence of strong community and parental support (social capital), Catholicity as a form of cultural capital, demanding and focused academic programmes, the influence of structured environments, student engagement with the aims of the schools and an 'inspirational ideology' and clear sense of an educational mission. However, this matrix is not a constant across all Catholic schools but is differentially constituted according to local circumstances. The effectiveness of the matrix is related to the historical and cultural heritages of particular schools, to the social and economic well-being of local communities, to the differential presence of committed teachers and of inspired educational leadership in specific schools and the strength of local Catholic support networks.

Of the fifty-eight Catholic secondary schools in this enquiry which entered students from inner-city and deprived urban locations for the GCSE examinations, thirty-three were achieving above-average results in their local areas, some at a very high level. Of the twenty-five whose profiles were below the local average at the time of the fieldwork (1997–9), five had achieved an above-average position by the summer of 2000. Overall, these Catholic urban schools demonstrated a strong academic profile, a visible and measurable success and, as a result, an increasing number of them were becoming over-subscribed by parents anxious to gain admission for their children. There are many reasons therefore for the Catholic community to celebrate the academic success of Catholic schools in urban areas. In assisting disadvantaged students to achieve GCSE qualifications (with their potential for employment and for social mobility), such schools are realising the foundational Catholic principle that 'first and foremost the Church offers its educational services to the poor'. Given that the Catholic schools in this enquiry offered their educational services also to those who were not Catholics, then it can be said that the academic achievements of such schools are making an important contribution to the common good and well-being of society and not simply to the advancement of the Catholic community. In their overall academic success Catholic schools can claim, in the main, to be fulfilling the imperatives of the parable of the talents: that human potentiality should be developed to the highest possible degree.

Ironically, however, academic success for Catholic schools is not without its problems. The very success of the highly achieving schools, leading as it does to more applications than can be accepted, generates the admissions dilemma and the problematics of interview selection. Are practising Catholics to be favoured over non-practising Catholics? Are well-presented and 'cooperative' students to be preferred to those lacking such qualities? Are middle-class or aspirant working-class (and employed) parents seen to be more reliable allies than those who are unemployed? This study does not provide evidence of discrimination in admissions but it does suggest that the preservation of the mission integrity of Catholic schools in urban areas, in terms of access to such schools, is a heavy responsibility for school leaders in these circumstances.

In more general terms, all Catholic schools are affected by the growing dominance of academic performance indicators over all the other outcomes of schooling. The pursuit of the higher percentage GCSE pass level, year upon year, has the potential to distort the Catholic educational mission from its Catholic purposes. Once again, whether this happens or not will depend to an important degree upon the Catholic school leader's stewardship of mission integrity. To adapt Bernstein's (1997) concept of visible and invisible pedagogy, the danger in the present context is that the visible pedagogy and visible outcomes of Catholic academic achievement may begin to overshadow the invisible pedagogy and relatively invisible outcomes of Catholic spiritual, moral and social formation. It is the particular responsibility of Catholic school leaders to try to ensure that this does not happen.

# 8 Market culture and Catholic values in education

The attempted colonisation of schools, colleges and universities in the 1980s and 1990s by the values, practices and discourse of market ideologies has presented Catholic school leaders in some countries with sharp challenges to the principles of a distinctive Catholic educational mission. Catholic schools, with other schools, have been caught up in a global ideological struggle between those who claim that the application of competitive market forces within education will be a revitalising reform for schooling, making it more efficient, effective and responsive to education 'consumers', and those who argue that it will be a distortion and corruption of what education is about.

Writers such as Chubb and Moe (1990, 1992) have celebrated the potential of market disciplines and market competition to enhance educational effectiveness:

> The whole world is being swept by a realization that (education) markets have tremendous advantages over central control and bureaucracy.[1]

Ranson (1993, p. 336) on the other hand has argued against the introduction of market values and practices into the world of education:

> Action in the market is driven by a single common currency – the pursuit of material interests. The only effective means upon which to base action is the calculation of personal advantage: clout in the market derives from the power of superior resources to subordinate others in competitive exchange.

Thus expressed, market values and practices in education appear to be at odds with some of the foundational values of the Catholic educational mission. If a market culture in education encourages the pursuit of material interests, what becomes of a Catholic school's prime commitment to religious, spiritual and moral interests? If calculation of personal advantage is necessary for survival in the market, how can Catholic schools remain faithful to values of solidarity and community? If schools in a market economy in education must show good 'company' results in academic success and growing social status, what becomes of the Catholic school principle of 'preferential option for the poor'? In a situation in which socially approved, visible outcomes become critical to the survival of schools, those which serve deprived and fragmented communities have few market assets. The temptation in a market economy for schooling is to try by manipulation of admissions policies and exclusion policies to maximise the number of potentially 'profitable' students and to reduce the number of challenging and uncooperative pupils. In other words, a more calculative and selective policy on who enters the school and who is retained by the school may begin to displace earlier policies of community service.

One answer to these questions would be to say that with good judgement and critically aware educational leadership Catholic schools in contemporary settings can find a workable synthesis between the demands of market survival (and even of market success) and the preservation of the integrity of the distinctive principles of Catholic schooling. Christian culture is aware of the injunction to render to Caesar the things that are Caesar's and to God the things that are God's, and a workable synthesis of market and mission in education might be regarded as a contemporary manifestation of that injunction. Catholic writers such as Novak (1993) believe that such a synthesis between market culture and the Catholic ethic can be found. It is wrong, in Novak's view, to assume that Catholic values and market values are incompatible in economic life or in the functioning of institutions.

What has to be found is a defensible synthesis between individual freedom and creative enterprise on the one hand and social, moral and community responsibility on the other hand. Novak would take the view that Catholic schools in a competitive market environment for education should establish such a legitimate synthesis in the conduct of their mission.

Other writers are more sceptical that such a synthesis or at least a legitimate one can be established in such conditions. Pring (1996, p. 65) argues that:

> The market model of individuals all pursuing their own respective interests leads not to an improvement of the general good but only

> to an improvement of the positional good of some vis-à-vis other competitors and also to a deterioration of the overall situation.

In other words, the individualistic competition ethic which is the driving force of market culture will operate in practice against conceptions of the common good. Given that Catholic education holds service to the common good as one of its primary aims, it is, in Pring's view, at odds with a marketised conception of schooling. Sullivan (2000, pp. 63–4) also suggests that the application of market and business values in Catholic schooling may:

> threaten to turn education into a commodity, to undermine collective action and to cause us to fail to understand how … individual choices cumulatively impact on the social fabric.

In 1997 the Catholic Bishops' Conference of England and Wales sought to give some guidance to the schools and colleges within its jurisdiction on the implications of the Church's social teaching for precisely these issues of policy and practice. This document, *The Common Good in Education*, may be regarded as a counter-cultural response to the rising dominance of market culture and its values in English and Welsh schooling. The bishops produced a powerful critique of market ideology in education:

> Education is not a commodity to be offered for sale. The distribution of funding solely according to the dictates of market forces is contrary to the Catholic doctrine of the common good. Teachers and pupils are not economic units whose value is seen merely as a cost element on the school's balance sheet. To consider them in this way threatens human dignity. Education is a service provided by society for the benefit of all its young people, in particular for the benefit of the most vulnerable and the most disadvantaged – those whom we have a sacred duty to serve. Education is about the service of others rather than the service of self.
>
> (Catholic Education Service 1997a, p. 13)

The Catholic bishops went on to suggest that all Catholic schools should show a commitment to the common good in education by reviewing their own admissions procedures, sharing specialist resources with other schools, acting collectively in staff development programmes, helping unpopular schools to improve their performance and their image and working together to try to ensure equity in funding.[2]

While the education policies of successive British governments encouraged Catholic schools to think of ways of being individually successful in a market economy for schooling, the Catholic bishops exhorted them to hold fast to common good values and to values of solidarity and professional community.

The Catholic headteachers in this study had to pursue their conceptions of the educational mission in the midst of these theoretical, ideological and theological controversies about market values and Catholic values. Unlike many protagonists in this larger debate, they encountered the immediate practical realities of market forces in education and of the challenges of survival, success and of mission integrity which they generated. The following sections give an account of how these headteachers positioned themselves in this context and of the various stances which they adopted in this contested situation.

## Individual advantage versus the common good: the temptations of grant-maintained status

> The Education Reform Act 1988 and Education (Schools) Act 1992 have set in train a transformation of our school system. They have created more choice and wider opportunities as a springboard to higher standards. Central to this has been the development of school autonomy, both within schemes of local management and increasingly as GM (Grant Maintained) schools outside local government.[3]

The official discourse of the British government's White Paper, *Choice and Diversity: a new framework for schools* (1992), had made it quite clear to all headteachers, governors and parents that a strong political imperative existed to encourage all maintained schools, including Catholic schools, to opt out of local government jurisdiction and to choose a direct and individually funded status known as grant-maintained. In an attempt to introduce greater diversity into the school system and greater consumer choice, the GM option was an important ideological strategy. As Edwards and Whitty (1997, p. 39) suggest, GM schools and the intended marketisation of education were closely linked:

> Potentially the largest move towards a market of autonomous and differentiated schools has been the creation of grant-maintained schools 'freed' from LEA control by the exercise of a collective consumer voice in favour of self-government.

To encourage both state and Catholic schools to seek freedom from the bureaucratic constraints of local education agencies and of diocesan authorities, considerable financial inducements were offered to schools to make the decision for what was called, without apparent irony, 'opting out'. As Simon and Chitty (1993, p. 44) noted:

> Several years' experience have now made it abundantly clear that schools becoming GMS have been treated far more generously than county schools ... GMS schools got on average four times as much in the way of capital grants than mainstream county schools.

As the Catholic community in England and Wales had significant financial responsibilities for the capital costs of their schools, the financial benefits associated with the option for GM status constituted a particular form of market education temptation. It was clear that the issue was not simply one of choosing a new administrative and financial status for a Catholic school. It also encoded moral and social choices between individual advantage and community common good.

This potential contradiction was articulated by the Catholic hierarchy who, through the agency of the Catholic Education Service, gave a formal response to the White Paper:

> We do not in principle oppose increased independence and self management for schools. However, the GM option is more than this. It intensifies financial and curricular inequalities between schools and creates new inequalities. It also supposes that schools derive their strength from their own autonomy, without any sense of having a wider responsibility (the common good). Moreover there is no reason to believe that the growth of the GM sector will do other than undermine the financial viability and reputation of those schools which remain outside the GM sector.
>
> (Catholic Education Service 1992, p. 7)

Catholic schools in England and Wales, especially during the period 1992 to 1997, were faced with a major educational, moral and religious dilemma. Should the governors, parents and headteachers make the decision for greater GM school autonomy and financial resources (with obvious individual advantages) or should they remain within the community of local authority and diocesan Catholic schools, as advised by the bishops (with possible disadvantages for their schools and their students)?

At the time of the research fieldwork for this study, the newly elected Labour government in the UK had abolished the status of GM schools and all of the schools were in the process of making decisions about their future status. However, it is very significant that when asked to consider the impact of market forces upon educational policy and practice in Catholic schooling many of the participating headteachers framed their answers in relation to the GM strategy. In other words, for these headteachers the GM school episode was a dramatic and concrete realisation of the impact of individualistic market values within the relatively insulated world of Catholic schooling.

Of the fifty-eight headteachers for whom the GM school option had been a possibility, sixteen were leading GM schools[4] at the time of the research and forty-two were leading voluntary-aided schools – which meant, in effect, that they had resisted the temptations of GM school market advantage for various reasons.

## Breaking free from the local state for funding equity

Those Catholic headteachers who defended most strongly the decision to opt out of the jurisdiction of the LEA and to accept GM status rejected the argument that they were seeking market advantages over their colleagues. Their rationale was that the option for GM status was a necessary strategy for obtaining funding equity with county (state) schools in those local authorities which for ideological reasons were hostile to the existence of church schools, particularly Catholic schools. The existence of such ideological hostility in the local state meant in practice, according to these headteachers, that Catholic schools were systematically underfunded for their operational costs and were generally unsuccessful in bids for capital expenditure. From this perspective, the GM option was not part of a marketing strategy but rather a strategy designed to obtain funding equity for the teachers and students in Catholic schools. It is significant that the headteacher who was the most powerful advocate of this position was responsible for a school located in a local authority which had historically demonstrated high levels of such hostility towards Catholic schools:

> Catholic schools and the voluntary sector have been second-class citizens, and grant-maintained status gave the opportunity for a level playing field to be funded and resourced at a level of entitlement. Catholics pay their taxes like any other – why should they be

> resourced at a lower level in education? There was a report prepared for secondary schools in this city on the differentials of funding between the voluntary and the county schools. It never saw the light of day! We went GMS on equality and entitlement. We have not taken a penny that would have been given to another school. We have taken it from the local bureaucracy in education which is totally overfunded.
>
> (Headteacher, St Pius X School)

A very similar argument was generated by four Catholic headteachers in another city whose schools were located within the jurisdiction of an LEA marked by ideological hostility to Catholic schools and by its associated underfunding. In this case, to avoid any charges of seeking individualistic market advantages over their colleagues, the four headteachers coordinated a strategy to opt for GM status at the same time. In one sense this was a collective vote of no confidence in the LEA:

> In this city there has been a lot of antipathy towards Catholic schools, covertly very often so that if, for example, there was any money available and we were asked to bid for it, Catholic schools just didn't get it. When you looked at the funding of schools and compared Catholic schools with county schools, we were usually at the bottom of the pile.
>
> (Headteacher, Sacred Heart of Mary School)

What these and similar accounts demonstrate is the need to take into account the contextual location of any school before arriving at a judgement about its relative performance or its policy decisions. In this case the GM option for Catholic schools was not a simple choice between individualistic market values and Catholic community values but a more complex decision mediated by local political, ideological and economic circumstances. The majority of the sixteen headteachers involved in the option for GM status believed that they were trying to obtain social justice (in the form of fair funding) for their schools and their students.

However, as other Catholic headteachers pointed out, whatever the rationale for taking the GM option, the effect in practice was to give such schools a competitive market advantage over other schools. The generous funding which accompanied GM status allowed schools to engage in major capital improvements of their sites and facilities and to spend more upon staff development, staffing establishment and other resources. More money was available for public relations activities with parents, including the production of glossy promotional materials. In short, while the Catholic GM option was frequently taken for what the headteachers believed were reasons of equity, the GM status, once acquired, introduced inequity among Catholic schools. This was strongly resented by those headteachers who remained loyal to the collective guidance of the Catholic bishops on this issue and who sought to persuade their school governors and parents to resist the temptations of the GM option.

## 'Opting out' of the Catholic community of schools: the critics

While the emphasis of official discourse was upon a strategy of 'opting out' of the control of the local educational state, to take the GM option was, in the opinion of many of the headteachers, to take a decision to opt out of the Catholic community of schools and of its diocesan administration. From this perspective, the GM option could never be a legitimate Catholic educational policy response whatever the injustices of the local situation. This argument was powerfully advanced by the headteacher of a GM school whose advice *against* taking this strategy had been overruled by a determined Chair of Governors (a priest) and by a majority vote of the parents:

> I think the bishops in *The Common Good* restated the principle of solidarity. We're hitting on something very important, because that principle of solidarity was very much affected by what was going on. The philosophy of Catholic schools sits uneasily in a free market economy … I think that being a grant-maintained school has undermined and threatened the solidarity of the Catholic schools.
>
> (Headteacher, St Gabriel School)

Similar arguments about the divisive effects of the GM option upon the community of Catholic schools were repeated in other accounts from the majority of headteachers who resisted the GM strategy. A particularly strong condemnation suggested that to take such an option was un-Christian:

> I think that the whole philosophy of grant-maintained schools was un-Christian. Some Catholic authorities saw it as a way to help them finance their schools but we've always been urged by the Archdiocese not to go grant-maintained … I think that when we

> talk about community we mean, among other things, the community of schools. By going grant-maintained that community spirit was broken.
>
> (Headteacher, Cardinal Hume School)

In reviewing the GM episode in the history of Catholic schooling in England, Arthur (1995) has concluded that it generated considerable internal tension and conflict within the educational community. A government strategy premised upon the 'need' for schools to break away from the constraints of bureaucracy, whether LEA or diocesan, to become more autonomous units in local education markets for schooling clashed with some traditional Catholic values. These included giving priority to community common good issues over private good issues and remaining loyal to the guidance of the Catholic hierarchy on what were legitimate policy decisions for schools.[5] Among the many outcomes of the struggles over GM school decisions in the Catholic community in England was the making visible of new forms of parental power. What Brown (1990) has referred to as 'the ideology of parentocracy' was crucially involved in the value conflicts related to the GM option. The GM episode in English Catholic schooling revealed that a new generation of parents had constituted itself, in certain areas, as a force to be reckoned with in policy decision making. Faced with an immediate conflict between options for the private good of their own children and Church-approved options for the common good in education, they were likely to choose the former. If necessary they were prepared to defy hierarchical authority on such questions.[6]

The interpretation of what this new form of Catholic parentocracy signifies is not straightforward. It could be seen as the end of a deferential lay tradition when faced with ecclesiastical authority and the beginning of more assertive and active participation by lay Catholics. From this perspective, a more educated and middle-class group of parents was prepared to exercise independent judgement on matters of educational policy. This could be claimed to be an exercise in the 'active citizenship' which was being officially encouraged by government agencies at this time. However, from another perspective it could be interpreted as the action of a particular interest group (i.e. parents are only part of the community of citizens) for the private interest of their own children. What was a matter of some concern to the Catholic hierarchy was the realisation that with the increase of parental empowerment in the specifics of educational decision making, Church-approved policies might be increasingly challenged. In so far as these active and empowered parents were inclined to favour a new, competitive, market-driven version of schooling, then serious ideological/theological divisions were being created within the Catholic community, bringing with them associated power struggles. These new power relations within the Catholic community in England presented serious challenges. Arthur (1994a, p. 188) has summarised the position well:

> The church's dispute with both government and some of its own members can be located in the differing interpretations of parental rights. The government's stress on parental involvement and choice gives predominance to the market and emphasises individual rights over the rights of the community as a whole. By contrast, the Church's distinctive mission places greater emphasis on the right of the whole Catholic community in determining the future of Catholic schools. The Church does not recognise that the rights of parents and pupils already placed in Catholic schools can over-ride the rights of the whole Catholic community.

These fundamental ideological/theological differences on the role of individual rights compared with community rights did not disappear from the politics of Catholic education with the ending of GM status in 1997/8. The GM episode in Catholic schooling was simply a dramatic manifestation of greater differentiation in values and behaviour within the Catholic community. Such differentiation can be expected to exercise its influence on the future of Catholic policy making in education.

## Market competition in Catholic schooling: an animating or a corrupting influence?

The Institute of Economic Affairs in London was particularly active in the early 1990s in publishing texts designed to construct a moral and ethical defence of market culture and mechanisms as essential elements of a 'free' society. Publications such as *The Moral Foundations of Market Institutions* (1992) and *God and the Marketplace* (1993) sought to justify the extension of market dynamics to a wider range of social institutions and publicly provided services. Among other things these publications attempted to convince religious believers and members of the various faith communities in the UK that there was no intrinsic contradiction between market values and religious values. It was recognised that some market advocates and ideologies had alienated the churches by an aggressive discourse:

> Neglect of moral issues has reinforced the tendency of churches to view the markets with suspicion, if not outright hostility. During the Thatcher years when successive administrations … sought to abandon collectivism and restore liberty in Britain, the churches typically withheld their blessing, implying that market competition was at best morally dubious and possibly wicked.[7]

A more measured approach, it was suggested, would show that the market entrepreneurial spirit and the religious spirit could be reconciled. The parable of the talents, after all, had indicated commendation for enterprise and condemnation for failure to use talents in the marketplace. Advocates of market forces in education such as Flew (1991) and Tooley (1994) argued that the application of market principles within the insulated and protected realm of schooling would have an animating effect which would increase efficiency and effectiveness to the benefit of more students and the satisfaction of the parents/consumers.

In response to these and other claims, the Catholic bishops of England and Wales issued in 1996 a guidance document *The Common Good and the Catholic Church's Social Teaching*. As one of the most recent formulations of Catholic social teaching with implications for educational policy it is worth quoting at some length:

> The Catholic Church in its social teaching explicitly rejects belief in the automatic beneficence of market forces. It insists that the end result of market forces must be scrutinised and if necessary corrected in the name of natural law, social justice, human rights and the common good. Left to themselves market forces are just as likely to lead to evil results as to good ones …
>
> The Church recognises that market forces when properly regulated in the name of the common good can be an efficient mechanism for matching resources to needs in a developed society … There is no doubt too that competition can often harness creative energy and encourage product innovation and improvement …
>
> We think it is time to re-emphasise in our society the concept of the common good. It provides the criteria by which public authorities can distinguish between those economic activities that can safely be left to market forces and those that require regulation, state intervention or full provision by the public sector … Catholic Social Teaching, while it recognises that there are at times merits in the market principle, resists the conclusion that that principle should be extended wherever possible.
>
> (pp. 18–20)

In essence, the position of the Catholic bishops was that the legitimate sphere for market forces and its associated values and practices was in the realm of commodity production and development, wealth creation and the provision of commercial services. What was to be resisted was the extension of market forces and market values into areas of 'common good' services for all citizens, such as health and education. Market competition in these sectors would, in the opinion of the bishops, be likely to lead to a polarisation of services and opportunities, a 'winner'/'loser' syndrome, the failure and subsequent closure of institutions in some communities which would militate against the interests of the poor and the powerless.

The Catholic headteachers participating in this study had to work out their notions of the legitimate role of market competition in education in the midst of this ideological/theological set of controversies at national level and the supply and demand dynamics of their particular local settings. As might be expected, this produced an interesting and varied range of responses to what was a central issue for most of them.

## Catholic schools and competition: recognising reality and avoiding hypocrisy

Very few of the headteachers were explicit defenders[8] of the values of a more competitive environment within the world of Catholic schooling but their most vigorous advocate suggested that this was a subject where large-scale hypocrisy operated to hide the true state of relations among Catholic schools and between Catholic schools and county schools. The headteacher of St Matthew's School was particularly explicit on this issue:

> I don't put a lot of credence on what the hierarchy says on this question. There are public statements but there is also private advice. I do think that a competitive edge is good. The people who gain of course are the pupils and they are the most important thing. They are getting a much, much better deal. The schools are not set up for the clergy or for the teachers. The competitive edge works wonders. Schools never have looked out for one another and of course, that's part of the sham … This is how the Church is – saying one thing, doing another. Schools have always been cut-throat.

The strong position taken by this headteacher denied that common good principles had ever seriously informed Catholic schooling practice at least in terms of competition for student enrolments. Added to this was the suggestion that Church policy in education was marked by internal contradictions between public statements and private practice. While no other headteacher made such robust statements, a small number argued that competition had always existed among Catholic schools and that high-status and successful schools (often religious order schools) had never shown any particular 'common good' concern for other Catholic schools in difficult circumstances. Those headteachers who welcomed the new visibility of market competition among Catholic schools and between Catholic schools and state schools took the view that this was a more honest and open situation than had been previously the case. In their opinion, the Catholic educational world had nurtured myths[9] about a 'community of schools' when in fact various forms of selection, competition and individual advantage existed below the surface of this rhetoric.

## Catholic schools and competition: pragmatic survivors

In analysing the responses of the sixty Catholic headteachers to increased market competition in schooling, the category which is called here *explicit pro-market* was small (five headteachers). A much larger number (twenty-five) took a stance which may be described as *pragmatic survivors*. Headteachers in this category characteristically made no philosophical or moral evaluation of increased market competition in Catholic education but generally focused upon what a school had to do to survive in the new competitive conditions. Included in the pragmatic category were those who simply remarked that if a school had a strong established reputation of 'success' then competition wasn't a worrying issue, and those whose schools were located in areas where they were a monopoly provider of Catholic schooling.

The pragmatic survivors among these Catholic headteachers clearly took the view that, rightly or wrongly, an internal market among all schools and among Catholic schools had been intensified by Conservative government action and that there was little prospect of this changing under the New Labour government of the late 1990s. In these circumstances there was little point in engaging in impotent criticism of these changed relations among schools. The responsibility of Catholic school leaders had to be to ensure the survival of their individual schools:

> Clearly there is a defined market and your budget is attached to pupil numbers. You've got to maximise your numbers … Market

> forces are operating and I think that the difficulty is that you can't ignore them … If you don't survive the end result is that you don't provide a Catholic education for the youngsters in your area.
>
> (Headteacher, St Richard School)

> I have heard other heads say 'I don't care where I get the students from as long as I get them into my school and I don't worry about the ethics of it' … With the formula being very much based on student numbers it is an issue of survival. It's not something that sits comfortably, but it's a reality and we face that day in and day out.
>
> (Headteacher, Our Lady of Lourdes School)

> There's a good relationship between the Catholic heads in the area but we have found that some schools quite definitely have regard to their own interests in admissions etc. They would definitely act in their own interest and I would be failing this school if I didn't, at the end of the day, put its interests first.
>
> (Headteacher, St Margaret Mary School)

> My impression is that now one is less willing to share information even with other Catholic heads. They are your competitors. We are judged in terms of material success and statistics. But you can't get away from that. It's there and you have to adopt it to survive.
>
> (Headteacher, Pope Pius XII School)

A central characteristic of the pragmatic survivor stance was the belief that there was no practical alternative to the present conditions of individual competitive relations among schools for parental regard and for student numbers. Some of these school leaders asserted that in their areas there was no collaboration among Catholic headteachers and no diocesan administrative attempts to regulate competitive behaviour. Others argued that good social and interpersonal relations might exist among Catholic headteachers, but, as one headteacher put it, this was 'to compensate for our secret feelings of competition'.

Given that the Catholic bishops of England and Wales had issued an important guidance on these precise matters in the document *The Common Good in Education* (1997) at the time when the fieldwork for this study was being undertaken, it is significant that few of the pragmatic survivors referred to it. Perhaps the comment of the headteacher of Pope Pius XII School that the document was 'idealistic' is indicative of the perspectives of the pragmatic survivors. The bishops might proclaim the virtues of community and common good action among

Catholic schools but they were themselves insulated from the day-to-day realities of competitive survival in the education marketplace. In so far as the headteachers in this category took such a stance, they were implicitly denying that there could be a distinctive Catholic alternative to the 'realities' of market forces and market values in education. On this there was not, in their view, a Catholic position, only a survival position. However, at least half of the participating sample (thirty headteachers) disagreed with this instrumentalist position and argued that various forms of a distinctive Catholic response to market forces in education did exist and should be implemented.

## Resisting market 'realities' and working for the common good

In their 1996 publication *The Common Good and the Catholic Church's Social Teaching* the Catholic bishops had attempted to formulate a distinctive Catholic position on the role of market forces in these terms:

> The Church recognises that market forces when properly regulated in the name of the common good can be an efficient mechanism for matching resources to needs in a developed society.
>
> (p. 19)

This key phrase 'properly regulated in the name of the common good' characterised the stance of the thirty headteachers in this study who may be called *market regulators*.[10] The Catholic market regulators sought to find alternatives to the 'winner'/'loser' syndrome in individualistic competitive relations among schools by finding a synthesis between the values of competition and the values of the common good.

For one group within this category the source of regulation could be found in informal professional relationships among Catholic headteachers (sometimes involving regular meetings) in which the members would work together to modify the impact of market forces on the schools. This could be done by exchange of information and by informal agreements about admissions policies, relations with parents and holding to notions of natural 'catchment areas' for recruitment despite the official existence of an open free market. In effect these Catholic headteachers were engaged in forms of covert subversion of the logic and dynamics of market competition in schooling.

> We communicate and keep in contact with each other, especially about admissions. We have done a sort of undercover arrangement

> in the past but now we actually put it in our documentation to parents, saying that we will be discussing and working together … That's cooperation rather than competition.
>
> (Headteacher, St Joan of Arc School)

> The Catholic secondary schools in this area do try to work together on admissions and on other big issues. For instance, on grant maintained status we decided that either we would all be grant-maintained or none of us would be.
>
> (Headteacher, St Mark School)

> There is a certain amount of competitiveness but I don't think competition is necessarily a bad thing … but on the other hand you've got to think about the morality of it and how much you engage in it … We try very hard to make sure that we're not pulling the other schools down by presenting ours in a good light.
>
> (Headteacher, Sacred Heart of Mary School)

Macbeth *et al.* (1995), in their important text *Collaborate or Compete? Educational Partnerships in a Market Economy*, point out that a more competitive environment does not invalidate processes of collaboration and may even in fact generate new forms of partnership in the face of new competitive challenges. There was evidence in this present study that a significant number of Catholic headteachers were prepared to regulate the impact of market forces in education by holding to old forms of collaboration and in some cases creating new ones in defence of professional collegiality and of the common good of the wider community of schools in a given area.

A second group of market regulators looked to the Catholic Church and in particular to the officials of its system of diocesan school administrations to provide effective leadership in the moral and practical regulation of market forces in education.[11] Such headteachers believed that the Catholic Church had to go beyond the issuing of principled statements such as *The Common Good in Education* and should show more involvement in working practically against the deleterious consequences of market forces in education. This group expected diocesan education officials and, in some cases, the local archbishop, to take action to regulate competition for student enrolments especially where such competition threatened the survival of individual Catholic schools in inner-city locations.

While it was recognised that diocesan officials and even archbishops could not overrule open recruitment policies which had the force of law, this group of headteachers argued that if there really was a distinctive Catholic schooling culture, with distinctive social and moral principles about the common good, then it should be possible for diocesan educational leaders to use moral persuasion as a countervailing strategy against extreme forms of market competition. What became apparent in this research study was that in some of the Catholic archdioceses involved, diocesan officials did attempt to use their influence to regulate the operation of market forces in education and to assist schools in difficulty. In other cases, however, local headteachers perceived their diocesan administrations as laissez-faire on these issues. This led to a feeling among the Catholic headteachers in this research that there was too much variation in policy and practice among diocesan administrators on the crucial question of how Catholic schools should act ethically and in a clearly Christian way, in the face of market competition.

In the Archdiocese of 'St Anthony' many of the headteachers commended the leadership given by the Diocesan Director of Schools in attempting to regulate and to ameliorate the worst effects of market competition among Catholic schools. For this Director such action was an expression of a distinctive Catholic culture of educational administration:

> We don't have a statutory jurisdiction … We have no locus officially in these things but whereas we don't have power, we do have influence and it's far better to exert an influence rather than a power. So we give a lot of advice and guidance and spend a lot of time dealing with areas of tension in the Catholic community … Financial resources you can't transfer by law, but human resources can be transferred and in this diocese we have 14 seconded headteachers into schools in difficulty.

The Archdiocese of 'St Anthony' provided an exemplar of diocesan influence and resources being used as some form of moral and practical regulation of the undesirable consequences of market culture in schooling. However, despite its best efforts one of its inner-city schools was closed during the research fieldwork period as a result of a public 'naming and shaming' campaign.

Diocesan school administrations operating on the principles of a Catholic conception of the common good in education could have been a powerful counter-culture force to the penetration of market values into the world of English Catholic schooling. In practice, they had only a limited and partial impact. While the attitudes of individual diocesan directors of schools were obviously a crucial variable in explaining this outcome, another crucial variable was their own limited resources. In an archdiocese with a jurisdiction for over 200 Catholic schools, a typical diocesan office might have five officials. It was virtually impossible in these circumstances to provide a sustained counter-cultural strategy in the face of the resources available to the central state in propagating the virtues (and rewards) of individualistic competitive behaviour in the education marketplace. This, unfortunately, was a David and Goliath situation in reverse!

The Catholic headteachers in this study recognised the difficulties faced by local diocesan administrations in constituting themselves as a counter-cultural force in education policy and practice. As a result there was evidence that Catholic headteachers were prepared to meet together in cluster and professional support groups more frequently than they had in the past. In all four of the major archdioceses involved in this research, there were examples of headteachers meeting together on a regular basis to discuss policy and practice issues and to give mutual support to each other. These groups were, in effect, *informal professional networks* based implicitly on notions that common good thinking in education must be defended against the inroads of competitive individualism. There was evidence that the headteachers of Catholic schools in difficulty found such groups a valuable source of support. However, Glatter (1995, p. 33) in reflecting upon the nature of partnership behaviour in market conditions for schooling, has argued that such grouping may be vulnerable:

> Without some kind of semi-permanent infrastructure to promote and facilitate collaboration ... the partnerships that do arise may well be more ad hoc, fragile and transient than is desirable.

It is precisely this form of infrastructure which has been established in the Archdiocese of Birmingham, which makes Catholic educational collaboration in that city particularly noteworthy, although surprisingly underreported.

## Organising for the common good: Birmingham's Catholic Secondary Partnership

Explicit condemnation of the potentially corrupting effects of market values and market forces in Catholic education characterised the responses of thirty of the headteachers involved in this study. Typical examples of such condemnation were:

> I think the whole thing is divisive. It will set schools against each other. Not only that, it will cause divisions and tensions within the

> staffroom ... There is very little flexibility if you accept the marketplace dynamic for carrying those pupils who need to be carried. The philosophy is 'shoot the wounded because they are holding the army back'.
>
> (Headteacher, St Robert Bellarmine School)

> I've tried to take up this issue of competition for pupil enrolments with my Catholic colleague headteachers but got absolutely nowhere. If we are in the mission of Catholic education, this 'community thing', then why are we competing in other schools' catchment areas? ... I think it is doing us great damage.
>
> (Headteacher, St Lawrence School)

Responses such as these made by headteachers in the Archdioceses of 'St Robert' and 'St Anthony' indicated that informal networks against market competition only existed in certain locations and even where they existed they might not be, in practice, very effective at ameliorating competitive relations among Catholic schools. The lack of a formal infrastructure for collaboration was apparent in three of the archdioceses involved in this enquiry. By contrast, the Archdiocese of Birmingham presented a remarkable example of a formal infrastructure in support of a Catholic partnership involving the ten secondary schools of the city.

Although at the time of the research fieldwork (1999) the Birmingham Catholic Secondary Partnership appeared to be a unique example of a formal educational collaboration based upon the principles of the common good, its actual origins in 1988 were related to a government funding project.[12] However, during the 1990s the Partnership widened its objectives and purposes and became more explicitly a 'common good' organisation in education, providing practical examples of how schools could collaborate with each other and, in another sense, providing a powerful symbolic critique of what many headteachers took to be the inevitable realities of marketplace competition in schooling.

The Birmingham Catholic Secondary Guarantee document published in 1998 stated the developed mission of the Partnership:

> Birmingham Catholic secondary schools are committed to working together in partnership to promote professional and curriculum development, thereby enhancing the quality of teaching and learning in our schools. We are committed to sharing our expertise so that we can enrich the education of all our students in an atmosphere of Christian love to the benefit of Catholic education in the City.

To support these intentions a Catholic Partnership Office had been established (based in one of the schools) which employed two full-time officers to provide the necessary infrastructural support to implement these principles. The ten schools of the Partnership had agreed a budget levy on each school for the maintenance of the infrastructure.

By 2000/1 the Partnership had extended its activities beyond joint programmes of staff and curriculum development and regulation of competitive marketing for students to include forms of support for schools in difficulty. As one school in the Partnership encountered recruitment and other difficulties in 2000, the members of the Partnership seconded staff to the school to assist it in its current problems. In other words, by 1999/2000 the Partnership was operating as a developed counter-cultural force to the 'win' or 'die' logic of market competition in schooling. It was a practical realisation of the principles of the common good in education as propagated by the Catholic bishops in 1997.

The experience of the Partnership from the perspective of one of its leading members ought to provide a model for Catholic schooling everywhere in its resistance to the divisive effects of individualistic competition in education:

> I do believe that if there is to be a real attempt to deliver the objectives set out in *The Common Good in Education* then it will only be achieved by the development of genuine partnerships of schools on a much greater scale and in a much more profound way than we have seen so far.[13]
>
> (Headteacher, St Basil School)

The Partnership headteachers in this study were enthusiastic about the concept and the practice:

> I think the Catholic Partnership is tremendous – it was one of the best things that happened in Birmingham. It was one of the best things that happened at St Scholastica's which could have been a very isolated school without it ... We met as a Board of the heads every half-term and any problems with competition would be ironed out.
>
> (Headteacher, St Scholastica School)

> If somebody is having a tough time with an Ofsted inspection, we as a group of heads can be a supportive group. If somebody has

> achieved considerable success, it can be shared. In other words, the success of the one can be shared for the success of the many.
>
> (Headteacher, St Clement School)

> In terms of competition, I am with the Catholic Partnership and part of what we are about is ensuring that we work collaboratively together. We want to get away from competition and work with collaboration.
>
> (Headteacher, St Cyril School)

> We have ten colleagues who've joined together in commitment to the Catholic education of all the children in the city. There is a sharing of values and even a sharing of children … In straightforward practical terms when they realised that our school was in difficulty they took action to help us.
>
> (Headteacher, St John of the Cross School)

> I was totally against the Thatcher years of competition between schools. I think some schools suffered badly under that competitive marketing strategy. We, as a Catholic Partnership, are not in competition with each other.
>
> (Headteacher, Epiphany School)

It is remarkable that in their 1995 survey of forms of collaboration and partnership in education, Macbeth *et al.* make no reference to the Partnership which had been in existence since 1988. Since this Partnership is arguably one of the most powerful exemplars of educational collaboration in England and Wales, its omission is all the more surprising. This may be an example of the way in which developments within the Catholic school system (and even its existence) are routinely ignored in 'mainstream' educational research and publication. Widespread ideas in the USA, the UK and elsewhere that Catholic schooling has now come 'out of the ghetto' may therefore be somewhat premature. Forms of intellectual and research ghettoisation may prove to be more enduring.[14]

The success of the Partnership, as validated by this research study, deserves to be known and studied and emulated beyond the confines of the Catholic educational community and there is now encouraging evidence of international interest in this Catholic counter-cultural achievement.[15]

Why should this development have occurred in the Archdiocese of Birmingham and not in the schools of the Archdioceses of 'St Anthony', 'St Robert' and 'St Thomas' where Catholic headteachers also encountered the tensions between individual competition and common good collaboration? A fortunate conjunction of circumstances in Birmingham appears to be the explanation. These included the inspirational leadership of the principal of a Catholic sixth form college in the city in the initial formation of the Partnership; the facilitating effects of the city's geography and transport links; an existing sense of community among the ten secondary schools; committed leadership from the designated Partnership Coordinators; and a geography of Catholic schooling which assisted the development of the project. A number of the Partnership headteachers pointed out that the locations of the Catholic schools involved meant that competition for student enrolments occurred 'only at the margins' and that this circumstance greatly assisted the process of Partnership formation. These headteachers recognised that Catholic schools in other settings might face more fragmented, individualised and competitive conditions than those which existed in Birmingham. In other words, the Birmingham headteachers were anxious not to appear 'holier than thou' in any comparisons with Catholic headteachers elsewhere.

## Organising against social exclusion: Birmingham's Zacchaeus Centre

Permanent exclusions of students from English schools for disruptive and unacceptable behaviour increased dramatically in the 1990s. Parsons (1999) has shown that in 1996–7 over 10,000 students were permanently excluded from secondary schools and rapid increases in the rates of exclusions were noted. Among the explanations given for the rise in student exclusions from secondary schools, a powerful one has been that such schools have been affected by market competitive pressures to obtain the best students, the best academic league table position and the best image in the locality. In order to obtain a good school reputation it has become increasingly necessary to exclude those students who obstruct the building of that reputation and the progress of other students. These pressures, and the actions of a more interventionist group of parents, have, it is argued, caused schools to resort to exclusions more frequently than in the past.

For Catholic schools this situation has generated some sharp dilemmas. On the one hand Catholic schools formally acknowledge their mission to the educational service of troubled youth and proclaim a Christian message of forgiveness and reconciliation and yet, on the other hand, they have to survive in an education marketplace where compassion does not feature among the performance indicators.

Many of the headteachers in this study claimed that their schools 'went the extra mile' with the persistently disruptive or even dangerous student. They claimed also that rates of permanent exclusions from Catholic secondary schools were lower than those in the county (state) sector, in their areas. In other words, they claimed that the mission principles of community and forgiveness were maintained as far as possible, except for extreme cases involving violence to other pupils and to teachers, drug dealing in school situations and the possession of weapons in school. Informal arrangements existed in some areas to encourage the transfer of difficult students to other Catholic schools but these arrangements depended upon the willingness of other headteacher colleagues to take such students and this was not always forthcoming.

Once again, the schools of the Birmingham Catholic Secondary Partnership had attempted to evolve a distinctive Catholic response to the challenges of disruptive students. In cooperation with Birmingham LEA, the ten Catholic secondary schools had established in 1995 a learning support unit, the Zacchaeus Centre. The intention of this Centre is primarily to try to prevent exclusions happening in the Partnership schools by receiving 'at-risk' students from the schools and working with them to try to help their specific difficulties. The programmes at the Centre are designed to show that Catholic educators care about the troubles of inner-city students and are trying to find resolutions of them which will permit the students to reintegrate with their original school. A generous staff–student ratio allows the time and space for problem discussion which is often not possible in a large secondary school.

The Director of the Centre explained its rationale in these terms:

> I think that the Centre was a way of saying, here we are, Catholic Christians. Christianity is to do with inclusivity, and what we were saying to our excluded students, and to our students on the point of exclusion was, 'You are not good enough to stay in the Catholic system.' That seemed to us to be utterly against what Christ had taught, so we felt that we must keep these students *included*, as far as possible.

In the opinion of external inspectors this Catholic partnership initiative (with strong support from the LEA) had proved to be an effective agency in reducing permanent exclusions in the schools:

> There is strong evidence to support the proposition that Zacchaeus assists a considerable number of pupils to be maintained within the

> school system who otherwise may have been permanently excluded.[16]

Developments such as the Zacchaeus Centre and other centres based upon it as a model[17] give some evidence that Catholic educational values of community, common good and reconciliation can generate alternative approaches to dealing with disruptive students other than simply ejecting them from schooling systems.

## Market competition and the common good in education: the Catholic 'third way'

Giddens (2000, p. 13), following the argument of Alan Ryan, points out that the 'third way' is a distinct and viable approach to social, political and economic issues and that in fact it is 'a reversion to a very old idea'. From this perspective:

> The third way attempts to avoid an excessive domination of the state … but does not accept that the market can be left to its own devices.

Applied to educational policy and practice the third way implies that schools should not be dominated by the ideologies and bureaucratic procedures of the central and the local state, but, on the other hand, they should not be left to the mercy of unregulated market forces in education. Some form of third way has to be found.

Vallely (1998) and others in *The New Politics: Catholic Social Teaching for the Twenty-First Century* argue that the Catholic Church had been proclaiming the virtues of the third way based upon ideas of the common good long before the term 'third way' became fashionable in social and political discourse. The Catholic Church has been a critic both of unrestrained capitalism and of unrestrained state control and it has historically called for the development of intermediate groupings and associations to be formed in social, economic and political life. In the conclusion of their scholarly review of the interactions of the school, the state and the market in education, Whitty *et al.* (1998 p. 134) produce a similar argument:

> We now need to experiment with and evaluate new forms of association in the public sphere within which citizen rights in education policy … can be reasserted against current trends towards

> both a restricted and authoritarian version of the state and a marketized civil society.

What this study has shown is some evidence of what these 'new forms of association' might be in educational policy and practice, albeit among school professionals rather than the whole constituency of citizens. At least half of the Catholic headteachers involved in this research were searching for forms of association and collaboration which would meet reasonable demands for efficiency and accountability on the one hand, while not involving the 'win or die' imperatives of unregulated market competition in schooling. Specifically in the Birmingham Catholic Secondary Partnership, a new form of professional association had emerged which demonstrated that the realisation of the 'third way' in school relations was possible.

It is also clear from this research that the rearticulation of common good principles in education by the Catholic Bishops of England and Wales had played a crucial part in strengthening collaborative networks among Catholic school leaders.

On the other hand, the fact that twenty-five of the Catholic headteachers in this study adopted a stance of 'pragmatic survivor' in the face of a marketised system of schooling suggests that the impact of Catholic third-way thinking in education is still limited.

A characteristic of Mrs Thatcher's ideological strategy for the marketisation of English society in the 1980s and 1990s was the assertion that 'there is no alternative'. In fact, as this study has shown, there are Catholic alternatives in the sphere of educational policy and practice. However, these alternatives need to be more widely known, studied and practised both within the Catholic educational community and in the wider society.

# 9 Spirituality, morality and personal and social justice

## The nurture of the spiritual

It can be argued that the prime purpose for the existence of Catholic schools is the spiritual, moral and social formation of young people within the specificities of Catholic religious culture and that all of their other activities exist to serve and support these ends. However, this proposition generates a host of related questions. Among them are questions such as 'what constitutes an appropriate spiritual, moral and social formation in Catholic education?' and 'how is it possible to know whether this has been achieved or not?'

Wright (1998, pp. 97–8) reflects upon some of the difficulties related to education as spiritual nurture:

> Since there is no universal understanding of the nature of spirituality[1] ... it becomes the responsibility of the school to make decisions regarding the spiritual tradition that informs the whole curriculum. A school with spiritual integrity must take this responsibility seriously.

For the Catholic schooling system, the spiritual, the moral and the social are necessarily interconnected as categories. There can be no authentic love of God (a manifestation of the spiritual) which is not, at the same time, linked to living a good life (a manifestation of the moral) and to loving and helping one's neighbour (a manifestation of social concern).

In Catholic religious culture, spirituality is understood to be an awareness of a transcendent God whose teachings and example generate a larger sense of purpose and meaning to the prosaic events of daily life. Spirituality shapes identity and gives a transcendent meaning to the purposes of life and to encounters with suffering and death. For Catholics, as Cardinal Hume (1997, p. 126) pointed out, the foundation stone of spirituality is prayer and reflection:

> To pray is to try to make ourselves aware of God and in that awareness respond to him. It is an attempt to raise our minds and hearts to God.

The nurture of spirituality in a Catholic school is supported by the centrality of religious education[2] and by collective worship, the regular celebration of the sacraments, the prayer life of the school and, crucially, by generating 'spaces for reflection' against the environmental press of constant busyness. These 'safe' or protected spaces are necessary, as Archbishop Nichols (1997, p. 100) has argued, to:

> open up the school community to a sense of the Absolute and so contribute to spiritual development.

One of the ironies and contradictions of contemporary work and education is that there is a widespread recognition of the value of reflection in professional practice (as in Schön's (1983) call for reflective practitioners and in Nichols' (1997) call for reflective spaces) just at the time when working conditions have intensified and when, for instance, school life is subject to more monitoring, accountability and inspection surveillance. Catholic schools, along with other schools in England and Wales, have been subjected to an intensified work and surveillance culture and this raises questions about what effect the new 'performativity' culture in schools is having upon the spiritual development of both teachers and students. In other words, it seems likely that contemporary school life is becoming colonised by a hegemony of performance indicators and likely therefore that the spaces for spiritual reflection and development are being reduced. The nurture of the spiritual has never been straightforward but contemporary conditions in school and society appear to make it even more problematic. In his perceptive review of new forms of cultural unbelief, Gallagher (1997, pp. 28–9) identifies the growing significance of 'secular marginalisation', a cultural phenomenon in which religion is no longer vigorously attacked by rationalist or atheist critics but rather simply ignored. From this perspective, secular marginalisation in the wider society begins to permeate the culture of faith-based schools:

> An obvious battleground here involves the relation between the official faith-vision of the school and the unofficial cultural agenda lived in the daily praxis of both school and society. In practice it can be seen as a zone of ambiguity, where the Christian ideals of the institution are subtly undermined by the pressures of competition

(from examinations to sport) or from the alternative curriculum of liberal relativism and self-fulfilment that is so easily absorbed from the wider culture – including of course the culture of the parents.

The present research enquiry was, in part, focused upon a tentative assessment of the extent to which secular marginalisation had permeated the culture of the participating Catholic secondary schools.

## Catholicity: a particular expression of spirituality

In considering the Catholic school's fundamental reasons for existing, the Sacred Congregation for Catholic Education proclaimed 'education in the faith' as a priority objective. What 'education in the faith' entails, what the evidence of its relative success or failure can be said to be, and what forms of Catholicity are actually realised in the living cultures of different types of Catholic school are currently topics for debate and for research in the UK and elsewhere. Groome (1996) has claimed that what makes a school culture distinctively Catholic is a sacramental life and a sacramental consciousness, i.e. an awareness of the presence of God as mediated by the sacraments, especially the celebration of the Mass. In addition to this a strong communal emphasis and a strong sense of the importance of tradition and history in the development of the Catholic Christian story are important defining features. Catholicity is the distinctive spiritual, religious and cultural habitus in which the presence of God is encountered.

To what extent in the past Catholic schools in England actually realised a culture of Catholicity of this type is difficult to assess given the paucity of systematic research with such a focus.[3] However, there are influential writers, both in the USA and in the UK, who claim that the distinctive culture of Catholicity is weakening both in the Church and in the Catholic schooling system as a result of the overzealous implementation of reforms arising from the Second Vatican Council in the 1960s. The chapter headings of Hitchcock's (1995) text, *Recovery of the Sacred*, demarcate the thesis of these conservative critics in the USA – 'The Chimera of Relevance', 'The Cult of Spontaneity', 'The Loss of History', 'The Death of Community', 'Folk Religion' and 'The Reformed Liturgy'. In Hitchcock's view, post-Vatican II Catholicism has lost a sense of the sacred in its pursuit of modernity, relevance and rational explicitness. The necessary insulating boundaries between the realm of the sacred (and of its attendant mysteries and rituals) have been, in Hitchcock's view, dangerously invaded by the practices of the mundane world. In particular contemporary Catholicism has sustained an impoverishment of its traditional cultural riches – symbolism and ritualism. Similar views have been echoed in the UK in Caldecott's (1998) text, *Beyond the Prosaic.*

The thesis of the weakening of Catholicity in Catholic secondary schools in England has been advanced by the work of James Arthur. As noted in Chapter 4, his research published in 1995 as *The Ebbing Tide: Policy and Principles of Catholic Education* argued that Catholic secondary schools in England had moved from a 'holistic model' (concerned with the classic transmission of Catholic religious and liturgical culture) to new 'dualistic' and 'pluralistic' models of schooling. In this analysis, the dualistic Catholic school separates the secular and religious elements of education, regarding the Catholic ethos of the school as something additional to its secular academic programme. The pluralistic Catholic school involves an explicit openness to the families and students of all Christian denominations and also to those of other faiths such as Islam.

For James Arthur, contemporary Catholic secondary schooling in England has been characterised by a decline in the number of schools of 'holistic' Catholic culture and an increase in the number of those with dualistic and pluralistic cultures. What this amounts to, it is argued, is an overall weakening of the distinctive culture of Catholicity in the Church's secondary schooling system and in particular of the sacramental life of schools and of the consciousness that goes with it. For Arthur, Catholicity is an ebbing tide in the cultures and practices of contemporary Catholic secondary schools and if these processes continue the schools will 'become institutions practically indistinguishable from those under LEA control'.[4]

The 'Ebbing Tide' analysis of 1995 provoked much controversy within the Catholic educational community in England. For some, it has given expression to their deepest fears that Catholic schools are undergoing processes of cultural incorporation. If this analysis is correct then the dualistic Catholic school is being incorporated into a secular academic success culture whereby the spiritual and religious messages of schooling have become merely contextual and not central to the educational programme. The schools are becoming more instrumental and less spiritual. In addition to this, those Catholic schools which for various reasons[5] have become more pluralistic in recruitment and culture are represented as being involved in processes of ecumenical or multi-faith incorporation which is weakening the distinctive nature of their Catholic ethos.

Those who have supported the analysis given in *The Ebbing Tide* argue that a great strength of Catholic religious and educational culture is the richness of its symbolic life and its ritual practices. This richness, in their view, should not be lost to Catholic school culture in the future in the mistaken pursuit of modernity, 'efficiency', pluralism or ecumenism. McClelland (1992, pp. 6–7) has argued that:

> The crucifix should not be discarded from classrooms as a gesture to religious pluralism. Neither should representation of saints be neglected ... in the interests of a false ecumenism. Nor should pious religious practices be abandoned on the altar of individual freedom. All these things are daily reminders of that communion of saints which lies at the heart of the theology of the Catholic school. Such schools will not overcome the materialism of the age ... (in this way).

Observations such as this and the research of James Arthur have stimulated a debate about what constitutes the Catholic ethos of a school. For some, the issue is necessarily tied to the proportions of Catholic students (practising or nominal) and the proportion of Catholic teachers present in a particular school or college. A high proportion of Catholics in a school, with a visible Catholic symbolic culture and an active sacramental life and liturgical practice, is the *sine qua non* of a strong Catholicity. For others, this is a narrow and mechanical view of Catholicity which makes it the prisoner of a cultural ghetto. From the perspectives of these critics, Catholic schools have to be open to the contemporary faith pluralism of many inner-city communities and should be of service to 'those who are far from the faith'.[6] Just as Catholic school leaders have to consider the legitimate balance between the demands of market survival and those of spiritual and moral mission, so too they have to consider what is the proper balance between the generation of a distinctive Catholic ethos and an openness to communities which are increasingly pluralistic in urban areas.

In 1996, Peter Hastings, a former Catholic secondary school headteacher in the English Midlands, published a strong criticism of what may be called traditional constructs of Catholicity. In a chapter entitled 'Openness and Intellectual Challenge in Catholic Schools' Hastings argued that much of the Catholicity of English schooling in the past was oppressive in its culture and immature in its religious and spiritual outcomes. For Hastings, the future of a mature and internalised Catholicity would have to be found in Catholic schools which practised spiritual and value openness and which generated cultures where intellectual challenge was the norm.

Similar arguments in favour of openness in Catholic education can be found in the work of Bernadette O'Keeffe, Deputy Director of the

Von Hügel Institute in the University of Cambridge. O'Keeffe (1992) believes that the future for Catholic schools in England (and by implication, elsewhere) must be in the direction of greater openness. Such openness is already a *de facto* feature of many Catholic schools in inner-city areas where substantial 'other faith' school populations exist. For O'Keeffe this should now become a principled development for the future where faith rather than denomination would seek to achieve the integration of differences into a collaborative and fruitful whole.[7] While a lively debate exists about the nature of spirituality and of Catholicity in contemporary Catholic schooling, the amount of assertion and counter-assertion is greater than the research evidence. *The Ebbing Tide*, which generated so much controversy in England, had, for instance, a very limited research base for the claims which it made.[8]

In 1995 the Catholic Bishops of England and Wales issued a discussion paper, *Spiritual and Moral Development Across the Curriculum*, to assist the professional development of Catholic teachers and school leaders on these contested issues. While emphasising that spiritual and moral development in Catholic schools was ultimately the responsibility of all teachers, all curriculum subject study and of the whole-school ethos, religious education and practice obviously had a leading influence:

> Spiritual development is, of course, inseparable from religious education, catechesis, worship and liturgy in which we try to introduce to the pupils the person of Jesus Christ and relate his teaching to their experience. It is in this context that the liturgical life of the school assumes its richest significance, where opportunities for prayer and reflection enable pupils to strengthen, in a very specific way, their life in Christ. The opportunities provided by a Catholic school … bring the spiritual life of the school to its most explicit expression.
>
> (Catholic Education Service 1995b, p. 16)

But what do we actually know, what *can* we know, about the 'explicit expression' of spiritual development among young people or about the spiritual vitality, 'effectiveness' and living Catholicity of individual Catholic schools? These matters, unlike the assessments made for specific curriculum subjects, are less amenable to the measurement of contemporary performance indicators. This is not to say that such phenomena are unknowable but it is to say that judgements about their relative 'success' or 'failure' have to be made with due recognition of the complexities involved and the provisional nature of the knowledge available.

Historically, headteachers and school principals, as leaders of Catholic schools, have been expected to be not only professional leaders but also faith leaders. These expectations were made explicit in the Vatican publication *Lay Catholics in Schools: Witnesses to Faith* (Sacred Congregation for Catholic Education 1982) and have been further developed by the publications of Catholic bishops conferences in various societies. In the present research study, the sixty Catholic secondary school headteachers who participated were, in effect, the stewards of the spiritual and Catholic development of their students. They were also possessed of much evidence on this subject, some of it formal and official (the OFSTED and diocesan reports) and some of it more informally derived from their years of professional observations of students within given school settings. Every headteacher participant was asked, during the interview, to comment upon their knowledge of spiritual development in their schools and more specifically to respond to Arthur's (1995) thesis that Catholicity was weakening in contemporary secondary schools. What follows gives some indication of the nature of these responses. An immediate objection to this procedure would be that Catholic headteachers, as faith leaders, are likely to give subjective and biased accounts of the spiritual and Catholic vitality of their own schools, overemphasising the positive features. While this possibility must, from a research integrity perspective, be fully acknowledged, the existence of a countervailing influence, i.e. the professional integrity of the headteachers as 'witnesses to truth', must also be acknowledged. In situations such as this, social and educational research has long recognised the value of triangulation procedures, i.e. cross-checking individual accounts by gathering data from a number of sources. Independent reports on spiritual development and on school ethos were available for the majority of schools from OFSTED inspectors and reports on spirituality, Catholicity and religious education from diocesan inspectors. Some main themes in these reports are presented before the headteacher interview accounts are considered.

## Spirituality and Catholicity through the eyes of external inspectors

Fifty-one reports from OFSTED were available to the researcher, as were forty-seven reports from Catholic diocesan inspectors. The OFSTED reports always included comments on spiritual development within each school but these were generally confined to brief observations upon the provision of collective worship and the extent to which spiritual values were realised in all subjects of the national curriculum.[9]

OFSTED inspectors frequently commented upon the existence of 'a distinctive Roman Catholic ethos' within the schools under examination. This might suggest that Arthur's (1995) thesis that distinct Catholicity in secondary schools is declining was not supported in these cases. However, it must be noted that the OFSTED reports gave little evidential detail about what constituted a distinctive ethos. A similar lack of detail and evidence could be noted in those OFSTED reports which moved beyond comments upon *provision* for spiritual development to judgements upon effectiveness and outcomes, e.g. as in statements such as 'pupils' spiritual development is excellent'.

Where OFSTED inspectors concentrated upon provision for spiritual development in these Catholic secondary schools, the picture which emerged was one of overall strength. Where they commented upon the permeation of spiritual values across all subjects of the curriculum, the picture was more variable.

As might be expected, the forty-seven reports of diocesan inspectors were more focused and detailed about religious education, spiritual development and the Catholic nature of the school. What emerges from a reading of these reports is strong evidence that the Catholic schools involved in this enquiry were taking the spiritual development of their students seriously and were attempting, by the provision of what might be called *Catholic resources for spirituality*, to facilitate such development. Catholic resources for spirituality in most of the schools, from the perspectives of diocesan inspectors, included the following:

- *Mission statement*: a carefully produced mission statement (often the result of much consultation) which clearly expressed spiritual values and which was used extensively to direct and shape the whole life of the school – 'a permeating Mission statement and not just a prospectus Mission statement'.
- *Catholic ethos*: a distinctive Catholic ethos constituted in part by the presence of Catholic religious symbols, icons and artefacts, in part by a distinctive vocational commitment among the teachers and in some cases by the continuing influence of the charisms of religious orders (sixteen references were made to charism influence.)
- *Faith leadership of headteachers*: a visible commitment by headteachers to the priority of the spiritual and religious life of the school by personal example, in professional and student leadership and by allocation of staff and resources in support of the spiritual and religious objectives of the school.
- *Liturgy, Masses and prayer life*: an active and participative liturgical culture, with regular celebration of the Mass and a prayer life for

teachers and students normalised as part of the everyday experience of school life. A dialogic induction of the student into Catholic religious practices, prayers and devotions.

- *School chapel, oratory, quiet room*: the existence of a school chapel, oratory or quiet room which could provide a protected space[10] for prayer and reflection and, in some cases, for the reservation of the Blessed Sacrament. (Twenty-four reports mentioned the importance of such protected spaces in assisting the spiritual development of teachers and students.) The use of spiritual retreats as an aid to spiritual development was commended in many schools.
- *Chaplaincy teams and spiritual life committees*: the existence of chaplaincy teams (including priests and lay men and women) was mentioned in twenty-four reports as constituting a major asset and resource for spiritual development in the schools. In a minority of schools, committees or working groups existed to keep under review issues of spirituality and Catholicity, often chaired by a senior staff member or school governor.
- *Religious education department*: religious education departments were frequently mentioned as a crucial agency (along with chaplaincy teams) for giving drive and inspiration in the spiritual life of schools. At their best, religious education departments acted in the role of spiritual mentors for teachers in other departments to assist them with prayer and liturgical issues and with the discernment of the spiritual aspects of their curriculum subject. However, the accounts given in the diocesan reports were variable. In some cases it appeared that other teachers regarded the spiritual life of the school as the responsibility of the religious education department as a spiritual 'add-on' to the National Curriculum provision. In other cases serious staffing and resource problems in religious education departments were noted, including difficulties in appointing heads of department and in recruiting and retaining qualified teachers of the subject.

Diocesan reports commented, in the main, upon the provision of resources to assist spiritual and Catholic development among the students and upon certain measurables such as the number of students entered for religious education as a subject and the percentage who were successful at GCSE level. It was noted in many reports that the time allocated to religious education as a subject had fallen below the 10 per cent recommended by the Catholic bishops.[11] In so far as the imposition of the National Curriculum upon Catholic schools has had a secularising and 'performativity' effect, one interpretation of this finding might be to say that religious education as a 'protected space' for the nurture of the spiritual is under threat. Diocesan inspectors rarely commented upon the actual impact as opposed to the likely impact of spiritual opportunities upon individual students. As the inspectors at St Lawrence School expressed it in their report:

> It is not possible, or indeed desirable, to measure the impact of the school framework of prayer on individuals. However, it is desirable that the effectiveness of its delivery is reviewed.
>
> (p. 8)

This observation raises some profound questions about how the outcomes of spiritual and Catholic opportunities for formation can be assessed and evaluated in Catholic schooling. Greeley (1998) has argued that the outcomes of Catholic spiritual, moral and social formation in schooling will only become fully apparent in the mature adult lives and behaviours of Catholic men and women. This is why oral history accounts, such as those used in Chapter 3 of this book, are so valuable. However, another approach is to suggest that Catholic school effectiveness in the spiritual realm may be assessed by looking at the vitality of the links between Catholic schools and their associated parishes. In some cases these are seen to be strong. The diocesan inspectors of St Clement's School reported, for instance:

> The school fosters links with its feeder parishes. The local parish priests are welcome to visit the school and meet their parishioners. Pupils train as altar servers, extraordinary ministers of the Eucharist, readers and cantors. They also write intercessory prayers and prayers of thanksgiving. The school is conscious of its responsibility to help form the next generation of Catholics. It encourages pupils to become active members of their own parish.
>
> (p. 14)

This degree of school–parish linkage at secondary school level appeared to be unusual. From the perspectives of conservative critics of Catholic schools there is too little evidence of such functioning relationships and this leads such critics to believe that the spiritual impact of Catholic schools is weakening or, in Arthur's (1995) terms, there is an ebbing tide of Catholicity within secondary schools in England. In an attempt to obtain further sources of evidence on these contested issues the sixty Catholic secondary school headteachers involved in the study were asked to give their considered professional judgements about the spirituality and Catholicity of their schools and students.

## Spirituality and Catholicity through the eyes of headteachers

As might be expected, the answers of the headteachers on matters relating to spiritual development, as opposed to academic achievement, were much more hesitant and tentative than most of their other responses. Some referred to the positive reports the school had received from OFSTED inspectors and from diocesan inspectors about spiritual development among the students, but this was nearly always qualified by a recognition that these reports were based upon one-week inspection visits only. The headteacher of St Matthew's School was characteristically frank on this issue:

> I don't really understand spirituality. I have to be honest. Spirituality has always been a bit of a mystery to me. What I do know is that we have a culture here where people learn to love one another. Some of them have to learn to love themselves first, quite frankly. That is terribly important.

In talking about spiritual development within their schools many headteachers made reference to the extent to which what has already been called Catholic resources for spiritual development were fully utilised in their institutions. These resources of chaplaincy, retreats, pilgrimages, chapels and quiet rooms, missions, liturgies, Masses and the work of religious education departments were cited as providing opportunities for young people to discover the presence of God in their lives and their communities.

But the difficult questions remained – how could they know if these opportunities were being taken up in a serious way and how could they discern any evidence relating to the spiritual 'effectiveness' of their educational programmes?

## Looking for outward signs of inward grace

The majority of the headteachers looked for outward signs of inward grace among their students in the realm of relationships, behaviour and involvement in good works. Many of these secondary schools were located in inner-city and deprived urban communities marked by violence, crime, drug and alcohol abuse and manifestations of racism. These distortions of human relations and of human beings might well have been reconstituted within the cultures of the Catholic schools serving these localities. The fact that, in the main, this was not happening in the schools of this research enquiry was attributed by the headteachers to the relative effectiveness of the spiritual and moral culture which the schools had been able to generate in opposition to various distortions in the wider community. From the perspectives of the headteachers these Catholic schools were agencies for the preservation and enhancement of virtue[12] and faith in the most unpromising settings. The work of spirituality could be discerned, in their view, in the way their students conducted themselves:

> Some work with the Jesuits in this area, some with local housing associations and with the homeless … Really positive living Christians … That if you like is getting into the good works side of things … But I don't accept that faith alone without good works will get you there.
>
> (Headteacher, St Vincent School)

> I see kids being respectful in the main to one another. I see an atmosphere of calmness about the place. I see relationships between people being far more positive than negative. I see examples of caring … I see the charities and the huge outpourings of help and money.
>
> (Headteacher, Cardinal Hume School)

> I think if you look at behaviour, relations with staff, response to spiritual activities within the school, extent of student involvement in liturgies – you can get a good measure of the spiritual life of your school community … We can intuitively and personally experience spiritual development.
>
> (Headteacher, St Clement School)

Other headteachers took the view that some indication of the spiritual vitality of a school could be discerned in the prayer life of the community and a general openness to spiritual values:

> They will turn to prayer very naturally … and they will come and ask you to pray.
>
> (Headteacher, Mary, Mother of God School)

> In the chapel there is a book in which the pupils themselves write their prayers … They are sincere, heartfelt concerns that the pupils have. It is very moving to read them. They never make fun of each other over this – it is accepted.
>
> (Headteacher, St Robert Bellarmine School)

> When a retired head from a local county school spent some time with us he reported that he was amazed at the spiritual openness of our pupils, the way they talk with the teachers about these ideas compared with the pupils in a neighbouring county school with similar intake.
>
> (Headteacher, Holy Cross School)

While these responses give some indication of the 'outward signs' that headteachers used in commenting on spiritual development in their schools, their characteristic stance was to say that spiritual development was not amenable to a contemporary target-setting and performance indicator culture which was currently dominating educational practice. In their view the spiritual nurture of young people was a manifestation of Bernstein's (1997) invisible pedagogy, i.e. an enterprise in which the results could only be seen in the long term in adult life. Nevertheless from such indicators as were available to them there emerged a general sense that the spirituality of Catholic schools was a living, counter-culture influence in the lives of many of their students despite urban problematics and the materialism of the wider society. Yet there was, at the same time, a recognition that the spiritual culture of Catholic schools was vulnerable. The serious nurture of the spiritual needed protected time and protected space over and against the relentless pressure of educational performance efficiency. The temptation to give more time and space to those activities which could generate short-term visible results was considerable. The possibility had to be faced that because spiritual development could not be quantified and entered on performance league tables, it might become a marginalised and weaker sector of a school's activities. The headteacher of St Joan of Arc School expressed this recognition of pressure and vulnerability:

> So much emphasis is now placed on your targets … focusing in on performance so we're all preoccupied with two things, performance targets and actual achievements, as if this was the only matter that engaged the Catholic school. We've got to keep reminding ourselves that this is not just why we are here.

## Catholicity: ebbing or renewing?

The question of what sort of Catholicity was being generated in the secondary schools involved in this enquiry stimulated much reflective comment from the participating headteachers. All of them were asked to compare the Catholicity of their own secondary schooling and formation with the Catholicity which they discerned in the contemporary schools for which they were responsible. A main theme which emerged from these discussions was a recognition that the Catholicity of their own secondary school formation had been, in general, one of strong, traditional Catholic habitus. Such Catholicity was marked by the regular celebration of the Mass, attendance at Benediction, the saying of the Rosary, the practice of Confession, the saying of the Angelus, prayers at the commencement and conclusion of lessons and the frequent presence of priests, nuns and teaching brothers as models of the spiritual life and as exemplars of vocational commitment to the service of others. This strong and distinctive Catholic school environment was generally reinforced by a family practice of regular attendance at Sunday Mass. Of the sixty headteachers in the sample, twelve had experienced a call to the religious life and were currently members of various religious congregations, and three were former members of religious orders. A significant number of the lay headteachers spoke of their work in terms of a lay vocation to teaching and of service to the young.

Despite their own experiences of classic Catholic spiritual and cultural formation in secondary schooling in the past, very few[13] of the headteachers endorsed the argument that Catholicity was ebbing out of contemporary secondary schools in England. The dominant view was that in keeping with the reforms of the Second Vatican Council of the 1960s, the expression of Catholic religious faith and of service to others was taking new forms in new circumstances. In their perceptions of the Catholicity of their individual schools they saw a renewal of Catholicity among young people and its expression in diverse ways. This was not the Catholicity as realised in the religious and cultural practices of their own youth but, in their estimation, evidence of the work of the Holy Spirit in their schools:

> I think lots of schools in the past could be considered to have a strong Catholic ethos because of statues, reciting prayers and learning the Catechism but I don't know if that made it necessarily Catholic. We're about promoting the basics in terms of Christian values, love of God and love of your neighbour. Jesus never made it difficult. It's only theologians who make it difficult … We often have a para-liturgy rather than a Eucharistic liturgy because we involve the pupils more and we feel that we can give them a very real experience of the liturgy.
>
> (Headteacher, Sacred Heart of Mary School)

> If you turned up at school on a Monday morning you were asked if you had been to Sunday Mass – there was a kind of rule of fear – that's changed … We have a new Catholicity that is rooted in the Gospel which needs to find new forms of community, of worshipping together and new ways of being family … What you try to hand on is a value, a sense of relationship, a sense of faith, a sense of transcendence and a critical awareness of what matters.
>
> (Headteacher, Holy Rosary School)

> There are other definitions of Catholicity of course, and I think that we ought not to forget that there are many Catholic schools worldwide where many of the pupils are not Catholic. There are other ways of looking at Catholicity, for example: Is this a school where the Gospel is proclaimed? Yes. Is this a school where there is prayer which is spontaneous and voluntary? Yes. Is this a school where pupils can find words for devotion? Yes. I think that a lot of the Catholicity of the past was found in the Catechism and the explicit formulations of the Church, whereas now we have to accept that Catholicity is a process of growing in understanding – it is more dynamic.
>
> (Headteacher, St Patrick School)

Such arguments in celebration of new forms of post-Vatican II Catholicity in the secondary schools of this research are unlikely to convince religious conservatives who see visible evidence that contemporary school Catholicity is ebbing away. From this perspective, the evidence of declining practice of the faith (in particular low levels of youth attendance at Sunday Mass) and a sharp fall in the number of vocations to the priesthood and the religious life demonstrate a weakening of the religious and spiritual habitus of Catholic schools – especially secondary schools. If the Holy Spirit is at work in the schools in new ways, as these headteachers assert, then why are the fruits of this work less evident than they were in the past?

The headteachers of the research schools were familiar with such criticisms, sometimes voiced by local priests or by members of the school governing body and regularly present in the Catholic popular press. Perhaps because of their familiarity with such criticisms, there was a high level of consensus in their responses to them. Four major themes could be discerned in their discourse on Catholicity, as follows.

### *Change is needed in the institutional Church and its liturgies*

From the perspectives of many of the headteachers there was too much disjuncture between the liturgical life of Catholic secondary schools which emphasised creativity, activity and participation by the young and the liturgical culture of local parishes and churches which in the main involved a ritual of prescribed responses and limited scope for participation. If there was a crisis about the active Catholicity of the young, then, in the view of the headteachers, the problem was located to an important extent in the parishes and not in the secondary schools:

> I dread to say this, but we also have problems with the church's liturgy at present. The church's liturgy is not on the whole geared to young people and I think this is a major problem with their Mass attendance … I talk to young people when we have our prayer leadership weekends and their greatest problem is their parish church – how young people are treated in church. I feel that the Church itself must have another look at liturgy and priests have to think again about what they are doing for young people.
>
> (Headteacher, St Mark School)

> If you look at the Catholic popular press, it is a recurring theme of people who write in to say 'it's not like it used to be'. I think that some people get a satisfaction in suggesting that they have the Holy Grail and the rest of the world is doomed. I would then turn this round and say that those who come out with this line ought to analyse what actually happens on a weekly basis in our churches. My own three children only go to church under duress. They wouldn't wish to be there. I think that the Church needs to appeal to the young people in a much more fundamental way.
>
> (Headteacher, St Basil School)

> If the institutional Church changed and made itself more user friendly to many of the adults who send their children to us, that would help. In our school we do our best to share our faith with the girls. What we find is a lack of knowledge and understanding and that is to do with the home and parish settings. In some of our parishes, we would be bored as adults. So God help these kids. If it's boring, why would you go?
>
> (Headteacher, St Colette School)

> It's the parishes who are failing us … for a child it must be an intensely boring experience.
>
> (Headteacher, Pope Pius XII School)

These powerful criticisms of the institutional Catholic Church and of the liturgical culture of many of its parishes in the three cities of this enquiry cannot lightly be set aside. They were voiced by a group of Catholic school leaders, all of whom were practising their faith and some of whom (the headteachers of St Mark and of St Colette) were members of religious orders. If their analysis has any validity then any perceived crisis in the Catholicity of the young people involved arises not primarily because of weaknesses in the schools but because of weaknesses in the *liturgical articulation* of secondary schools and their feeder parishes.

### *Family support for Catholicity is declining*

The headteachers in this study had generally attended Sunday Mass in their youth as part of an accepted family practice of Mass attendance. They now encountered situations in their urban communities where the very concept of 'family' and of 'parents' had become much more diffuse, varied and problematic. As family structures and family life had changed radically for many of their students, so too had the notion of family religious practice. It had declined sharply. Even in schools with 100 per cent Catholic enrolments (as judged by baptismal status), most headteachers estimated a rate of religious practice among the students of only 10 per cent and even lower, where 'practice' was defined as Sunday Mass attendance. While it was accepted that this was in part the expected outcome of 'adolescent rebellion', it was also interpreted as evidence of religious apathy or loss of faith in the home:

> The Catholicity unfortunately that is outside the gate, is the Catholicity that is ebbing. Therefore the Catholicity of the schools may ebb too … I think part of the reason is the breakdown of family life. I think this is so tragic.
>
> (Headteacher, Holy Family School)

> My implication is that there is something failing all round. There is something failing within the family. We're in the 1990s. I don't think that it's necessarily the Catholic schools 'with their wishy-washy

> liberalism and Weaving the Web religious programmes' that have contributed to it. I think it is more complex than that.
>
> (Headteacher: Corpus Christi School)

> It is impossible for a Catholic school to totally reverse what pupils perceive as being society's values and indeed their own parents' values.
>
> (Headteacher, Cardinal Hume School)

This last observation resonates with the arguments advanced in Bernstein's (1970) classic paper, 'Education cannot compensate for Society'. In this paper Bernstein criticised the unrealistic expectations of social reformers that schooling alone could achieve significant transformations of social structures and social relations and produce fundamental cultural change. The responses of the Catholic headteachers in the present study have, in effect, constituted a Catholic version of this thesis, i.e. 'Catholic schools (alone) cannot compensate for a fragmented, secular and materialist Society'.

### *Vocations exist in new forms*

In only three of the schools (Pope Pius VII, St Anthony of Padua and St Pius X) was there any evidence[14] of recent vocations to the priesthood and the religious life. Two of these schools had strong elements of traditional Catholic habitus and both had headteachers who were members of religious orders. The characteristic response of headteachers in other schools was to argue that judging Catholic secondary schools by the number of vocations to service in the institutional Church was too narrow an approach to contemporary conceptions of vocation:

> It's harking back to a time that has gone. Each Christian and Catholic has to carry with them the church and we are not today gauging 'vocation' around the life of the priest or the religious because you can actually fulfil your role in other ways.
>
> (Headteacher, St Colette School)

> Society has changed now and there are lots of ways of living out your commitment to God and to other people that wasn't possible in the past. Particularly for women there are now more opportunities.
>
> (Headteacher, Mary, Mother of God School)

In talking about Catholicity, many of the headteachers made distinctions between the institutional or clerical Church and the Church understood as the People of God in service to others. While some of them regretted the decline of vocations to the institutional Church, they saw a growing sense of a lay vocation to service among their students. For them, the concept of vocation still existed but was increasingly expressed in lay forms. In that sense they believed that Catholic secondary schools had a crucial role to play in recontextualising the idea of vocation for young people and in presenting to them opportunities for service in the local community, the nation and the wider world.

### *The Catholic secondary school is the living church and parish for young people*

This statement occurred so many times during the course of the interviews that it began to acquire the quality of a headteacher credo. These school leaders were convinced that Catholic secondary schools were not only a desirable part of 'the saving mission of the Church' but, in contemporary conditions, an essential part. Many of them knew enough of the history of Catholic schooling in England to make reference to the classic statement by the Catholic bishops of the 1850s that the building of schools should take precedence over the building of churches for the advancement of the Catholic mission. For these headteachers the spiritual, religious, moral and social work of contemporary Catholic schools was now crucial for the future of the Catholic Church in England. It would be possible to fill the rest of this book with quotations elaborating that position but limitations of space make it necessary to present only a representative sample:

> If the Catholic Church is about preaching the Gospel then it should see that the contact that the schools have with young people is its most important resource in spreading the message of the Gospel and it should see that this is where Gospel values are being inculcated.
>
> (Headteacher, St Flannan School)

> It is not that religion is ebbing out of Catholic schools – it is something within society itself. One could reverse the statement and say that the only hope that we have is the Catholic school … the role of the Catholic school is perhaps more important today than it ever was.
>
> (Headteacher, St Dominic School)

> I think that it's an important fact that if we had no Catholic secondary schools we might have no Catholic population at all with any knowledge of the Faith in the new millennium.
>
> (Headteacher, St Cyril School)

> It places a greater responsibility on our schools because we are their parish. The local church isn't because they stop going there when they are 13. We *are* the parish.
>
> (Headteacher, Corpus Christi School)

> We are the church – that's why Catholic schools are so important. What goes on in parishes week by week is to an ageing and diminishing population. The church isn't the building – it's a faith community. That is why the work we do in Catholic secondary schools is so important.
>
> (Headteacher: St Basil School)

In his recent reflections upon taking seriously the idea of Catholic school as Church, Sullivan (2000) has argued that contemporary conditions made the role of headteachers as faith leaders even more important than it had been in the past. In addition to currently prioritised notions of 'management literacy' and 'ICT literacy' for school leaders, Sullivan points out that there is a clear need among Catholic headteachers and school leaders for a greater degree of 'theological literacy'.[15] In other words, if Catholic secondary schools in England have become *de facto* the church and the parish for many young people in urban areas, then this requires new initiatives from the institutional Church and its educational agencies. Among these would be the provision of professional development courses for headteachers and teachers, with a spiritual focus, and changes in the formation programmes of priests, religious and chaplains who will be working in partnership with secondary schools.[16]

Overall, the view of the headteachers in this study was that Catholicity was ebbing out of homes and parishes in the inner-city and deprived urban areas in which most of them were located and that this weakening of faith practice in the wider community presented new challenges to the schools. However, most of them were confident that their schools were finding imaginative and relevant ways of nurturing spirituality and of renewing Catholicity in difficult circumstances. At the heart of this renewal were two complementary strategies. The first was the maintenance of protected time and protected space for the nurture of reflection and prayer. The second was the generation of a liturgical culture which was creative and participative for young people and which provided the impetus for involvement in good works in the local community and beyond.

## Issues of morality and personal and social justice

Bryk (1988, p. 274) has argued that:

> A set of moral ideals provides the organizational linchpin that ties the structural features of Catholic high schools to their normative environments. The good Catholic school is impelled by fundamental beliefs about the dignity and worth of each person and a vision of a just social world.

The previous chapters have shown the various ways in which the Catholic school leaders involved in this research attempted to promote the moral formation of their students as good people (principles of personal morality) and as good citizens (principles of social morality). The moral life of the research schools was characterised by serious attention to issues of moral integrity, concepts of 'right' and 'wrong' in moral conduct, the formation of personal and social responsibility, the inculcation of a sense of conscience and compassion and a commitment to the service of others. The reports of external inspectors, both OFSTED and diocesan, attested to the seriousness with which these Catholic schools pursued both personal moral ideals and ideals of social justice.

The moral and social justice programmes of the schools had to be attempted against the grain of an external social and cultural milieu that was inimical to many of these school-generated ideals. A wider environment marked by moral relativism, individual hedonism, consumerism, and by class, race and gender inequalities and distortions of relationships, set the challenges for the schools. These Catholic schools were involved in an attempt to transmit ideas about 'the dignity and worth of persons' and of 'a just social world' to young people who saw little evidence of this in their own urban communities.

The first challenge which the headteachers recognised was what can be called the *school–community disjuncture* in moral and social culture, i.e. the juxtaposition of different normative environments in the urban context. The second challenge, specific to Catholic schools, was the *Church–youth disjuncture* in moral culture. Catholic secondary schools were faced with a difficult role in mediating between the institutional Catholic Church with its clear prescriptions for moral behaviour and a generalised youth culture and mass media culture which was questioning and relativistic about many moral issues.

The headteachers were aware that attempting to bridge these moral, social and cultural disjunctures was a demanding responsibility:

> I think the most difficult thing for me in this area is the moral upbringing of the children because it is against all Christian morality. This is ingrained within the families and to be able to cut through this is very difficult … The children have to be really strong in order to break away from the immediate culture which exists here in the inner-city.
>
> (Headteacher, St Mark School)

> I do know that what does happen here is that it is a haven for working class youth. It gives them a sense of community and a sense of society and social cohesion which possibly they won't find anywhere else.
>
> (Headteacher, Holy Redeemer School)

> I don't know how many of the girls have had an abortion but I know that some have and certainly their mothers for whatever reason. You cannot condemn them through your teaching. You've got to be very sensitive but the teaching will be the ideal as put forward by the Catholic Church.
>
> (Headteacher, Mary, Mother of God School)

> The boys have a strong sense of Catholic community … But they are not impressed by the Church as an institution and they are not impressed by its personal moral teachings related to sex.
>
> (Headteacher, Pope Paul III School)

> My concept of Catholicity is that it must change. It has to be concerned with social justice much more and sex a lot less.
>
> (Headteacher, Ascension School)

Much of the moral teaching of these Catholic schools focused upon the principle of respecting the dignity and worth of individuals. Taking this principle seriously raised questions about economic and social relations in society and in the global economy, about institutional cultures and the treatment of persons and about personal morality including sexual relations. The headteacher of Ascension School was not alone in suggesting that the emphasis of 'dignity of the person' moral teaching needed to be more strongly placed on social structural and economic issues and not simply upon the regulation of sexual behaviour.[17]

Taking 'dignity of the person' as a central moral principle also raised a set of other questions about how their own schools operated in practice. These questions related to race and gender issues in the schools and crucially to whether or not their own students experienced 'dignity of the person' as a reality in the school culture.

## Racism and the Catholic school

In 1989 the Pontifical Commission for Justice and Peace at the Vatican issued a guidance document for all Catholics on matters concerning race relations. This document, *The Church and Racism: towards a more fraternal society*, included, among other things, a commitment to the eradication of racism within its own institutions:

> The Church wants first and foremost to change racist attitudes, including those within her own communities.[18]
>
> (p. 44)

It also included a call for Catholic schools to play a leading role in working against racism in its various manifestations. What the impact of this document has been on the institutional practices of the Catholic Church and the educational cultures of Catholic schools internationally remains uncertain because very little research has been undertaken on race relations within Catholic schools.[19] It seems likely that given the cosmopolitan and multi-ethnic nature of many Catholic schools and a formal religious commitment to 'love of neighbour' and to 'dignity of the person', it has been assumed that racism is not a problem within the Catholic school – whatever may be the case in the external world. The fact that the Catholic bishops and schools of South Africa took leading roles in resistance to apartheid as a racist policy (Christie 1990) has helped to confirm the image of Catholic schools as relatively racist-free institutions. This image was reinforced by the majority of the Catholic headteachers with whom this issue was raised.[20] The dominant view was that although a number of the schools were located in communities known to be marked by racist organisations and activity, this external racism did not significantly affect the internal culture of the schools or the relationships within them.

Characteristic responses were:

> This is one of the most multicultural schools in the country, with 30 per cent black Afro-Caribbean, about 25 per cent white, 10 per cent Vietnamese and the rest Asian, largely Indian … We interview

> every parent and we make it quite clear that racism, bullying, violence won't be tolerated. Despite this there are some incidents of racism of course but overall it's not something we have to worry about in terms of what is going on in the school.
>
> (Headteacher, St Martin de Porres School)

> One of the things that the OFSTED report commented upon was the apparent lack of racism in the schools and I am happy to say that there have been few incidents of racism that I've had to deal with.
>
> (Headteacher, St Sebastian School)

> Every school has racist incidents where pupils are into name-calling but it's dealt with. We've got a clear policy on it … I've never really experienced in this school any really vicious racism.
>
> (Headteacher, St Patrick School)

In general, only three headteachers whose schools were multi-ethnic in student population made any extended responses to issues about racism. For the headteachers of Catholic secondary schools with all-white populations, racism did not appear to be a salient educational issue. In a review of research undertaken among Catholic schools in England in the 1980s it was noted that, 'in predominantly white secondary schools … there were few new initiatives and … many schools did not see dealing with racism as part of their task'.[21] This still appears to be the case in the 1990s.

One headteacher, who chaired a Justice and Peace Working Party on Countering Racism in Catholic Schools, was particularly critical of what he saw as a culture of silence among his colleagues on racism questions:

> I know that Heads won't generally engage openly and officially and have real discussion about these issues … They're in denial in effect … But the fact is they will be excluding more black boys in particular. They know also that if their school becomes more black, then the white kids won't want to come.
>
> (Headteacher, St Bernard School)

These challenging observations raised the vexed question of institutional or community racism and the conduct of the Catholic school. In only five interview situations did headteachers volunteer comments on these issues. In two schools (St Cyril and St Martin de Porres) reviews of institutional practice were in progress. In two other schools (St John of the Cross and St Bernard) the headteachers acknowledged that white racism in their local communities had affected their white student enrolments and in one case had brought a school to a serious enrolment crisis. The evidence available in this research is very limited on questions of racism and the Catholic schools participating, and therefore any conclusions can only be tentative. A 'no problem here'[22] response characterised most of the interviews. However, a critical minority believed that there was too much silence on this issue among Catholic educators. If the Catholic system of schooling was to be true to its own declared anti-racist principles then this minority believed that more open discussion and more in-depth research enquiry was needed on racism and the Catholic school.

This latter view has been endorsed by the Catholic Bishops of England and Wales who, in their consultative paper *Catholic Schools and Other Faiths* (1997b), argued that:

> All Catholic schools, regardless of their location, will need to give full attention to matters concerning multi-culturalism and racism.
>
> (p. 22)

The bishops were particularly sensitive to the situation that Catholic schools in multi-racial areas were, in some cases, more predominantly white in student composition than neighbouring county or state schools. This had led to accusations of institutional racism in Catholic school admissions. While these charges could be countered by an insistence that Catholicity and not ethnicity was the determinant of school admission policies, the sensitivity of these issues in some multi-racial communities was acknowledged.

## Gender, leadership and Catholicism

In Chapter 6 some analysis of the discourse of the twenty-four women headteachers in the sample was given on concepts of leadership and mission in Catholic education and on particular commitments to the education of young women. In this section some indication is given about how these women school leaders personally experienced the strong patriarchal traditions and practices of Catholic culture and about what changes in this culture they believed to be necessary in the future.

The most distinctive responses on this subject were given by women religious sisters (or former sisters) who were in charge of ten of the schools (nine girls' schools, one mixed school). Among these sister headteachers there were some who believed that Catholic patriarchy must be challenged and, in the long term, changed:

> I think that schools are an expression of Church and certainly are responsible for the future of the Church … there's a contentious issue here, and I'm not even meant to discuss this, which is to do with the position of women in the Church and the fact that I am head of an all-girls school. What is the contribution that women can make to the future of the Church? How can they be involved in the priesthood in its broadest sense? It may well be that we need to change the theology of the priesthood.
>
> (Headteacher, Holy Rosary School)

> The Church has to listen to what women are saying and if it doesn't, it will die. If you go to any parish in this city, the majority of people who are attending the liturgy are women. What does that say about us as a church? I say to the pupils that if they see the Church (as patriarchal and authoritarian) they have to be part of it, to change it.
>
> (Headteacher, St Colette School)

> The priests are probably quite happy for a woman religious to be head of this school. I think they are nervous of secondary school girls anyway, but perceiving me as a strong headteacher is another thing. It might challenge some of their views. Strong women are often seen as being 'aggressive' by the clergy.
>
> (Headteacher, Sacred Heart of Mary School)

The sister–headteachers in this study generally projected a sense of confidence in their leadership role and, in some cases, an ability to be critical about aspects of the patriarchal culture of Catholicism. Their confidence arose partly from the fact that they were responsible for leadership in large urban schools with visible 'success' profiles and partly from their sense of wider support from the religious congregations of which they were members.[23] These were, in the main, strong (not aggressive!) women who experienced a relative sense of autonomy in the administration of their schools. A number of them remarked that while some Catholic priests had exercised undue authority over women primary school headteachers, this was a much less frequent occurrence at secondary school level. This situation also appeared to be the case in the schools of the fourteen lay women headteachers (seven girls' schools, six mixed schools, one boys' school). None of these headteachers raised issues of patriarchy in relationships or governance as constituting a serious problem for their educational leadership. No wider critique of the patriarchal traditions of the Catholic Church was forthcoming from this group. The only source of what might be called a feminist critique of the Church came from the interview discourse of some of the sister–headteachers.

Does this show that the women headteachers in this sample do not see the patriarchy of Catholicism as an important issue for educational discussion – or does it show that they have adopted a 'culture of silence' on patriarchy and Catholicism as ordained by the Pope?[24]

It was noted in Chapter 3 that one of the unintended consequences of a Catholic convent school education in the past had been the formation of a number of prominent feminists. Perhaps the existence of all-girls schools[25] (a Catholic tradition) headed up by strong women headteachers produces a situation in which a feminist consciousness will develop for some young women and for some headteachers despite (or perhaps because of) the strong patriarchal associations of Catholicism.

## Mission principles: the perspectives of students

If the spirituality, morality and justice commitments of Catholic schooling are strongly grounded upon a 'dignity of the person' principle, then the students in Catholic schools can be expected to experience this as a reality. As indicated in Chapter 5, a small-scale attempt to sample student opinions on this issue was undertaken in five inner-London schools. Focus-group discussions were held with two groups of five students in each school from Year 10 (14–15 years). The schools were asked to select five model students and strong school identifiers (informally called 'the saints') and five who were regarded as troublesome school resistors ('the sinners'). Given photocopies of their schools' mission statements they were asked to reflect upon the extent to which the principles proclaimed to the world had been realised in their own experience of Catholic schooling.[26]

The views portrayed here cannot be taken as definitive comments about the mission integrity of Catholic schools. They represent the perspectives of only fifty Year 10 students in five London secondary schools. However, they do raise issues which all Catholic schools engaged in self-evaluation of the practice of their mission principles might want to reflect upon.

With these limitations in mind, it can be noted that six themes emerged from the focus-group discussions with students, as follows.

### *Dignity of the person*

This principle, mentioned in most of the school mission statements, was endorsed as a reality by the majority of students. As might be expected, its existence was most positively celebrated by the 'saints':

> No-one is discriminated against because of gender, race, ability or religious experience ... We are taught to respect others.
>
> (Female student)

Nevertheless, even the 'saints' noted that the culture of respect for persons depended crucially upon teacher behaviour as well as student behaviour:

> Some teachers make it hard for you to respect them because of what they do and say.
>
> (Female student)

### *Forgiveness and justice*

There was more disagreement about the presence of these qualities in the practice of the schools. Given the complex nature of these concepts this is hardly surprising. While there was significant endorsement across the five schools that forgiveness and justice were real in the schools, the 'sinners' (perhaps by definition!) believed that the record was far from perfect:

> There is no justice. People get blamed for a lot of things they didn't do. I don't feel as if teachers have any faith in me.
>
> (Female student)

> Where it says (in the mission statement) 'being forgiving', I don't think that is true because I did a very bad thing in Year 7 and the Deputy Head still to this day holds it against me.
>
> (Female student)

> Once the school knows something about you, they will put you down – they will make your life hell.
>
> (Male student)

These comments can of course be dismissed as special pleading by known school 'sinners'. On the other hand, they may be evidence that it is easier to write 'forgiveness and justice' in the mission statements of

Catholic schools than to live it in the day-to-day tensions of school life in urban areas.

### *Racism*

In only two cases was some reference made by students to the presence of racism which undermined a 'dignity of the person' school ethos. These observations were countered in the majority of cases by students who spontaneously noted a multi-ethnic and multi-cultural harmony in their schools.

### *Bullying*

Only in one boys' school, St Lawrence, located in an area marked by an external gang culture and overt conflict in the community, was any reference made to bullying. Most students commented on the absence of bullying and the generally harmonious atmosphere in their schools.

### *Quality of teaching*

For many students, 'dignity of the person' had a very concrete realisation, i.e. they expected to receive good teaching, in well-organised classes, by teachers who obviously wanted them to be successful in their studies. The students believed that their schools' mission statements which referred to academic achievements were valid in their experience. They generally commended the commitment of their teachers and they were confident that they would be academically successful. Only at St Lawrence were negative comments made about the quality of teaching and this was attributed by the students to the school operating with a rapidly changing series of supply teachers.[27]

### *Catholicity*

In general the students spoke positively of their experience of Catholic religious teaching and liturgy in the schools. Once again, the exception to this was St Lawrence, where there were negative experiences. Seven students in other schools spontaneously argued that their schools should be more explicitly religious than they were:

> We should have more gathered Masses for the whole school, to reflect and pray.
>
> (Female student)

> We do have the traditions of the Catholic faith and I think we celebrate it well but we should pray more often and not only on main events.
>
> (Female student)

> I think what would make this a better school is if all the teachers were Catholic and we went to Mass more.
>
> (Male student)

> I think that the school could stress the Catholic Faith more by making sure that all pupils keep up the Faith.
>
> (Male student)

These comments came, as might be expected, from the schools' designated 'saints'.

In contrast to this, the 'sinners' provided other perspectives which suggested that a school ethos which was too religious and virtuous might be experienced as oppressive:

> The mission statement is not true about 'encouraging personal development' because this school wants you to be something you're not. It tries to make you a perfect person, even if you can't be one.
>
> (Male student)

> I was only baptised to get into this school and to please my Nan. I only go to church for weddings and funerals but apart from that it bores the brains out of me.
>
> (Female student)

This small project in listening to the student voice on matters of mission integrity in Catholic schooling gives some encouragement to those who argue that post-Vatican II Catholic schooling is living the mission in its day-to-day practice. However, more extensive and systematic research is required before mission integrity can be celebrated as a general feature of Catholic schooling.

## Overview

This has been the longest chapter in this book because it deals with those issues which Catholics claim are most distinctive of their schooling cultures. Issues of spirituality, Catholicity, morality and personal and social justice have been examined across the sixty schools from the perspectives of the headteachers and external inspectors, from state agencies and from Church agencies. From five schools in London, the perspectives of fifty senior students have also been examined.

In overall terms the picture which emerges has more positives than negatives on the issues considered. In other words, the mission integrity and distinctiveness of these schools appears to be relatively strong, given the challenges which they face in an a-religious and materialist society and given the specific urban dislocations which characterise many of the communities which they serve. Nevertheless, there is also the sense that their mission of spirituality, Catholicity, morality and justice is vulnerable. It is maintained by the professional and faith commitment of a particular generation of school leaders and teachers working with a strong conception of a lay vocation. Will this be maintained and renewed in the next generation?

It is maintained against the curriculum and assessment pressures and constraints of an interventionist secular state in education. Will such pressures work to undermine Catholic school distinctiveness in the future?

It is maintained in urban communities experiencing economic and social change, demographic change, change in family life and organisation and change in patterns of religious practice. As the resources of the institutional Church weaken in terms of priests, members of religious orders and cultural and economic capital, can Catholic schools sustain the educational mission to the urban poor?

The following chapter will reflect upon these issues and others generated by the research.

# 10 Catholic schools

## The renewal of spiritual capital and the critique of the secular world

Bourdieu (1986) has referred to three forms of capital which need to be considered in analysing any educational system, i.e. economic capital, whose effects are mediated by social class inequalities in the lives of students; social capital constituted in different access to supportive social networks; and cultural capital viewed as language, knowledge and 'style' differentially available to students in their homes. To this may be added, for the analysis of faith-based schooling systems, the concept of *spiritual capital*. Spiritual capital is defined here as *resources of faith and values derived from commitment to a religious tradition.*[1] Bourdieu argues that cultural capital is a power resource which can have an existence independently of economic capital[2] and this argument can be extended to include spiritual capital. Spiritual capital can be a source of empowerment because it provides a transcendent impulse which can guide judgement and action in the mundane world. Those within education whose own formation has involved the acquisition of spiritual capital do not act simply as professionals but as professionals and witnesses.

The Catholic schooling system internationally has benefited from the presence of significant spiritual capital among its school leaders. This leadership cadre has been recruited from priests, teaching Brothers and Sisters of various religious orders and from lay men and women who have acquired a sense of educational vocation through their own Catholic schooling and college experiences. In terms of the maintenance and enhancement of the Catholic educational mission, this cadre of leaders (despite the individual failings of some of its members) has been overall a powerful asset for the system – the animating spiritual capital of Catholic schooling.

This study has analysed the dilemmas arising for some Catholic secondary school leaders in urban areas in England as they face the contemporary challenges of mission, market and morality in rapidly changing conditions. Among the major challenges that have been highlighted are nurturing spirituality in the young against external pressure for secularism, hedonism and materialism; renewing and revivifying Catholicity to meet the needs of contemporary adolescents; mediating between the moral teachings of the institutional Church and the mores of youth culture; teaching the importance of personal and social justice and the dignity of the person; strengthening Catholic values of community, solidarity and the common good in the face of the imperialism of market values and competitive individualism in education; and holding to traditional Catholic concepts that academic success and empowerment are intended to be used in the service of others.

While variations in the responses to these challenges of the sixty schools have been demonstrated, what emerges overall is a recognition that the majority of these Catholic school leaders have drawn upon their resources of spiritual capital in discerning the way forward and in giving leadership on the educational policies and practices of their schools. Using their understanding of the fundamental principles of the Catholic faith and of its associated moral and value positions, the Catholic headteachers of this study have, in the main, attempted to maintain the mission integrity of Catholic schooling in the face of many external pressures which could compromise that integrity. The sources of their own spiritual capital have included the significant effects of their own secondary schooling and college experiences (the influence of religious orders being prominent), a family background of prayer and regular attendance at Mass, their own current prayer life and religious practice, and professional opportunities for development and reflection upon the spiritual context of Catholic schooling.

As this study has shown, future generations of school leaders and teachers in Catholic education are unlikely to benefit from this matrix of sources for spiritual capital. The reduced influence of the religious orders in schooling and in teacher formation and radical changes in the religious life of families have resulted in a weakening of this matrix. There is evidence[3] that many candidates for the headship of Catholic schools in England can now talk confidently about achievements in test scores and examinations, business planning and budgets, marketing and public relations, but are relatively inarticulate about the spiritual purposes of Catholic schooling. This is a major contradiction in a system of schooling which exists to give the nurture of spirituality a top priority and it demonstrates that the traditional spiritual capital of Catholic school leadership is a declining asset. This would not matter so much if extensive action for the renewal of such capital was being undertaken in courses and programmes offered by Catholic professional development agencies in England. However, there is little evidence yet that such provision is being made on the scale required by contemporary conditions.[4]

This study argues that the spiritual capital of the Catholic schooling system in England (and by implication elsewhere) is what has provided the dynamic drive of its mission in the past and helped it to preserve, in the main, its mission integrity in the challenges of the present. The renewal of its spiritual capital thus becomes the crucial question for the continuance of its *distinctive* mission in the future. This is a major conclusion of the research project.

'Transmission of the charism' is one way of speaking about and implementing the processes which are needed in Catholic education. A number of religious orders, e.g. the Jesuits, the Salesians, the De La Salle and the Christian Brothers, the Marists, the Sisters of Notre Dame, the Faithful Companions of Jesus and the Sisters of Mercy, have organised programmes for the spiritual formation of their lay successors as headteachers and teachers. However, there is also considerable scope for what may be called the *transmission of a lay charism* to a new generation of educators. Programmes using experienced or recently retired Catholic headteachers as mentors for new Catholic educators have much potential. With a specific focus upon the ways in which spirituality can relate to educational policy and practice, such programmes can be a valuable counter-cultural agenda to that provided by secular courses of headteacher 'training'. Such charism transmission now seems essential for the future of Catholic education.

It could be argued that a limitation of this research and of its conclusions regarding spiritual capital arises from its concentration upon school leadership roles, in particular those of headteachers. While headteachers in English Catholic schools are significant influences upon mission, ethos and effectiveness, they are only part of the larger enterprise of the Catholic school. The writer accepts that limitations of research resources have resulted in limitations of the analytical scope of this study. It is fully recognised that the resources of spiritual capital in Catholic schooling extend well beyond that possessed by individual headteachers. Spiritual capital is also constituted in school governing bodies, in classroom teachers, in priests and school chaplains, in parents and not least in the students themselves. A comprehensive analysis of the resources of spiritual capital in contemporary Catholic schooling would require examination of all these constituencies and of their future roles in spiritual regeneration. There have been indications during this research of the crucial importance of these other constituencies in the renewal of Catholic schooling. Among developments reported by headteachers as significant in the spiritual lives of the schools were the impact of Christian teachers of other denominations,[5] the importance of lay school chaplains and the contributions of senior students ready to take the leading role in the enhancement of the religious and spiritual programmes of the school. In other words, while the spiritual capital of Catholic schooling from traditional sources may be in decline there is some evidence that it is being renewed from other sources, when these sources are used creatively.

Wilson (1999), in his analysis of the decline of religious certainty in Europe, nevertheless concludes his influential book *God's Funeral* with the observation that 'the immense strength of the Catholic idea played a demonstrable role in the collapse of the Soviet Communist system' (p. 354). If the great challenge to Catholicism in the past, i.e. that of communist atheism with imperialist intentions, has declined, a new challenge and a new imperialism has emerged, i.e. that of global capitalist values. Soros (1999) has charted the nature of this new cultural and economic imperialism and has concluded 'that market values have assumed an importance at the present moment in history that is way beyond what is appropriate and sustainable' (p. 46).

Usher and Edwards (1994, p. 175), in their study of the effects of globalisation upon education, have argued that national objectives in education will soon be limited to 'fulfilling the requirements of the economy under conditions of global competition'. However, what is remarkable about the growing literature on globalisation and education, including the work of Usher and Edwards (1994), Green (1997) and others, is that the role of religion is generally ignored. The fact that world-based religions such as Catholic Christianity and Islam are international power sources which have missions other than those of economic globalisation appears to be marginalised in the globalisation analyses and debates. This is yet another example of the effects of secular marginalisation upon contemporary intellectual culture which this book hopes to challenge. There can be no comprehensive understanding of the economic, social and cultural effects of globalisation which does not take fully into account the countervailing influences of major religious cultures and organisations.

One of the countervailing institutions against the hegemony of market materialism, individual competitiveness and commodity worship is the Catholic Church and its various agencies internationally. Among these, Catholic schools are crucial in the contemporary struggle for the formation of young people and for the shaping of their consciousness.[6] Such schools strive to renew a culture of spirituality, virtue and service to the common good in an increasingly materialist and individualistic global market.

In *Religion and the Secular City* Cox (1984, pp. 170–1) made the prescient observation that:

> If freedom once required a secular critique of religion, it can also require a religious critique of the secular.[7]

The very existence of Catholic schools and indeed of all faith-based schools constitutes part of the religious critique of the secular, without which both culture and freedom would be diminished.

# Appendix 1

## Research school details

*Table A1.1* Archdiocese of St Anthony and Archdiocese of St Thomas

| *School* | *Size* | *Gender* | *FSM (%)★* | *GCSE (%)★★* | *Catholic pupils (%)* | *Catholic teachers (%)* |
|---|---|---|---|---|---|---|
| St Eugene | 620 | Girls | 57 | 32 | 56 | 58 |
| St Stephen, Martyr | 250 | Mixed | 45 | 9 | 33 | 42 |
| Carthusian Martyrs | 1,100 | Mixed | 44 | 32 | 85 | 47 |
| Mary, Mother of God | 900 | Girls | 47 | 60 | 99 | 50 |
| Bishop Anselm | 1,030 | Girls | 54 | 43 | 75 | 50 |
| St Alphonsus | 970 | Boys | 43 | 25 | 90 | 66 |
| Holy Angels | 530 | Girls | 51 | 49 | 90 | 50 |
| St Lawrence | 673 | Boys | 55 | 21 | 55 | 52 |
| St John Fisher | 590 | Mixed | 40 | 46 | 100 | 65 |
| St Lazarus | 570 | Mixed | 64 | 18 | 80 | 33 |
| St Margaret Mary | 560 | Girls | 30 | 53 | 98 | 50 |
| Holy Rosary | 750 | Girls | 23 | 69 | 100 | 70 |
| St Joan of Arc | 1,050 | Girls | 20 | 67 | 100 | 66 |
| Pope Pius XII | 790 | Boys | 13 | 85 | 100 | 70 |
| Pope Paul III | 1,150 | Boys | 10 | 60 | 100 | 60 |
| St Francis | 1,062 | Boys | 22 | 63 | 85 | 70 |
| St Vincent | 790 | Boys | 36 | 34 | 90 | 50 |
| Sacred Heart of Mary | 600 | Girls | 27 | 47 | 100 | 58 |
| Holy Family | 600 | Girls | 28 | 64 | 100 | 70 |
| St Gabriel | 918 | Mixed | 33 | 48 | 94 | 80 |
| Corpus Christi | 586 | Mixed | 50 | 32 | 90 | 33 |

*Table A1.1* Continued

| *School* | *Size* | *Gender* | *FSM (%)★* | *GCSE (%)★★* | *Catholic pupils (%)* | *Catholic teachers (%)* |
|---|---|---|---|---|---|---|
| St Mark | 610 | Mixed | 47 | 40 | 100 | 66 |
| St Matthew | 724 | Boys | 50 | 53 | 85 | 50 |
| St Patrick | 485 | Mixed | 35 | 49 | 95 | 51 |
| St Sebastian | 500 | Boys | 45 | 18 | 70 | 40 |
| St Peter Damian | 640 | Boys | 35 | 28 | 90 | 60 |
| St Genevieve | 770 | Girls | 36 | 36 | 82 | 60 |
| Pope Pius VII | 920 | Boys | 7 | 50 | 95 | 80 |
| Holy Redeemer | 980 | Mixed | n/a | n/a | 70 | 50 |
| St Bernard | 1,100 | Mixed | n/a | n/a | 65 | 50 |

*Note*: These are the 'Research Names' of the schools and *not* the actual names.

★ Free school meals entitlement

★★ General Certificate of Secondary Education, A★–C passes

*Table A1.2* Archdiocese of St Robert

| *School* | *Size* | *Gender* | *FSM (%)*★ | *GCSE (%)*★★ | *Catholic pupils (%)* | *Catholic teachers (%)* |
|---|---|---|---|---|---|---|
| Holy Disciples | 670 | Girls | 60 | 29 | 85 | 70 |
| St Monica | 1,150 | Girls | 32 | 54 | 100 | 50 |
| St Jude | 278 | Mixed | 71 | 6 | 95 | 75 |
| Our Lady of Lourdes | 1,100 | Girls | 62 | 26 | 98 | 75 |
| St Robert Bellarmine | 720 | Mixed | 55 | 26 | 98 | 80 |
| St Rita | 339 | Mixed | 71 | 6 | 92 | 60 |
| St Finbarr | 830 | Mixed | 36 | 29 | 87 | 60 |
| St James | 800 | Mixed | 51 | 16 | 90 | 80 |
| St Flannan | 562 | Boys | 76 | 3 | 85 | 53 |
| St Richard | 960 | Boys | 47 | 20 | 99 | 75 |
| St Anthony of Padua | 1,197 | Mixed | 35 | 21 | 99 | 65 |
| St Brendan | 1,357 | Boys | 58 | 26 | 90 | 65 |
| Holy Cross | 1,466 | Mixed | 22 | 42 | 99 | 52 |
| English Martyrs | 426 | Mixed | 42 | 10 | 90 | 67 |
| St Dominic | 620 | Mixed | 67 | 23 | 90 | 60 |
| Cardinal Hume | 1,160 | Boys | 38 | 28 | 99 | 68 |
| St Colette | 1,130 | Girls | 25 | 54 | 100 | 80 |
| St Pius X | 1,210 | Boys | 21 | 46 | 100 | 70 |
| St Helena | 1,108 | Girls | 48 | 39 | 95 | 73 |
| St Claire | 889 | Mixed | 43 | 27 | 90 | 80 |

*Note*: These are the 'Research Names' of the schools and *not* the actual names.

★ Free school meals entitlement

★★ General Certificate of Secondary Education, A★–C passes

*Table A1.3* Archdiocese of St James

| *School* | *Size* | *Gender* | *FSM (%)★* | *GCSE (%)★★* | *Catholic pupils (%)* | *Catholic teachers (%)* |
|---|---|---|---|---|---|---|
| St Ciaran | 950 | Mixed | 34 | 24 | 99 | 50 |
| St Bede | 580 | Mixed | 46 | 36 | 50 | 45 |
| St Cyril | 880 | Mixed | 35 | 38 | 50 | 60 |
| St Clement | 926 | Mixed | 10 | 61 | 95 | 52 |
| St Basil | 1,300 | Mixed | 25 | 44 | 88 | 63 |
| St Martin de Porres | 620 | Mixed | 50 | 25 | 33 | 60 |
| Ascension | 620 | Mixed | 60 | 33 | 51 | 53 |
| Epiphany | 1,230 | Mixed | 33 | 33 | 100 | 90 |
| St John of the Cross | 460 | Mixed | 60 | 10 | 35 | 40 |
| St Scholastica | 950 | Girls | 20 | 70 | 99 | 53 |

*Note*: These are the 'Research Names' of the schools and *not* the actual names.

★ Free school meals entitlement

★★ General Certificate of Secondary Education, A★–C passes

# Appendix 2

## Headteacher interview schedule

Catholic secondary schools in urban areas: contemporary challenges and responses

This interview schedule, covering twelve areas for discussion, was sent to the participating headteachers in advance of the actual interview. It was pointed out that the twelve areas were a suggested agenda and that the participants could add to or delete from the list as they judged appropriate. It was emphasised that the interview was intended to be a dialogue based upon an agreed list of strategic issues.

Area 1 Your own Catholic and professional background and view of schooling; conceptions of mission and leadership.
Area 2 Socio-economic context of the school and local reputation: pupil characteristics, e.g. free school meals, % Catholic, ethnicity, etc.
Area 3 Mission statement of the school; progress and problems.
Area 4 Academic results, value-added profile, OFSTED reports, admission arrangements.
Area 5 Spiritual, moral and social development; inspection reports and evaluations.
Area 6 Catholic ethos and nature of Catholicity; chaplaincy, percentage of Catholic teachers.
Area 7 Discipline and pupil exclusions; trends.
Area 8 Market forces in education; competition and collaboration; relationships with other schools.
Area 9 Relations with governors, LEA, parishes, parents, diocese.
Area 10 Finances, resources and local management of schools.
Area 11 Distinctive pressures on Catholic headteachers.
Area 12 Reforms needed to assist the mission of Catholic schools in urban areas.

# Appendix 3
## Headteacher details

*Table A3.1*

| *Archdiocese* | *Men* | *Women* | *Years of experience* | | *Lay* | *Religious* |
|---|---|---|---|---|---|---|
| | | | *Less than 5* | *More than 5* | | |
| St Anthony & St Thomas | 16 | 14 | 14 | 16 | 25 | 5 |
| St Robert | 13 | 7 | 8 | 12 | 14 | 6 |
| St James | 7 | 3 | 2 | 8 | 9 | 1 |

Twelve headteachers were members of religious orders drawn from:

The Society of Jesus
The Sisters of Mercy
The Sisters of Notre Dame (two)
The Salesian Sisters of Don Bosco (two)
The Salesian Fathers of Don Bosco
The Brothers of Christian Instruction
The Faithful Companions of Jesus (two)
The Congregation of La Sainte Union
The Sisters of Charity of St Paul

Three headteachers were former members of religious orders drawn from:

The Society of the Sacred Heart
The Christian Brothers
The De La Salle Brothers

# Notes

## Introduction

1 One example of this is the amount of attention that Catholic schools are now receiving in the British media as a result of their relative academic success and high placements in the league tables of examination and test achievements.
2 This would be the case, for instance, for Catholic schools in Africa and in India.
3 Archbishop Pittau (2000), Secretary of the Vatican Congregation for Catholic Education, has recently pointed to the extensive nature of Catholic school provision worldwide, including as it does 84,000 primary/elementary schools and 34,000 secondary/high schools operating in a wide range of socio-economic and cultural settings and serving almost 50 million students internationally. Given the global nature of the Catholic educational mission it is remarkable how little attention it has received from educational researchers.

## 1 The Catholic school: the sacred and the secular

1 See Morris (1994, 1998a, 1998b) and Catholic Education Service (1995a).
2 Arthur (1995, p. 119) notes that: 'As recently as March 1989 the Association of Metropolitan Authorities passed a resolution which found voluntary aided schools "damaging" to the interests of education in some localities'. Some radical Labour councils in London and Liverpool were hostile to the existence of Catholic schools on ideological grounds, despite the fact that many Catholics were Labour voters.
3 The title of Hornsby-Smith's early study, *Catholic Education; The Unobtrusive Partner* (1978), conveys a sense of the marginality of the Catholic sector in the 1960s and 1970s in educational policy terms.
4 See Grace (1998b).
5 Quoted in Durkheim (1971, pp. 24–5). This was first published in 1912
6 Ibid, p. 422.
7 Ibid., p. 415.
8 Ibid, p. 419.
9 See Thatcher (1993, p. 626). In this infamous assertion Margaret Thatcher demonstrated a form of aggressive individualism totally at odds with the principles of Catholic religious and social teaching.

10 It should be made clear that Durkheim was commenting upon the role of religion in the societies which he studied. His own personal stance was secular and he looked forward to the time when the idea of society would replace that of religion and the church as a unifying social and moral force.

11 Quoted in Arthur (1995, p. 15).

12 Ibid, p. 34.

13 For the uneasy relation between English Catholicism and the Irish, see Hickman (1995).

14 See McClelland (1962) and Selby (1974).

15 The mission of leadership for upper- and middle-class Catholic youth was particularly evident in the educational work of the Benedictines, the Dominicans, the Jesuits, the Society of the Sacred Heart, The Institute of the Blessed Virgin Mary and the Ladies of Mary, among others.

16 In the provision of Catholic grammar schools many religious orders were involved, including (for boys) The Christian Brothers, The De La Salle Brothers, the Franciscans, the Jesuits, the Oratorians, the Marists, the Salesians and the Xaverians, and (for girls) the Faithful Companions of Jesus, the Dominican Sisters, the Sisters of Notre Dame, the Sisters of St Paul, the Sisters of La Retraite and the Ursulines, among others. Many of the headteachers interviewed later in this study had received their secondary education and spiritual formation in schools run by these orders.

17 For a similar argument see Abbs (1995).

18 From a secular perspective, religious ideas cannot be accepted as a revelation of truth from a divine source but rather as an ideology in the service of religious interest groups. It should be noted however that Hirst does not utilise the concept of ideology in his writings.

19 In the last instance, the protection of notions of intellectual integrity and of the relative autonomy of the learner is a major responsibility of education professionals in all categories of school and college. Whether external conditions allow them to exercise that responsibility is another matter.

20 'Hidden curriculum' refers to the ways in which school ethos, organisation and practice educate pupils in addition to the outcomes of the formal taught and visible curriculum.

21 For an important discussion of concepts of indoctrination, see Snook (1972) and Astley (1994). Astley points out that until this century, indoctrination had the neutral meaning of teaching or instruction. It acquired pejorative associations later. In a pejorative sense, it has frequently been applied to Catholic education, implying that it has been a process for the imprinting of the mind with dogma and catechism. Given the large number of lapsed Catholics in contemporary society this suggests that the idea of Catholic indoctrination is not true, or if true, has not been very effective.

22 See, for instance, Winter (1985).

23 For a review of available studies, see Chapter 4.

24 See Mayer (1929) and Donlon (1952). For a valuable recent collection of the writings of Thomas Aquinas, see McInerny (1998), and for new reflections upon his continuing relevance for education see Arthur *et al.* (1999).

25 Writing of 'some consequences of the failure of the Enlightenment Project', MacIntyre (1981) argues that

> the problems of modern moral theory emerge clearly as the product of the failure of the Enlightenment project. On the one hand the

> individual moral agent, freed from hierarchy and teleology, conceives of himself and is conceived of by moral philosophers as sovereign in his moral authority. On the other hand the inherited, if partially transformed rules of morality have to be found a new status, deprived as they have been of their older teleological character and their even more ancient categorical character as expressions of an ultimately divine law. If such rules cannot be found a new status which will make appeal to them rational, appeal to them will indeed appear as a mere instrument of individual desire and will.
>
> (p. 62)

The implication of MacIntyre's argument is that secular rules of morality have failed to find a new status (comparable with the 'will of God') and that therefore a state of moral anomie in modern society has resulted.

26 Taylor's major text, *Sources of the Self*, argues for the necessity of an ontological basis for ethics and morality: 'one or another ontology is in fact the only adequate basis for our moral responses, whether we recognise this or not. A thesis of this kind was invoked by Dostoyevsky and discussed by Leszek Kolakowski in a recent work: "If God does not exist, then everything is permitted"' (p. 10).

27 See Flannery A (1998, pp. 725–37).

28 See, for instance, the accounts of Catholic schooling in Chapter 3.

29 Catholic schools for Catholics only had been the cultural norm of the pre-Vatican II era in the USA, the UK and Ireland, Australia and in Europe, although in 'mission countries' in Africa, India and Asia in general, the Church recognised that Catholic pupils might be a minority of the school population. The principle of openness articulated in post-Vatican II documents was more radical. The *Catholic School* document (1977) under the heading 'Openness to non-Christians' argued that: 'In the certainty that the Spirit is at work in every person, the Catholic school offers itself to all, non-Christians included …' (p. 66). This principle of openness has been repeated in the most recent statement of the Vatican Congregation for Catholic Education (1998, p. 44): '[The Catholic school] fulfils a service of public usefulness and although clearly and decidedly configured in the perspective of the Catholic faith is not reserved to Catholics only, but is open to all those who appreciate and share its qualified educational project'.

30 The principle of 'working for the common good' has a long Catholic history emanating from the writings of St Thomas Aquinas, mediated by Catholic philosophers such as Maritain and expressed in various modern documents of the Church.

31 For an account of this research, see Chapter 4.

32 Pope John Paul quoted in Carr (1999, p. 173).

33 The act of discernment is central to the *Spiritual Exercises* of St Ignatius Loyola. Letson and Higgins (1995, p. 110) argue that the spirit of discernment 'in effect means the capacity to see with lucid self-knowledge what is necessary to be done'. This is obviously a quality needed by contemporary Catholic educators.

34 The 1998 document notes a reductionist tendency in educational policy and discourse: 'there has also been a noticeable tendency to reduce education to its purely technical and practical aspects' (p. 40).

35 The inspiration to do this came from Durkheim's (1977, p. 26) perceptive observation: 'From their origins, the schools carried within themselves the germ of that great struggle between the sacred and the profane, the secular and the religious'.

## 2 The field of Catholic education: perspectives from Bourdieu and Bernstein

1 In addition to Harker's (1990) collection of essays on Bourdieu, valuable reviews are given in Swartz (1997) and in Grenfell and James (1998).
2 See, for instance, Duffy (1997) on popes and anti-popes. A recent study by Collins (1997) traces the struggles between papal monarchism and a collegial view of authority within the Catholic Church.
3 Two studies were particularly influential at this time, i.e. Greeley and Rossi (1966) and Greeley *et al.* (1976). In particular, the conclusions of Greeley and Rossi (1966, p. 85) were widely quoted: 'We can go so far as to say that for all practical purposes the religious impact of Catholic education is limited to those who come from highly religious families.'

Later research cast doubt upon these conclusions and by 1989 Greeley had revised his views on the religious effectiveness of Catholic schools. For a useful review of the issues see Fahy (1992).
4 Swartz (1997, p. 92).
5 Kenneth Baker, Secretary of State for Education, quoted in Chadwick (1997, pp. 54–5).
6 Grant-maintained status for schools was a strategy introduced by Conservative governments in England to allow schools to become (after a parental ballot) independent of the local education authority, and in a direct funding relation with the state. The policy involved, in its early stages, considerable financial inducements to become, in Margaret Thatcher's phrase, 'state-independent schools'. Such a strategy for Catholic schools was problematic for the Catholic hierarchy on both political and moral grounds. The political dilemma was that Catholic GM schools might become too independent of the hierarchy and of diocesan administration and policy. The moral dilemma was that the extra resources to establish individual GM schools might be at the expense of the larger community of Catholic schools or of other schools in the locality and contrary to notions of the common good.
7 See, for instance, the Catholic Education Service, *A Response to the White Paper*, 24 September 1992, p. 7: 'We do not in principle oppose increased independence and self-management for schools. However, the GM option is more than this. It intensifies financial and curricular inequalities between schools and creates new inequalities. It also supposes that schools derive their strength from their own autonomy, without any sense of having a wider responsibility (the common good).' For an earlier discussion of these issues, see Grace (1995).
8 Quoted in Arthur (1995, p. 149).
9 This was explicitly stated by Pope John Paul II in an address to the Catholic Bishops of England and Wales in 1988: 'Everyone involved in the provision and management of Catholic schools is required to cooperate under the leadership of the bishops so that these schools may fulfil their mission both now and in the future. For some people this will mean the sacrifice of

personal preferences in favour of the common good' (quoted in Hume 1989, p. 355).

10 See 'Vaughan Deadlock Resolved', in *Briefing 89*, Vol. 19, No. 17, p. 359.

11 Swartz (1997, p. 213).

12 See Swartz (1997, pp. 114–16) for a discussion of the distinctions between culture and habitus. Bourdieu stresses that habitus is a way of 'conceptualising culture as practice'.

13 The habitus generated by Jesuit pedagogy is described in detail in Durkheim's classic text *The Evolution of Educational Thought* (1977, pp. 227–64). For English Jesuit schools and colleges, see Roberts (1996). Literary and autobiographical accounts are given in Hastings (1970) and in Joyce (1985).

14 Burgess (1983, p. 49) notes that 'there was evidence of divisions and of different schools being created on one site'.

15 This chapter has examined Bourdieu's elaboration of the concept of habitus. However, it should be noted that earlier writers had used the concept in analysing Christian education. For instance, Durkheim (1977, p. 29) noted that: 'Christianity was aware that the forming of a man was not a question of decorating his mind with certain ideas, nor of getting him to contract certain specific habits: it is a question of creating within him a general disposition of the mind ... Christianity consists essentially in a certain attitude of the soul, in a certain *habitus* of our moral being. To nurture this attitude in the child will thus henceforth be the essential aim of education.'

16 Note, however, the work of Swope (1992) in his pioneering study of base Christian communities in Chile which used concepts derived from Bernstein.

17 The now widespread discourse of curriculum 'delivery' is one of the clearest indicators of commodification in education.

18 Bernstein (1996, p. 20).

19 Bernstein (1996, p. 27).

20 Ibid.

21 See Walsh (1983) and Davis (1999).

22 Bernstein (1990, p. 86).

23 Honourable exceptions to this may be found in the work of Andrew Greeley, Anthony Bryk and Joseph O'Keefe in the USA, in the work of Michael Hornsby-Smith and Bernadette O'Keeffe in the UK, and in the work of Lawrence Angus and Patrick Fahy in Australia.

24 For a variety of applications in other fields, see Grenfell and James (1998).

## 3 Images of Catholic schooling: pre-Vatican II

1 As Fardon (1999, p. 104) remarks: '*Natural symbols* is a defence, both passionate and reasoned, of the importance of ritual to social life.'

2 Working-class accounts of the experience of Catholic schooling tend to appear in autobiographical/novel forms such as Frank McCourt's *Angela's Ashes*, Seamus Deane's *Reading in the Dark*, Billy Hopkins' *Our Kid* and Michael Carson's *Sucking Sherbert Lemons.*

3 All biblical quotations are taken from the *Ignatius Revised Standard Version, Catholic Edition, 1966.*

4 The words of this traditional Catholic hymn capture the dominating patriarchal habitus of pre-Vatican II Catholicism. Much was made of 'Faith of our Fathers', whereas in many Catholic homes it was 'Faith of our Mothers' which kept Catholic practice alive.

5 See, for instance, Billy Hopkins' account in *Our Kid*: 'the rote learning and memorisation of the Penny Catechism continued unabated and Miss Eager employed every method she knew, from persuasion, bribery and pleading to unbridled use of the strap, in order to cram Catholic doctrine into her pupils' unwilling heads. "Which are the four sins crying to heaven for vengeance?" she asked one day. "Wilful murder" said Stan White … "Sin of Sodom" said Joey Flewitt. "Please miss, what is the Sin of Sodom?" "Never you mind" said Miss Eager, blushing. "What's the third, Campbell?" "Oppression of the poor" replied Campbell, whose family was on the means test. "Defrauding labourers of their wages is the fourth" said Henry Sykes' (pp. 177–8).

6 For an example of this argument, see Hitchcock (1995).

7 Warner (1990, p. xxi) gives one example of this sense of struggle for purity: 'The price the Virgin demanded was purity and the way the educators of Catholic children have interpreted this, for nearly two thousand years, is sexual chastity. Impurity, we were taught, follows from many sins, but all are secondary to the principal impulse of the devil in the soul – lust.'

8 A very powerful denunciation of Catholicism's association with right-wing, racist and fascist regimes is given in the reflective account of Francis Pound (Sullivan 1996, p. 87) in the New Zealand Oral History collection: 'In my university years I was involved with anti-Vietnam protests and found that the views of the official Church … were on the side of the right wing … I remember Bishop Liston denying priests who had spoken out against the Vietnam war, the right to preach. From that moment I knew that the Church was on the side of reaction … One only has to think of the church's attitudes to homosexuality, abortion, contraception and women … I can't get out of my mind that the Vatican signed a concordat with the Italian fascists and that Pope Pius did not condemn Nazi genocide of the Jews, gypsies, homosexuals or leftists … The Catholic Church was always, and still is in places … revoltingly anti-Semitic. Without the age-old Christian persecution of the Jews there would have been no mass murder of six million Jews in our century.'

9 A similar point is made by Marina Warner in her 1991 reflective account: 'If you look at the history of Catholic thinking, this emphasis on the tremendous sinfulness of the flesh can be laid at Augustine's door. It is one of the tragedies of history that Augustine prevailed to the extent that he did … Many theories were produced (about evil). To put it crudely, Augustine's was that the root of all evil was concupiscence and that woman was the inspiration of this concupiscence. Like Eve, woman moves man to sin.'

10 See Calvez and Perrin (1961, p. 138).

11 Calvez and Perrin (1961, pp. 114–15) comment on 'the pre-eminence of the common good' in Catholic social teaching.

12 A number of reflective accounts make reference to the convent school cult of St Maria Goretti, martyred at 16 in defence of her virginity.

13 From the Litany of Our Lady, quoted in Tolerton (1994, p. 24).

14 The Baltimore catechism of 1885 had, for instance, this sequence:

Q571 How do you show that Protestant Churches have not the marks of the true Church?

A Protestant churches have not the marks of the true Church because (1) They are not one either in government or faith, for they have no chief head and they profess different beliefs; (2) They are not holy, because their doctrines are founded on error and lead to evil consequences: (3) They are not catholic or universal in time, place or doctrine. They have not existed in all ages nor in all places … etc.

15 Quoted in Gwynn, D. (1950) 'The Irish Immigration', in G. A. Beck (ed.) *The English Catholics, 1850–1950*, London: Burns & Oates, p. 266.

16 It is significant that Cardinal Manning wrote in 1890: 'The million of Irish Catholics in England are not only alienated from our laws and legislation but would upset the ink-bottle over the Statute Book. So long as this habit of mind lasts we shall never have a Civil priesthood; and so long as our priesthood is not Civil it will be confined to the sacristry … by our own incapacity to mix in the Civil life of the country' (quoted in Gwynn 1950, pp. 266–7 op. cit.).

17 For a powerful account of the experience of a pre-Vatican II Catholic education in the USA, see McCarthy's (1963) account, *Memories of a Catholic Girlhood*. This includes the classic passage about the existence of God: '"My child" he said gravely, "do you doubt the existence of God?" "Yes" I breathed in exultant agony, knowing that it was true … Very gently, seeing that this was what I seemed to want of him, he recited for me the five a posteriori proofs of God's existence: the argument of the unmoved Mover, the argument of efficient causes, the argument of the Necessary Being implied by contingent beings, the argument of graduated perfections, the argument of the wonderful order and design in the universe … The gist was clear to me. It was that every effect must have a cause and the cause was, of course, God. The universe could not exist unless some self-sufficient Being had created it and put it in motion … "Why, Father" I asked finally "does everything have to have a cause? Why couldn't the universe just be there, causing itself?"' (pp. 104–5).

## 4 Catholic schools post-Vatican II: a review of research studies

1 It is recognised that there are many 'minor studies' in the form of unpublished doctoral and masters' theses on various aspects of Catholic education. For bibliographic collections of these, see Traviss (1989) and Hunt (1998) for the USA and Atherton and Grace (1999) for the UK and Ireland.

2 As O'Keefe (1999a, p. 361) notes, with a Catholic population of 60 million the USA has 8,233 Catholic schools and 235 higher education institutions.

3 The phrase 'preferential option for the poor' originated from the Conference of Latin American Bishops at Medellín in 1968. This principle was a rearticulation and reformulation of an historical commitment by the Catholic Church to the service of the poor – see Dorr (1983). For an extended discussion of its contemporary implications, see Vallely (1998).

4 The designation of Catholic schools in the USA as 'private' arises from the fact that they are not state supported and therefore have to charge admission fees. However, the connotations of 'private', at least in the UK, with

elite, high-status pupil populations, does not apply, in general, to American Catholic schools.

5 See Fahy (1992, pp. 67–70).

6 The issue of what proportion of Catholic pupils is necessary to maintain a 'Catholic ethos' in a school is one that is constantly debated in the Catholic education community. In general, in the UK, it is thought to be unwise to allow the proportion of Catholic pupils to go below 50 per cent. However, there are very different attitudes to this question in the international settings of Catholic education and in relation to internal contexts, e.g. inner-city locations.

7 See Greeley (1982, p. 108): 'The success of Catholic schools with the multiply disadvantaged is the single most important finding in the present research.'

8 It can be argued that many religious orders bring with them a cultural capital of bookishness and disciplined use of time and that these qualities help to constitute the habitus of the schools under their control.

9 See Bryk *et al.* (1993, p. 337): 'Despite often heroic efforts by individual Catholic religious and laypeople, inner-city Catholic schools are closing at an alarming rate. This trend, first noticed in the late 1960s, shows no sign of abating.'

10 McLaren (1993, p. 253) calls for more study of and understanding of the role of ritual in Catholic schooling: 'The quality of our everyday rituals, including, if not especially, our classrooms rituals, is critically important and needs realistic and sensitive consideration, especially in terms of ritual's relationship to the learning process'. See Lesko (1988) for an empirical study of ritual in one Catholic school.

11 Paulo Freire, writing as a Professor of Education at the Catholic University of Sao Paulo, Brazil, argued that a new form of 'church' was emergent in Latin America and with it new forms of Catholic organisation and action. The 'Prophetic Church' (as opposed to the traditional or the modernising church) had the potential to provide an education for liberation and for justice. See Freire (1984).

12 Their conclusion that the result of the research 'dictates abandonment of the myth of public schools as integrative and equalizing, while private schools are segregative and unequalizing' (p. 197) was particularly provocative.

13 For an elaboration of the concept *social capital*, see Coleman (1988).

14 The relatively small size of Catholic secondary schools when compared with state/public secondary schools appears to be a crucial factor in helping to explain their general possession of a strong internal sense of community and a distinctive ethos. Bryk *et al.* (1993, pp. 75–6) noted for the USA that: 'The average Catholic high school enrolls 546 students, the average public school has 845 students … The major difference between the sectors is the relative absence of large Catholic secondary schools. Over 85 per cent of Catholic secondary schools enroll fewer than 900 students. In the public sector however 40 per cent of the schools have enrollments greater than 900.'

15 See Bryk *et al.* (1993, p. 378): 'We agree with Coleman that Catholic high schools benefit from a form of social capital, but we locate that capital in the relations among school professionals and with their parent communities.'

16 Students' religious and moral maturity as arising from their Catholic education can be expected to show itself in the maturing of their discourse on religious and moral matters. Qualitative methods which involve the recording and analysis of this discourse seem likely to give us greater insight than the ticked categories of questionnaires.
17 Callery (1998, p. 82) notes that: 'Catholic schools are at present attempting to develop a culture which includes educating their children about the history of racism in Australia and the consequences of this racism for Aboriginal Australian and Torres Strait Islanders'. This is clearly an important focus for future research studies in Australia.
18 See Naylor (2000).
19 Perhaps stung by this claim, the Catholic Bishops' Conference of England and Wales published an important policy statement on Catholic education in 1997 under the title *The Common Good in Education* and also in 1997, the Catholic Education Service published a collection of addresses by Catholic bishops on issues affecting Catholic education. See *Partners in Mission* (1997b).
20 However, it must be noted that fifth-year pupils were under particular examination pressures and this may account for their perceptions.
21 For another example of this, in relation to Poland, see Litak and Tulasiewicz (1988).
22 Quoted in Chadwick (1994, p. 147).
23 For another important discussion of the issues related to Northern Ireland, see Sutherland (1988).
24 See *A Struggle for Excellence: Catholic Secondary Schools in Urban Poverty Areas* (1997a), a research study commissioned by the Catholic Bishops' Conference in which Bernadette O'Keeffe played a leading role.
25 For a discussion of this issue in relation to Catholic schools in the USA, see O'Keefe (2000).
26 Quoted in *The Church and Racism* (1989, pp. 14–15).
27 See, for instance, Hogan and Williams (1997).
28 For a listing of research theses on Catholic education in Ireland see Atherton and Grace (1999).
29 See, for instance, Cariola (1971) and Richmond (1988). At the Fourth General Conference of Latin American Bishops (Santo Domingo, 1992), the bishops reaffirmed their commitment to the 'preferential option for the poor' in education and called for more public financing in support of the Catholic schooling system in Latin America.

## 6 Mission and leadership: concepts and challenges

1 Two of the participating institutions were Catholic sixth form colleges. To preserve their identities they are referred to in the following chapters as 'schools'.
2 See Bendix (1969, ch. X) for a full discussion of charismatic leadership and influence.
3 Quoted in Flannery (1998, p. 685).
4 For one example of this, see the journal of Catholic education *Networking, Catholic Education Today* Vol. 2, No. 1, September/October 2000.
5 See Badger (2000) for an example of this type of case study, although the focus for this study was a joint Anglican–Catholic secondary school.

6 The problematic nature of this judgement is fully recognised by the researcher. The judgement is based upon the extent to which headteachers conveyed a sense of committed endorsement (or nominal endorsement) of faith leadership during the course of the interview. Some headteachers may be more fluent at 'faith' presentation of self than others.

7 As Beck (1998, p. 7) notes, 'Her Majesty's Chief Inspector of Schools, Chris Woodhead, has seemed not merely to be deaf to those whose views differ from his own but increasingly to revel in a posture of intransigence.'

8 'Performativity', according to Lyotard (1984), refers to a generalised use in modern states of technicist and reductionist measures when evaluating the outcomes of institutions and policies.

9 Groome (1998, pp. 242–3) makes important distinctions between the authority of tradition within Catholicism and 'tradition as authoritarian', preventing individuals from thinking for themselves. Both of these elements have been present in Catholic culture.

10 Davies (1994, p. 1) warns against the emergence of new forms of authoritarianism in contemporary education arising from the effects of market culture and certain forms of managerialism.

11 It must be made clear that the analysis is based upon what the headteachers *said* about their conceptions of school leadership. Whether these constructs were realised in the day-to-day practice of the headteachers cannot be confirmed. As one of the headteachers observed about her own leadership style, 'you should ask the teachers'. This entirely correct suggestion for research triangulation could not be undertaken because of resource limitations.

12 The general or secular literature on school leadership makes much of the importance of 'purposeful' leadership. The Catholic version of this might be more specifically expressed as mission-focused leadership.

13 This group of ten represented the religious and educational charisms of the Faithful Companions of Jesus (two), La Sainte Union (one), Sisters of Notre Dame (two), Sisters of Mercy (one), Salesian Sisters (two), Society of the Sacred Heart (one) and Sisters of St Paul (one).

14 This was true for twelve of the twenty-four women in the sample. For men, fifteen out of thirty-six adopted a clearly collegial leadership discourse.

15 The emphasis on the importance of education for girls was linked to the traditions of particular religious orders of women, e.g. Sisters of Notre Dame, Society of the Sacred Heart.

16 It is accepted that other headteachers (men and women) may have been fully committed to educational opportunities for girls without explicitly stating this during the interviews. Reference is made here to those who particularly emphasised a commitment to the education of girls in explaining their own sense of mission in schooling.

## 7 The use of talents: Catholic theories of academic 'success' or 'failure'

* It will be apparent to the reader that this chapter has benefited from a critical reading by Professor Harvey Goldstein. The responsibility for the final version is, however, mine.

1 Personal communication from Professor Harvey Goldstein, March 2001.

2 Greeley argued that Catholic schools were effective contexts for the socialisation of black and Hispanic students just as they had been for the Irish, Italian and Polish immigrants of an earlier era. From Greeley's perspective the internal cultures of Catholic schools provided settings which 'worked' for the children of the urban poor.

3 The concept of a Catholic matrix for achievement is that of the present writer, i.e. as a summary statement for the findings of Bryk *et al.* (1993). Bryk and his colleagues do not use this construct in their own text.

4 A recent study by Sander (2000) has shown that Catholic high schools (in the USA) have 'a relatively large positive effect on the amount of time spent doing homework', especially for students from ethnic minority backgrounds.

5 Walsh (1993, p. 92) warns us, however, that 'inspirational ideologies' are not without their own problems: 'It is also important soberly to remember the shadow side of ideology and religion, the fundamentalism, fanaticism or just plain simple-mindedness that goes with the closure of thought into total systems'. All faith-based schooling systems have to face this as a potential danger.

6 Morris (1997, p. 390) acknowledges this: 'My study is limited. The findings are based on case studies of two schools in one shire county … Similar studies will be required in various parts of the country.'

7 Theory is used here in the sense indicated by Fay (1987, pp. 177–8): 'Theories are constructions which attempt to make sense of a mass of data … which try to fit what is thought to be the case into a coherent pattern … There is no reason to expect that there will be only one way to organize this material into such a pattern. Instead, there may be a number of competing theories.'

8 Goldstein observes that both of these measures are misleading indicators of a school's academic effectiveness – 'neither A-C nor A-G grades are good measures of effectiveness since neither is value-added'. Personal communication, March 2001.

9 Two of the cooperating 'schools' were in fact sixth form colleges and did not enter students on a large scale for the GCSE examinations.

10 The exceptions to this were St Clement and Pope Paul III, both of which were located in more attractive urban/suburban settings.

11 Particular public attention had been given to this school because of its academic success record with boys of Afro-Caribbean origin.

12 This classic argument has been reiterated in the recent work of Mortimore and Whitty (2000).

13 These comments refer to the work of Coleman and Hoffer (1987). However, the work of Bryk *et al.* (1993) did take into account the prior achievement of students, see ch. 7 'The Transition to High School'.

14 An internal contradiction in this interview account has to be noted because the headteacher referred later to the use of achievement information from primary schools as part of the process.

15 For a detailed account of this, see Bryk *et al.* (1993, chs 8 to 11).

16 What appears to be happening in the USA, the UK and elsewhere is that the academic success of Catholic urban schools is being appropriated by government agencies and by ideological agencies of the New Right as a stick to beat public/state schools and public/state systems of schooling. This is not welcomed by Catholic educators and these appropriations

dramatically oversimplify the different contexts for schooling and the conclusions which can be drawn.

17 This research enquiry did not have access to prior achievement data for the students of the participating schools.

18 It is likely for instance that Catholicity in contemporary urban settings has a changing social class location. See the work of Archer (1986) and of Hornsby-Smith (1999) for the UK and of Riordan (2000) for the USA.

19 A regular series of recruitment visits to teacher education colleges in Ireland had, in the view of this headteacher, been crucial in strengthening both the pedagogic quality of the teachers and also of their Catholic commitment. The Irish mission to England had in this sense been reconstituted in a new way!

20 This observation was made by a number of headteachers of schools with an improved profile of academic results. These headteachers were prepared to act (despite the difficulties) against teachers where evidence indicated unacceptable professional performance. In doing so they claimed that the interests of the students had to take precedence over the interests of teachers. As Christian school leaders in these circumstances they were often accused of lack of compassion for teachers in difficulty.

21 Other headteachers drew attention, where appropriate, to a strong academic success record in religious education. Several of the schools operated a policy of entering all students for the religious education examinations as a sign of its importance in the academic programme of the school.

22 'Star performers' is a media designation for such schools. Harvey Goldstein suggests that all such improvement profiles have to be cross-referenced to changing patterns of student intake (personal communication, March 2001).

23 In this school, three teachers left as a result of 'negotiations'. At St Matthew's School, two teachers left. In general, staff restructuring was not extensive but the negotiated departure of staff who resisted new teaching and learning approaches was regarded as crucial by the headteachers concerned.

24 This statement by the headteacher conflicted with the message given in the school's prospectus which stated that 'the main aim of Corpus Christi School is to educate the pupils in accordance with the principles of the Catholic Faith'.

25 A significant difference between the headteachers focused on the need to be a current classroom practitioner. Fourteen believed this to be essential to the educational leadership role. Ten took the view that headteachers must have demonstrated high teaching competence in the past but did not need to be (and in some cases, should not be) current classroom teachers.

26 It is apparent from this study and from studies in the USA that the fate of Catholic inner-city schools depends to an important degree on the attitude taken (and subsequent policy decisions) of the local archbishop. While some Catholic archbishops appear to have a policy that Catholic schools in such settings must be maintained whatever the cost, as a sign of the Church's commitment to the poor, other archbishops appear to be influenced by more hard-headed arguments relating to finance and organisational logistics.

27 Many of these Catholic urban schools faced problems of teacher supply and of headteacher supply. For a recent research study of this problem in

London see *Teacher Supply and Retention in London 1998–1999 Report*, TTA, London (2000).

28 The standards achieved by Catholic primary schools and the attitudes taken by primary headteachers towards particular Catholic secondary schools were regarded by the secondary headteachers as crucial to the improvement or decline of their schools. For one study of the challenges facing Catholic primary schools in urban areas see Catholic Bishops' Conference of England and Wales (1999).

## 8 Market culture and Catholic values in education

1 Chubb and Moe (1992, pp. 45–6).

2 For a further development of these ideas, see Grace (2000).

3 White Paper, 'Choice and Diversity' (1992, p. 19).

4 Of these sixteen grant-maintained schools, twelve were in London.

5 For a further discussion, see Grace (2001).

6 See Arthur (1995, ch. 5).

7 *God and the Marketplace* (1993, p. vi).

8 Only five of the Catholic headteachers in this study were explicit defenders of more competitive market values in education. However, in the opinion of the headteacher of St Matthew's School this was because the others were not telling the truth!

9 For a discussion of myths about schools as communities, see Fielding (1999).

10 For an earlier discussion of this stance among both state and Catholic school leaders, see Grace (1995, pp. 133–7).

11 The headteacher of Holy Angels School suggested that the diocesan administration, working with the LEA, should control and regulate student enrolments for each school to ensure a fairer distribution of student ability levels across all schools.

12 The Partnership began as a collective secondary school grouping to make a joint bid for funds made available for the Technical and Vocational Educational Initiative in the late 1980s. Nevertheless, according to its first Coordinator, 'the Partnership always saw itself as acting from a firmly faith-based position' (personal communication).

13 The Birmingham Catholic Secondary Partnership has influenced other partnership formations in Catholic education, including a Primary Partnership in that City (involving fifty-three schools) and partnerships in Manchester, Liverpool, Durham and Darlington.

14 For a discussion of reasons for this situation, see Marsden (1997).

15 In presentations at international conferences the present writer has encountered high levels of professional and academic interest in the Birmingham Partnership experience.

16 Report by HMI D. Moore to the Department for Education and Employment, 24 February 1998.

17 A similar Catholic unit, the Bartimaeus Centre, modelled on the Birmingham centre, has been established by eight Catholic secondary schools in Liverpool.

## 9 Spirituality, morality and personal and social justice

1 Wright (1998, p. 24) contrasts *anthropological* approaches to spirituality, 'understood as that area of human awareness, experience and inner feeling that illuminates the purpose and meaning of life, offers a glimpse of transcendence, reflects the longing for perfection and deals with matters at the heart and root of existence', with *theological* approaches which relate all of this to a sense of God.

2 'The centrality of religious education' in Catholic education is a formal statement of principle. In practice, religious education in some Catholic schools may now be undoing a process of de-centring, caused by secular pressures of the National Curriculum and by difficulties in recruiting and retaining specialist teachers.

3 Novels and oral history accounts give us some insight into the Catholicity experiences of an earlier generation of pupils. See Chapter 3 of this study.

4 p. 253.

5 Catholic secondary schools which could be described as 'pluralistic' were, in the present study, generally located in inner-city communities with multi-faith populations. Such schools had significant numbers of students from Islamic or Hindu backgrounds.

6 'Those who are far from the faith' can be interpreted to mean that Catholic schools should be of service, not only to other Christian believers but also to those of other faiths.

7 The Catholic hierarchy in England and Wales has been cautious in the extent of 'openness' in Catholic schooling. Bishop Nichols (1997, p. 58), addressing Catholic educators on the Church's mission in a multi-faith society, pointed out that 'Catholicism ... is not a denomination ... it is a response to the revealed truth.'

8 The study used limited empirical data derived from research into Catholic schools in one English county, Oxfordshire.

9 It was generally noted that spiritual values permeated the teaching of certain arts subjects such as English and History but were much less evident in the sciences and mathematics.

10 The difficulty of retaining 'protected spaces' for prayer and reflection in Catholic secondary schools became evident in this research. With increasing numbers of students and pressures on space there was a temptation to convert 'sacred space' (used intermittently) to 'secular space' used regularly for lessons.

11 The Catholic Bishops of England and Wales have attempted to give religious education a protected timetable space by suggesting that 10 per cent of timetabled time should be allocated to the subject. There was evidence in many schools that time allocations to religious education were falling below this figure.

12 Bottery (2000) points to a resurgence of interest in 'virtue theory' in education, particularly that associated with the Catholic philosopher MacIntyre (1981). From this perspective 'Creating the virtuous individual, the good citizen, can only be done through a society's narrative and norms, and the youth of society and their thought bedded within a set of principled dispositions. Only when these dispositions are firmly in place should they engage in principled interrogation of life's problems and dilemmas' (Bottery 2000,

p. 42). Many of the Catholic schools in this present enquiry were attempting to implement such virtue theory in difficult urban settings. See also the work of Carr (1991) for an important discussion of educating the virtues.

13 Only five of the headteachers endorsed 'the ebbing tide of Catholicity' thesis.

14 The interview schedule contained no direct question about vocations to the institutional Church. The intention here was to discover if headteachers would refer to such vocations as part of their evaluation of the religious effectiveness of the school.

15 St Mary's College, Strawberry Hill, now offers an MA in Catholic School Leadership with a strong 'theological literacy' emphasis. Many courses on faith leadership in the Catholic school are offered by higher education institutions in the USA, including Boston College, Fordham University, New York, and the University of San Francisco.

16 While the involvement of local priests and members of religious orders in the work of the schools was commended by many headteachers, some of them suggested that priests needed more seminary formation on relating to secondary school students.

17 For a detailed summary and commentary on the Catholic Church's teaching on sexual behaviour, see Lawler *et al.* (1998).

18 Stephen Corriette, Director of the Catholic Church's Association for Racial Justice in England and Wales, has argued that not enough action has been taken to eradicate racism within the Church's own culture and structures. (See the *Guardian* 16 October 2000).

19 For one important study in the USA, see Irvine and Foster (1996).

20 Questions about racism could not be asked in every interview because of time constraints. However, headteachers were always invited to add issues for discussion which they believed should be considered.

21 O'Keefe and O'Keeffe (1996, p. 304). There have also been complaints that ethnic monitoring in Catholic schools has tended to be preoccupied with the position and progress of black students. Representatives of the Irish community in the UK have claimed that the position of students of Irish descent needs more focused attention (see *Catholic Times* 24 December 2000).

22 'No Problem Here' was a characteristic stance identified by Chris Gaine in his research in all-white schools in the 1980s. It appears to have continued into the 1990s. See Gaine (1987).

23 For some interesting comparative data on women religious in the USA see Casey (1993, ch. 3).

24 During the fieldwork for this study, the *Catholic Herald*, 31 July 1998, under the headline 'British nun's books burned in USA as Vatican bans sale', reported the destruction of Sister Lavinia Byrne's book, *Woman at the Altar.* It reported that this had been done because the book infringed the Pope's prohibition of discussion of women's ordination.

25 The other side of the Catholic single-sex tradition of secondary schooling, i.e. the existence of all-boys schools, may, however, renew patriarchy and sexism in various ways.

26 The focus-group meetings began with general discussion of the students' experiences in the light of the principles in the mission statements of their schools. This was followed by some written comments from the students.

27 The students at St Lawrence showed considerable insight into the problems of their school, particularly regarding issues of teacher supply, quality and retention in tough inner-city areas.

## 10 Catholic schools: the renewal of spiritual capital and the critique of the secular world

1 Spiritual capital, in this definition, is a resource of faith and values possessed by all faith-based schools and not only by Catholic ones.
2 However, much of Bourdieu's work is directed to show that in practice these two forms of capital are highly interrelated.
3 During the course of the fieldwork, the researcher received such evidence from a range of individuals involved in the selection and appointment of new headteachers in Catholic schools.
4 This comment relates to the situation in the UK. There is more evidence of this provision in higher education institutions in the USA and Australia.
5 There has been a traditional Catholic preoccupation with the percentage of Catholic teachers in each secondary school. This research has shown that this is a simplistic approach to the question of school ethos. Teachers of other Christian denominations were widely reported by the headteachers as being significant spiritual assets for the schools when compared with luke-warm or nominal Catholic teachers.
6 Catholic schools may be viewed as agencies for the renewal of spiritual capital among the young, i.e. working against the materialistic spirit of global capitalism.
7 Quoted by Purpel (1989). I am grateful to David Purpel for the location of this quotation.

# Bibliography

Abbs, P. (1995) 'The Spiritual in Art and Culture', *The Salisbury Review*, June, pp. 27–31.

Angus, L. (1988) *Continuity and Change in Catholic Schooling: An Ethnography of a Christian Brothers' College in Australian Society*, London: Falmer Press.

Archer, A. (1986) *The Two Catholic Churches: A Study in Oppression*, London: SCM Press.

Arthur, J. (1994a) 'Parental Participation in Catholic Schooling: A Case of Increasing Conflict', *British Journal of Educational Studies*, Vol. 42, No. 2, pp. 174–90.

Arthur, J. (1994b) 'Trusteeship and the Governance of Roman Catholic Voluntary Aided Schools', *Law and Justice*, No. 120/121, pp. 3–11.

Arthur, J. (1995) *The Ebbing Tide: Policy and Principles of Catholic Education*, Leominster: Gracewing Publications.

Arthur, J., Walters, J. and Gaine, S. (1999) *Earthen Vessels: the Thomistic tradition in education*, Leominster: Gracewing Publications.

Astley, J. (1994) *The Philosophy of Christian Religious Education*, Alabama: Religious Education Press.

Astley, J. and Francis, L. (eds) (1994) *Critical Perspectives on Christian Education*, Leominster: Gracewing Publications.

Atherton, M. and Grace, G. (1999) Doctoral and Masters' theses and dissertations on Catholic education in the UK and Ireland, London: Institute of Education/CRDCE.

Atkinson, P., Davies, B. and Delamont, S. (eds) (1995) *Discourse and Reproduction: Essays in Honor of Basil Bernstein*, Cresskill, NJ: Hampton Press.

Badger, J. (2000) 'The Transmission of Values in a Church School: Consensus and Contradiction', Unpublished D.Phil. thesis, University of Oxford.

Baker, D. and Riordan, C. (1998) 'The "Eliting" of the Common American Catholic School', *Phi Delta Kappan*, September.

Baker, K. (1993) *The Turbulent Years*, London: Faber.

Beales, A. C. F. (1950) 'The Struggle for the Schools', in G. A. Beck (ed.) *The English Catholics, 1850–1950*, London: Burns Oates.

Beck, G. A. (1964) 'Aims in Education: Neo-Thomism', in T. H. B. Hollins (ed.) *Aims in Education*, Manchester: Manchester University Press.

Beck, J. (1998) *Morality and Citizenship in Education*, London: Cassell.

Bendix, R. (1969) *Max Weber: an intellectual portrait*, London: Methuen.

Bennett, J. and Forgan, R. (eds) (1991) *There's Something About a Convent Girl*, London: Virago Press.

Berger, P. (1973) *The Social Reality of Religion*, London: Penguin.

Bernstein, B. (1970) 'Education cannot compensate for Society', *New Society*, Vol. 387, pp. 344–7.

Bernstein, B. (1990) *The Structuring of Pedagogic Discourse*, London: Routledge.

Bernstein, B. (1996) *Pedagogy, Symbolic Control and Identity: theory, research and critique*, London: Taylor & Francis.

Bernstein, B. (1997) 'Class and Pedagogies: Visible and Invisible', in A. H. Halsey *et al.* (eds) *Education: Culture, Economy and Society*, Oxford: Oxford University Press.

Birmingham Partnership (1998) *The Birmingham Catholic Secondary Guarantee*, Birmingham: Partnership Office.

Bottery, M. (2000) *Education, Policy and Ethics*, London: Continuum.

Bourdieu, P. (1986) 'The Forms of Capital', in J. McPherson (ed.) *Handbook of Theory and Research for the Sociology of Education*, New York: Greenwood Press.

Bourdieu, P. (1989) 'Social Space and Symbolic Power', *Sociological Theory*, Vol. 7, pp. 14–25.

Bourdieu, P. (1990) *The Logic of Practice*, Oxford: Polity Press.

Boylan, P. (1996) 'Whither the Tide?', *Mentor*, Vol. 2, No. 1.

Bridges, D. and McLaughlin, T. (eds) (1994) *Education and the Market Place*, London: Falmer Press.

Brothers, J. (1964) *Church and School*, Liverpool: Liverpool University Press.

Brown, P. (1990) 'The "Third Wave": Education and the Ideology of Parentocracy', *British Journal of Sociology of Education*, Vol. 11, pp. 65–85.

Bryk, A. (1988) 'Musings on the Moral Life of Schools', *American Journal of Education*, Vol. 96, No. 2, pp. 256–90.

Bryk, A., Lee, V. and Holland, P. (1993) *Catholic Schools and the Common Good*, Cambridge, MA: Harvard University Press.

Burgess, R. (1983) *Experiencing Comprehensive Education: A study of Bishop McGregor School*, London: Methuen.

Byrne, L. (1994) *Woman at the Altar*, London: Mowbray.

Caldecott, S. (ed.) (1998) *Beyond the Prosaic*, Edinburgh: T & T Clark.

Callery, K. (1998) 'Pastoral Care and Leadership in Catholic Education', in P. Duignan and T. d'Arbon (eds) *Leadership in Catholic Education: 2000 and Beyond*, Strathfield, NSW: Australian Catholic University.

Calvez, J.-Y. and Perrin, J. (1961) *The Church and Social Justice*, London: Burns & Oates.

Cariola, P. (1971) 'The Thought of the Church and the Future of Catholic Education in Latin America', *Religious Education*, Vol. LXVI, p. 421.

Carr, D. (1991) *Educating the Virtues*, London: Routledge.

Carr, D. (1999) 'Catholic Faith and Religious Truth', in J. Conroy (ed.) *Catholic Education: Inside Out, Outside In*, Dublin: Lindisfarne Books.

Carr, D., Haldane, J., McLaughlin, T. and Pring, R. (1995) 'Return to the Crossroads: Maritain Fifty Years On', *British Journal of Educational Studies*, Vol. XXXXIII, No. 2, pp. 162–78.

Carson, M. (1992) *Sucking Sherbert Lemons*, London: Black Swan Books.

Casey, K. (1993) *I Answer with my Life: Life Histories of Women Teachers Working for Social Change*, New York: Routledge.

Catholic Bishops' Conference of England and Wales (1996) *The Common Good and the Catholic Church's Social Teaching*, London: CBC.

Catholic Bishops' Conference of England and Wales (1997a) *A Struggle for Excellence: Catholic Secondary Schools in Urban Poverty Areas*, London: CES.

Catholic Bishops' Conference of England and Wales (1997b) *Catholic Schools and Other Faiths*, London: CBC.

Catholic Bishops' Conference of England and Wales (1999) *Foundations for Excellence: Catholic Primary Schools in Urban Poverty Areas*, London: CES.

Catholic Education Service (1992) *A Response to the White Paper*, London: CES.

Catholic Education Service (1995a) *Quality of Education in Catholic Secondary Schools*, London: CES.

Catholic Education Service (1995b) *Spiritual and Moral Development Across the Curriculum*, London: CES.

Catholic Education Service (1997a) *The Common Good in Education*, London: CES.

Catholic Education Service (1997b) *Partners in Mission: a collection of talks by Bishops on issues affecting Catholic education*, London: CES.

Chadwick, P. (1994) *Schools of Reconciliation: Issues in Joint Roman Catholic-Anglican Education*, London: Cassell.

Chadwick, P. (1997) *Shifting Alliances: Church and State in English Education*, London: Cassell.

Christie, P. (1990) *Open Schools: Racially Mixed Catholic Schools in South Africa, 1976–1986*, Johannesburg: Raven Press.

Chubb, J. and Moe, T. (1990) *Politics, Markets and America's Schools*, Washington, DC: The Brookings Institute.

Chubb, J. and Moe, T. (1992) *A Lesson in School Reform from Great Britain*, Washington, DC: The Brookings Institute.

Cibulka, J., O'Biren, T. and Zewe, D. (1982) *Inner-City Private Elementary Schools*, Milwaukee: Marquette University Press.

Codd, J. (1990) 'Making Distinctions: The Eye of the Beholder', in R. Harker *et al.* (eds) *An Introduction to the work of Pierre Bourdieu*, London: Macmillan.

Coleman, J. (1988) 'Social Capital in the Creation of Human Capital', *American Journal of Sociology*, Vol. 94, pp. 95–120.

Coleman, J. and Hoffer, T. (1987) *Public and Private High Schools: the Impact of Communities*, New York: Basic Books.

Coleman, J., Hoffer, T. and Kilgore, S. (1982) *High School Achievement: Public, Catholic and Private Schools Compared*, New York: Basic Books.

Collins, P. (1997) *Papal Power*, Blackburn, Victoria: Harper Collins.

Conference of Latin American Bishops (1993) *Santo Domingo Conclusions*, London: CAFOD/CIIR.

Conference of Major Religious Superiors (1988) *Inequality in Schooling in Ireland*, Dublin: CMRS.

Conference of Major Religious Superiors (1991) *The Catholic School in Contemporary Society*, Dublin: CMRS.

Conference of Major Religious Superiors (1992) *Education and Poverty*, Dublin: CMRS.

Conference of Religious of Ireland (1994) *Women for Leadership in Education*, Dublin: CRI.

Congregation for Catholic Education (1998) *The Catholic School on the Threshold of the Third Millennium*, Vatican City: Libreria Editrice Vaticana.

Conroy, J. (ed.) (1999) *Catholic Education: Inside Out/Outside In*, Dublin: Lindisfarne Books.

Convey, J. (1992) *Catholic Schools Make a Difference: Twenty Five Years of Research*, Washington, DC: National Catholic Educational Association.

Cox, H. (1984) *Religion and the Secular City*, New York: Simon and Schuster.

Daniels, P. (2000) 'Have We Seen the Death of Dialogue?', in M. Hornsby-Smith (ed.) *Catholics in England 1950–2000*, London: Cassell.

Davies, J. (ed.) (1993) *God and the Market Place: Essays in the Morality of Wealth Creation*, London: Institute of Economic Affairs.

Davies, L. (1994) *Beyond Authoritarian School Management*, Ticknall: Education Now Books.

Davis, R. (1999) 'Can there be a Catholic Curriculum?', in J. Conroy (ed.) *Catholic Education: Inside Out/Outside In*, Dublin: Lindisfarne Books.

Deane, S. (1997) *Reading in the Dark*, London: Vintage Books.

Denzin, N. and Lincoln, Y. (eds) (1998) *Collecting and Interpreting Qualitative Materials*, London: Sage.

Donlon, T. C. (1952) *Theology and Education*, Iowa: W M Brown.

Dorr, D. (1983) *Option for the Poor: 100 Years of Vatican Social Teaching*, Dublin: Gill and MacMillan.

Douglas, M. (1966) *Purity and Danger: An Analysis of Concepts of Pollution and Taboo*, London: Routledge & Kegan Paul.

Douglas, M. (1973) *Natural Symbols: Explorations in Cosmology*, Harmondsworth: Penguin.

Drudy, S. and Lynch, K. (1993) *Schools and Society in Ireland*, Dublin: Gill and MacMillan.

Duffy, E. (1997) *Saints and Sinners: A History of the Popes*, New Haven, CT: Yale University Press.

Duignan, P. and d'Arbon, T. (eds) (1998) *Leadership in Catholic Education*, Strathfield, NSW: Australian Catholic University.

Durkheim, E. (1971) *The Elementary Forms of the Religious Life: A Study in Religious Sociology*, London: Allen and Unwin.

Durkheim, E. (1977) *The Evolution of Educational Thought*, London: Routledge & Kegan Paul.

Eagleton, T. (1967) 'Catholic Education and Commitment', *Catholic Education Today*, Vol. 1, No. 1, pp. 8–10.

Edwards, T. and Whitty, G. (1997) 'Marketing Quality: Traditional and Modern Versions of Educational Excellence', in R. Glatter, P. Woods and C. Bagley (eds) *Choice and Diversity in Schooling*, London: Routledge.

Egan, J. (1988) *Opting Out: Catholic Schools Today*, Leominster: Gracewing Publications.

Fahy, P. (1992) *Faith in Catholic Classrooms*, Homebush, NSW: St Paul Publications.

Fardon, R. (1999) *Mary Douglas: An Intellectual Biography*, London: Routledge.

Fay, B. (1987) *Critical Social Science: Liberation and its Limits*, Cambridge: Polity Press.

Feheney, M. (ed.) (1998) *From Ideal to Action: The Inner Nature of a Catholic School Today*, Dublin: Veritas.

Feheney, M. (ed.) (1999) *Beyond the Race for Points: Aspects of Pastoral Care in a Catholic School Today*, Dublin: Veritas.

Fielding, M. (1999) 'Communities of Learners: Myth: Schools are Communities', in B. O'Hagan (ed.) *Modern Educational Myths*, London: Kogan Page.

Flannery, A. (1998) *Vatican Council II: The Conciliar and Post Conciliar Documents: Vol. 1*, new revised edition, New York: Costello Publications and Dublin: Dominican Publications.

Flew, A. (1991) 'Educational Services: Independent Competition or Maintained Monopoly?', in D. Green (ed.) *Empowering the Parents: How to break the Schools' Monopoly*, London: Institute of Economic Affairs.

Flynn, M. (1975) *Some Catholic Schools in Action*, Sydney: Catholic Education Office.

Flynn, M. (1979) *Catholic Schools and the Communication of Faith*, Sydney: Society of St Paul.

Flynn, M. (1985) *The Effectiveness of Catholic Schools*, Homebush, NSW: St Paul Publications.

Flynn, M. (1993) *The Culture of Catholic Schools*, Homebush, NSW: St Paul Publications.

Freire, P. (1973) *Pedagogy of the Oppressed*, Harmondsworth: Penguin.

Freire, P. (1984) 'Education, Liberation and the Church', *Religious Education*, Vol. 79, No. 4, pp. 524–45.

Freire, P. (1990) *Education for Critical Consciousness*, New York: Continuum.

Freire, P. (1993) *Pedagogy of the City*, New York: Continuum.

Freire, P. (1994) *Pedagogy of Hope*, New York: Continuum.

Gaine, C. (1987) *No Problem Here: A Practical Approach to Education and Race in White Schools*, London: Hutchinson.

Gallagher, M. P. (1997) 'New Forms of Cultural Unbelief', in P. Hogan and K. Williams (eds) *The Future of Religion in Irish Education*, Dublin: Veritas.

Gamble, A. (1998) *The Free Market and the Strong State*, London: Macmillan.

General Council of the De La Salle Brothers, Rome (1997) *The Lasallian Mission of Human and Christian Education*, Oxford: De La Salle Publications.

Giddens, A. (1998) *The Third Way: the Renewal of Social Democracy*, Cambridge: Polity Press.

Giddens, A. (2000) *The Third Way and its Critics*, Cambridge: Polity Press.

Glaser, B. and Strauss, A. (1967) *The Discovery of Grounded Theory: Strategies for Qualitative Research*, Chicago: Aldine.

Glatter, R. (1995) 'Partnership in the Market Model: Is It Dying?', in A. Macbeth *et al* (eds) *Collaborate or Compete? Educational Partnerships in a Market Economy*, London: Falmer Press.

Glatter, R., Woods, P. and Bagley, C. (eds)(1997) *Choice and Diversity in Schooling*, London: Routledge.

Goffman, E. (1961) *Asylums*, Harmondsworth: Penguin.

Goldstein, H. *et al.* (1993) 'A Multilevel Analysis of School Examination Results', *Oxford Review of Education*, Vol. 19, pp. 425–33.

Grace, G. (1978) *Teachers, Ideology and Control: a study in urban education*, London: Routledge & Kegan Paul.

Grace, G. (1995) 'The Dilemmas of Catholic Headteachers', in *School Leadership: Beyond Education Management*, London: Falmer Press.

Grace, G. (1998a) 'Realising the Mission: Catholic Approaches to School Effectiveness', in R. Slee, G. Weiner and S. Tomlinson (eds) *School Effectiveness for Whom?*, London: Falmer Press.

Grace, G. (1998b) 'Critical Policy Scholarship: Reflections on the Integrity of knowledge and research', in G. Shacklock and J. Smyth (eds) *Being Reflexive in Critical Educational and Social Research*, London: Falmer Press.

Grace, G. (1998c) 'The Future of the Catholic School: An English Perspective', in J M Feheney (ed.) *From Ideal to Action: The Inner Nature of a Catholic School Today*, Dublin: Veritas.

Grace, G. (2000) *Catholic Schools and the Common Good: what this means in educational practice*, London: London Institute of Education/CRDCE.

Grace, G. (2001) 'The State and Catholic Schooling in England and Wales: Politics, Ideology and Mission Integrity', *Oxford Review of Education*, Vol. 27, No. 4.

Gramsci, A. (1971) *Selections from the Prison Notebooks*, trans. Q. Hoare and G. Nowell Smith, London: Lawrence and Wishart.

Gray, J. (1992) *The Moral Foundations of Market Institutions*, London: Institute of Economic Affairs.

Greeley, A. (1982) *Catholic High Schools and Minority Students*, New Brunswick, NJ: Transaction Books.

Greeley, A. (1989) 'Catholic Schools: A Golden Twilight', *Catholic School Studies*, Vol. 62, No. 2, pp. 8–12.

Greeley, A. (1998) 'Catholic Schools at the Crossroads: An American Perspective'. in J. M. Feheney (ed.) *From Ideal to Action: The Inner Nature of a Catholic School Today*, Dublin: Veritas.

Greeley, A. and Rossi, P. (1966) *The Education of Catholic Americans*, Chicago: Aldine.

Greeley, A., McCready, W. and McCourt, K. (1976) *Catholic Schools in a Declining Church*, Kansas City: Sheed and Ward.

Green, A. (1997) *Education, Globalization and the Nation State*, London: Macmillan.

Grenfell, M. and James, D. (1998) *Bourdieu and Education: Acts of Practical Theory*, London: Falmer Press.

Groome, T. (1996) 'What Makes a School Catholic?', in McLaughlin, T., O'Keefe, J. and O'Keeffe, B. (eds) (1996) *The Contemporary Catholic School: Context, Identity and Diversity*, London: Falmer Press.

Groome, T. (1998) *Educating for Life: A spiritual vision for every teacher and parent*, Allen, TX: Thomas More Press.

Habermas, J. (1978) *Knowledge and Human Interests*, London: Heinemann.

Haldane, J. (1999) 'The Need of Spirituality in Catholic Education', in J. Convey (ed.) *Catholic Education: Inside Out/Outside In*, Dublin: Lindisfarne Books.

Hall, V. (1994) 'Making it Happen: A Study of Women Headteachers of Primary and Secondary Schools in England and Wales', Paper presented at AERA Conference, New Orleans.

Halsey, A., Lauder, H., Brown, P. and Stuart Wells, A. (eds) (1997) *Education: Culture, Economy and Society*, Oxford: Oxford University Press.

Harker, R. (1990) 'Bourdieu – Education and Reproduction', in R. Harker, C. Mahar and C. Wilkes (eds) *An Introduction to the Work of Pierre Bourdieu*, London: Macmillan.

Hastings, A. (1991) *A History of English Christianity 1920–1990*, London: SCM Press.

Hastings, M. (1970) *Jesuit Child*, London: Michael Joseph.

Hastings, P. (1996) 'Openness and Intellectual Challenge in Catholic Schools', in T. McLaughlin *et al.* (eds) *The Contemporary Catholic School*, London: Falmer Press.

Hesketh, A. and Knight, P. (1998) 'Secondary School Prospectuses and Educational Markets', *Cambridge Journal of Education*, Vol. 28, pp. 21–36.

Hickman, M. (1995) *Religion, Class and Identity: the state, the Catholic Church and the education of the Irish in Britain*, Aldershot: Avebury.

Hickman, M. (1999) 'The Religio-Ethnic Identities of Teenagers of Irish Descent', in M. Hornsby-Smith (ed.) *Catholics in England 1950–2000*, London: Cassell.

Hirst, P. (1974) *Moral Education in a Secular Society*, London: University of London Press.

Hirst, P. (1976) 'Religious Beliefs and Educational Principles', *Learning for Living*, Vol. 15, pp. 155–7.

Hirst, P. (1994) 'Christian Education: A Contradiction in Terms?', in J. Astley and L. Francis (eds) *Critical Perspectives on Christian Education*, Leominster: Gracewing Publications.

Hitchcock, J. (1995) *Recovery of the Sacred: Reforming the Reformed Liturgy*, San Francisco: Ignatius Press.

Hogan, P. and Williams, K. (eds) (1997) *The Future of Religion in Irish Education*, Dublin: Veritas.

Hopkins, B. (1998) *Our Kid*, London: Headline Books.

Hornsby-Smith, M. (1978) *Catholic Education: The Unobtrusive Partner*, London: Sheed and Ward.

Hornsby-Smith, M. (1987) *Roman Catholics in England: Studies in Social Structure*, Cambridge: Cambridge University Press.

Hornsby-Smith, M. (1991) *Roman Catholic Beliefs in England*, Cambridge: Cambridge University Press.

Hornsby-Smith, M. (ed.) (1999) *Catholics in England 1950–2000: Historical and Sociological Perspectives*, London: Cassell.

Hornsby-Smith, M. (2000) 'The Changing Social and Religious Content of Catholic Schooling in England and Wales', in M. Eaton, J. Longmore and A. Naylor (eds) *Commitment to Diversity: Catholics and Education in a Changing World*, London: Cassell.

Hume, B. (1977) *Searching for God*, London: Hodder and Stoughton.

Hume, B. (1989) 'Catholic Schools Today: The Crucial National Issues', *Briefing 89*, London: Catholic Media Office.

Hume, B. (1997) 'The Church's Mission in Education', in *Partners in Mission: a collection of talks by Bishops on issues affecting Catholic education*, London: Catholic Education Service.

Hunt, T. (1998) *Doctoral Dissertations on Catholic Schools in the United States 1988–1997*, Washington: NCEA.

Hunt, T., Oldenski, T. and Wallace, T. (eds) (2000) *Catholic School Leadership*, London: Falmer Press.

Irvine, J. and Foster, M. (eds) (1996) *Growing Up African American in Catholic Schools*, New York: Teachers College Press.

Joyce, J. (1985) *A Portrait of the Artist as a Young Man*, London: Jonathan Cape.

Lauder, H. and Hughes, D. (1999) *Trading in Futures: Why Markets in Education don't work*, Buckingham: Open University Press.

Lawler, R., Boyle, J. and May, W. (1998) *Catholic Sexual Ethics: a summary, explanation and defense*, Huntington, IN: Sunday Visitor Publishing.

Lawton, D. (1994) *The Tory Mind on Education 1979–94*, London: Falmer Press.

Lesko, N. (1988) *Symbolizing Society: Stories, Rites and Structure in a Catholic High School*, Lewes: Falmer Press.

Letson, D. and Higgins, M. (1995) *The Jesuit Mystique*, London: HarperCollins.

Litak, S. and Tulasiewicz, W. (1988) 'Christianity: National Identity and Education in Poland', in W. Tulasiewicz and C. Brock (eds) *Christianity and Educational Provision in International Perspective*, London: Routledge.

Lodge, D. (1980) *How Far Can You Go?*, Harmondsworth: Penguin.

Lynch, K. (1989) *The Hidden Curriculum: reproduction in Education*, London: Falmer Press.

Lyotard, F. (1984) *The Postmodern Condition: A Report on Knowledge*, Minneapolis: University of Minnesota Press.

MacBeath, J. (ed.) (2000) *Effective School Leadership: Responding to Change*, London: Paul Chapman.

Macbeth, A., McCreath, D. and Aitchison, J. (eds) (1995) *Collaborate or Compete? Educational Partnerships in a Market Economy*, London: Falmer Press.

MacIntyre, A. (1981) *After Virtue: A Study in Moral Theory*, London: Duckworth.

MacIntyre, A. (1988) *Whose Justice? Which Rationality?*, London: Duckworth.

MacIntyre, A. (1990) *Three Rival Versions of Moral Enquiry*, London: Duckworth.

Maguire, M., Ball, S. and Macrae, S. (1999) 'Promotion, Persuasion and Class-taste in the UK Post-compulsory School', *British Journal of Sociology of Education*, Vol. 20, No. 3, pp. 291–308.
Maritain, J. (1948) *The Person and the Common Good*, London: Geoffrey Bles.
Maritain, J. (1961) *Education at the Crossroads*, New Haven, CT: Yale University Press.
Maritain, J. (1964) *The Aims of Education*, New Haven, CT: Yale University Press.
Marsden, G. (1997) *The Outrageous Idea of Christian Scholarship*, New York: Oxford University Press.
Marshall, J. (1999) 'Catholic Family Life', in M. Hornsby-Smith (ed.) *Catholics in England 1950–2000*, London: Cassell.
Mayer, M. (1929) *The Philosophy of Teaching of St Thomas Aquinas*, New York: Bruce.
McCarthy, M. (1963) *Memories of a Catholic Girlhood*, Harmondsworth: Penguin.
McCourt, F. (1997) *Angela's Ashes: A Memoir of a Childhood*, London: Flamingo.
McDonagh, J. (1991) 'Catholic Education and Evaluation', in N. Brennan (ed.) *The Catholic School in Contemporary Society*, Dublin: Conference of Major Religious Superiors.
McInerny, R. (1998) *Thomas Aquinas: Selected Writings*, London: Penguin.
McLaren, P. (1993) *Schooling as a Ritual Performance*, 2nd edition, London: Routledge.
McLaughlin, T. (1990) 'Parental Rights in Religious Upbringing and Religious Education Within a Liberal Perspective', Ph.D. thesis, University of London.
McLaughlin, T. (1992) 'The Ethics of Separate Schools', in M. Leicester and M. Taylor (eds) *Ethics, Ethnicity and Education*, London: Kogan Page.
McLaughlin, T. (1996) 'The Distinctiveness of Catholic Education', in *The Contemporary Catholic School*, London: Falmer Press.
McLaughlin, T., O'Keefe, J. and O'Keeffe, B. (eds) (1996) *The Contemporary Catholic School: Context, Identity and Diversity*, London: Falmer Press.
McClelland, V. (1962) *Cardinal Manning*, Oxford: Oxford University Press.
McClelland, V. (1992) 'The Concept of Catholic Education', *Aspects of Education*, Vol. 46.
McMahon, J., Neidhart, H. and Chapman, J. (eds) (1997) *Leading the Catholic School*, Richmond, Victoria: Spectrum Publications.
Morris, A. B. (1994) 'The Academic Performance of Catholic Schools', *School Organisation*, Vol. 14, No. 1, pp. 81–9.
Morris, A. B. (1995) 'The Catholic School Ethos: Its Effect on Post-16 Student Academic Achievement', *Educational Studies*, Vol. 21, No. 1, pp. 67–83.
Morris, A. B. (1997) 'Same Mission, Same Methods, Same Results? Academic and Religious Outcomes from Different Models of Catholic Schooling', *British Journal of Educational Studies*, Vol. 45, No. 4, pp. 378–91.
Morris, A. B. (1998a) 'Catholic and Other Secondary Schools: An Analysis of OFSTED Inspection Reports 1993–1995', *Educational Research*, Vol. 40, No. 2, pp. 181–90.
Morris, A. B. (1998b) 'So Far, So Good: Levels of Academic Achievement in Catholic Schools', *Educational Studies*, Vol. 24, No. 1, pp. 83–94.

Mortimore, P. and Whitty, G. (2000) 'Can School Improvement Overcome the Effects of Disadvantage?', in T. Cox (ed.) *Combating Educational Disadvantage*, London: Falmer Press.

Mortimore, P., Sammons, P., Stoll, L., Lewis, D. and Ecob, R. (1988) *School Matters: The Junior Years*, Wells: Open Books.

Myers, K. and Goldstein, H. (1998) 'Who's Failing?', in L. Stoll and K. Myers (eds) *No Quick Fixes: Perspectives on Schools in Difficulty*, London: Falmer Press.

Naylor, A. (2000) 'Teacher Education in Catholic Colleges in England: Historical Context, Current Perspectives and Future Directions', in M. Eaton, J. Longmore and A. Naylor (eds) *Commitment to Diversity: Catholics and Education in a Changing World*, London: Cassell.

Nichols, V. (1997) 'Spiritual and Moral Development and the Catholic School', in *Partners in Mission*, London: Catholic Education Service.

Novak, M. (1993) *The Catholic Ethic and the Spirit of Capitalism*, New York: Free Press.

O'Hagan, B. (ed.) (1999) *Modern Educational Myths*, London: Kogan Page.

O'Keefe, J. (1996) 'No Margin, No Mission', in T. McLaughlin *et al.* (eds) *The Contemporary Catholic School*, London, Falmer Press.

O'Keefe, J. (1999a) 'Visionary Leadership in Catholic Schools', in J. Conroy (ed.) *Catholic Education: Inside Out/Outside In*, Dublin: Lindisfarne Books.

O'Keefe, J. (1999b) 'Research on Catholic Education: A View from Australia', *Catholic Education*, Vol. 2, No. 3.

O'Keefe, J. (2000) 'The Challenge of Pluralism: Articulating a Rationale for Religiously Diverse Urban Roman Catholic Schools in the United States', *International Journal of Education and Religion*, Vol. 1, pp. 64–88.

O'Keefe, J. and O'Keeffe, B. (1996) 'Directions for Research in Catholic Education in the USA and the UK', in T. McLaughlin *et al.* (eds) *The Contemporary Catholic School*, London: Falmer Press.

O'Keeffe, B. (1986) *Faith Culture and the Dual System: A Comparative Study of Church and County Schools*, Lewes: Falmer Press.

O'Keeffe, B. (ed.) (1988) *Schools for Tomorrow: Building Walls or Building Bridges*, London: Falmer Press.

O'Keeffe, B. (1992) 'Catholic Schools in an Open Society: The English challenge', in V. McClelland (ed.) *The Catholic School and the European Context*, Hull: Hull University Press.

O'Keeffe, B. (1997) 'The Changing Role of Catholic Schools in England and Wales: From Exclusiveness to Engagement', in J. McMahon *et al.* (eds) *Leading the Catholic School*, Richmond, Victoria: Spectrum Publications.

O'Keeffe, B. (1999) 'Reordering Perspectives in Catholic Schools', in M. Hornsby-Smith (ed.) *Catholics in England 1950–2000: Historical and Sociological Perspectives*, London: Cassell.

Oldenski, T. (1997) *Liberation Theology and Critical Pedagogy in Today's Catholic Schools*, New York: Garland Publishing.

Organization for Economic Co-operation and Development (1991) *Reviews of National Policies for Education: Ireland*, Paris: OECD.

O'Sullivan, D. (1996) 'Cultural Exclusion and Educational Change: Education, Church, and Religion in the Irish Republic', *Compare*, Vol. 26, No. 1, pp. 35–49.

Parsons, C. (1999) *Education, Exclusion and Citizenship*, London: Routledge.

Paterson, L. (1991) 'Trends in Attainment in Scottish Secondary Schools', in S. Raudenbush and J. D. Willms (eds) *Schools, Classrooms and Pupils: International Studies of Schooling from a Multilevel Perspective*, San Diego: Academic Press.

Paterson, L. (2000a) 'Catholic Education and Scottish Democracy', *Journal of Education and Christian Belief*, Vol. 4, No. 1, pp. 37–49.

Paterson, L. (2000b) 'Salvation through Education? The Changing Social Status of Scottish Catholics', in T. Devine (ed.) *Scotland's Shame? Bigotry and Sectarianism in Modern Scotland*, Edinburgh: Mainstream.

Pittau, G. (2000) 'Education on the Threshold of the Third Millenium: Challenge, Mission and Adventure', *Catholic Education*, Vol. 4, No. 2, pp. 139–52.

Pontifical Commission for Justice and Peace (1989) *The Church and Racism*, London: Catholic Truth Society.

Pope John Paul II (1994) *Crossing the Threshold of Hope*, London: Jonathan Cape.

Pope Leo XIII (1891) *Rerum Novarum*, Vatican City: Libreria Editrice Vaticana.

Pope Paul VI (1975) *Apostolic Exhortation: Evangelii Nuntiandi*, Vatican City: Libreria Editrice Vaticana.

Pope Pius XI (1931) *Quadragesimo Anno*, Vatican City: Libreria Editrice Vaticana.

Pring, R. (1996) 'Markets, Education and Catholic Schools', in T. H. McLaughlin *et al.* (eds) *The Contemporary Catholic School*, London: Falmer Press.

Purpel, D. (1989) *The Moral and Spiritual Crisis in Education*, New York: Bergin and Garvey.

Ranson, S. (1993) 'Markets or Democracy for Education', *British Journal of Educational Studies*, Vol. XXXXI, No. 4, pp. 333–52.

Raudenbush, S. and Bryk, A. (1986) 'A Hierarchical Model for Studying School Effects', *Sociology of Education*, Vol. 59, pp. 1–17.

Richmond, R. (1988) 'Christian Denominations and the Development of Private Education in Chile', in W. Tulasiewicz and C. Brock (eds) *Christianity and Educational Provision in International Perspective*, London: Routledge.

Riordan, C. (2000) 'Trends in Student Demography in Catholic Secondary Schools 1972–1992', in J. Youniss and J. Convey (eds) *Catholic Schools at the Crossroads*, New York: Teachers College Press.

Roberts, I. D. (1996) *A Harvest of Hope: Jesuit Collegiate Education in England 1794–1914*, St Louis: The Institute of Jesuit Sources.

Rudduck, J. and Flutter, J. (2000) 'Pupil Participation and Pupil Perspectives: Carving a New Order of Experience' *Cambridge Journal of Education*, Vol. 30, No. 1, pp. 75–89.

Rudduck, J., Chaplain, R. and Wallace, G. (1996) *School Improvement: what can pupils tell us?*, London: David Fulton.

Rutter, M., Maughan, B., Mortimore, P. and Ouston, J. (1979) *Fifteen Thousand Hours: Secondary Schools and their effects on Children*, London: Open Books.

Sacred Congregation for Catholic Education (1977) *The Catholic School*, Homebush, NSW: St Paul Publications.

Sacred Congregation for Catholic Education (1982) *Lay Catholics in Schools: Witnesses to Faith*, London: Catholic Truth Society.

Sadovnik, A. (ed.) (1995) *Knowledge and Pedagogy: The Sociology of Basil Bernstein*, Norwood, NJ: Ablex Publishing.

Sammons, P., Hillman, J. and Mortimore, P. (1995) *Key Characteristics of Effective Schools*, London: Office for Standards in Education.

Sander, W. (2000) 'Catholic High Schools and Homework', *Educational Evaluation and Policy Analysis*, Vol. 22, No. 3, pp. 299–311.

Schön, D. (1983) *The Reflective Practitioner*, New York: Basic Books.

Selby, D. E. (1974) 'The Work of Cardinal Manning in the Field of Education', Ph.D. thesis, University of Birmingham.

Simon, B. and Chitty, C. (1993) *SOS: Save Our Schools*, London: Lawrence and Wishart.

Singh, P. and Luke, A. (1996) 'Editor's Preface' to B. Bernstein, *Pedagogy: Symbolic Control and Identity*, London: Taylor & Francis.

Slee, R., Tomlinson, S. and Weiner, G. (eds) (1998) *School Effectiveness for Whom?*, London: Falmer Press.

Snook, I. A. (ed.) (1972) *Concepts of Indoctrination*, London: Routledge & Kegan Paul.

Soros, G. (1999) *The Crisis of Global Capitalism*, London: Little, Brown.

Stoll, L. and Myers, K. (eds) (1998) *No Quick Fixes: Perspectives on Schools in Difficulty*, London: Falmer Press.

Sullivan, J. (ed.) (1996) *Catholic Boys*, Auckland: Penguin.

Sullivan, J. (2000) *Catholic Schools in Contention*, Dublin: Veritas.

Sutherland, M. (1988) 'Religious Dichotomy and Schooling in Northern Ireland', in W. Tulasiewicz and C. Brock (eds) *Christianity and Educational Provision in International Perspective*, London: Routledge.

Swartz, D. (1997) *Culture and Power: The Sociology of Pierre Bourdieu*, Chicago: University of Chicago Press.

Swope, J. (1992) 'The Production, Recontextualising and Popular Transmission of Religious Discourse in Eight Basic Christian Communities in Santiago, Chile', Ph.D. thesis, University of London.

Taylor, C. (1989) *Sources of the Self: the Making of the Modern Identity*, Cambridge: Cambridge University Press.

Thatcher, M. (1993) *The Downing Street Years*, London: HarperCollins.

Thomas, W. I. (1932) *The Child in America: Behaviour Problems and Programs*, New York: Knopf.

Tolerton, J. (ed.) (1994) *Convent Girls*, Auckland: Penguin.

Tooley, J. (1994) 'In Defence of Markets in Educational Provision', in D. Bridges and T. McLaughlin (eds) *Education and the Market Place*, London: Falmer Press.

Traviss, M. P. (1989) *Doctoral Dissertation on Catholic Schools, K-12 1976–1987*, Washington: National Catholic Educational Association.

Treston, K. (1997) 'Ethos and Identity: Foundational Concerns for Catholic Schools', in R. Keane and D. Riley (eds) *Quality Catholic Schools*, Brisbane: Catholic Education Office.

Tucker, B. (ed.) (1968) *Catholic Education in a Secular Society*, London: Sheed and Ward.

Tulasiewicz, W. and Brock, C. (eds) (1988) *Christianity and Educational Provision in International Perspective*, London: Routledge.

Usher, R. and Edwards, R. (1994) *Postmodernism and Education: Different Voices, Different Worlds*, London: Routledge.

Usher, R. and Scott, D. (eds) (1996) *Understanding Educational Research*, London: Routledge.

Vallely, P. (ed.) (1998) *The New Politics: Catholic Social Teaching for the Twenty-First Century*, London: SCM Press.

Vatican Congregation for Catholic Education (1988) *The Religious Dimension of Education in a Catholic School*, Dublin: Veritas.

Vitullo-Martin, T. (1979) *Catholic Inner-City Schools: The Future*, Washington, DC: US Catholic Conference.

Wallace, T. (2000) 'We are Called: The Principal as Faith Leader in the Catholic School', in T. Hunt *et al.* (eds) *Catholic School Leadership*, London: Falmer Press.

Walsh, P. (1983) 'The Church Secondary School and its Curriculum', in D. O'Leary (ed.) *Religious Education and Young Adults*, Slough: St Paul Publications.

Walsh, P. (1993) *Education and Meaning: Philosophy in Practice*, London: Cassell.

Warner, M. (1990) *Alone of All Her Sex: The Myth and Cult of the Virgin Mary*, London: Picador.

Weber, M. (1930) *The Protestant Ethic and the Spirit of Capitalism*, London: Allen and Unwin.

Wexler, P. (1997) *Holy Sparks: Social Theory, Education and Religion*, London: Macmillan.

White, A. (1999) *Frost in May*, London: Virago Press.

White, J. (1995) *Education and Personal Well-Being in a Secular Universe*, London: London Institute of Education.

Whitty, G., Power, S. and Halpin, D. (1998) *Devolution and Choice in Education: The School, The State and the Market*, Buckingham: Open University Press.

Willms, J. D. (1984) 'School Effectiveness within the Public and Private Sectors: An Evaluation', *Evaluation Review*, Vol. 8, pp. 113–35.

Willms, J. D. (1992) 'Pride or Prejudice? Opportunity Structure and the Effects of Catholic Schools in Scotland', *International Perspectives on Education and Society*, Vol. 2, pp. 189–213.

Wilson, A. N. (1999) *God's Funeral*, London: John Murray.

Wilson, V. (1997) 'Focus Groups: A Useful Qualitative Method for Educational Research?', *British Educational Research Journal*, Vol. 22, No. 2, pp. 209–24.

Winter, M. (1985) *Whatever Happened to Vatican II?*, London: Sheed and Ward.

Wright, A. (1998) *Spiritual Pedagogy*, Abingdon: Culham College Institute.

Wright Mills, C. (1973) *The Sociological Imagination*, Harmondsworth: Penguin.

Youniss, J. and Convey, J. (eds) (2000) *Catholic Schoools at the Crossroads: Survival and Transformation*, New York: Teachers College Press.

Youniss, J. and McLellan, J. (1999) 'Catholic Schools in Perspective: Religious Identity, Achievement and Citizenship', *Phi Delta Kappan*, October.

Youniss, J., Convey, J. and McLellan, J. (eds) (2000) *The Catholic Character of Catholic Schools*, Notre Dame, IN: University of Notre Dame Press.

# Name index

# Subject index